THE HISTORICAL ATLAS
OF EASTERN
AND WESTERN
CHRISTIAN MONASTICISM

Juan María Laboa

THE HISTORICAL ATLAS OF EASTERN AND WESTERN CHRISTIAN MONASTICISM

with articles by
Richard Cemus, s.j., Pascaline Coff, o.s.b., Zoran Krstić,
Ljubomir Maksimović, Gaetano Passarelli, Sava, bishop of Šumadija,
Columba Stewart, o.s.b., Anthony-Emile Tachiaos, Christo Ternelski,
Vassia Velinova, Mirjana Živojinović

THE LITURGICAL PRESS
Collegeville, Minnesota

www.litpress.org

On the cover:
illustrations from the book

French, Italian, and Spanish text translated by
Matthew J. O'Connell
and
Madeleine Beaumont

The authors of individual articles are indicated in the Contents by the following abbreviations:
Richard Cemus, S.J. (R.C.)
Pascaline Coff, O.S.B. (P.C.)
Zoran Krstić (Z.K.)
Juan María Laboa (J.M.L.)
Ljubomir Maksimović (Lj.M.)
Gaetano Passarelli (G.P.)
Sava, bishop of Šumadija (S.v.Š.)
Columba Stewart, O.S.B. (C.S.)
Anthony-Emile Tachiaos (A.-E.T.)
Christo Ternelski (C.T.)
Vassia Velinova (V.V.)
Mirjana Živojinović (M.Ž.)

© 2001 by Editoriale Jaca Book s.p.a., Milano. All rights reserved.

1   2   3   4   5   6   7   8

Library of Congress Cataloging-in-Publication Data

Atlas historique du monachisme d'Orient et d'Occident. English.
    The historical atlas of Eastern and Western Christian monasticism / Juan María Laboa,
editor ; with articles by Richard Cemus . . . [et al.].
        p. cm.
    Includes bibliographical references and indexes.
    ISBN 0-8146-2778-1 (alk. paper)
        1. Monasticism and religious orders—History—Maps. 2. World.   I. Laboa, Juan María.
II. Cemus, Richard, 1954–.   III. Title.

G1046.E4.H5 2003
271'.0022'3—dc21

2003055008

CONTENTS

VI. The Development of Monasticism in the West

VII. A Millennium of Christian Monasticism in the East

VIII. A Millennium of Christian Monasticism in the West

INTRODUCTION

"You made my heart for yourself, Lord, and it is restless until it rests in you." Thus did St. Augustine "confess" and express with simplicity the innermost experience of humanity down through history. The creator, who has made human beings in the divine image, has lovingly placed in their hearts a longing for the source from which they came, a restless search for truth, the hope of a definitive, illuminating encounter.

The human person is the great pilgrim, the great seeker, who is capable of traveling the roads of life without wearying, once she or he has encountered this primordial spark of divine love. In their awareness that their house of clay encloses and conceals something greater and more lasting, human beings endeavor in countless ways to purify what is earthly in themselves and discover the divine. How splendid is the history of this immense people who down the centuries, in countless different ways, have endeavored to bring to light within them that which connects them with their creator! In their interior deserts, so many unknown valiant women and men, whose virtues have flourished in hiding, have struggled tenaciously and constantly to know and love God, while rejecting and abandoning everything that could delay that encounter.

To love means, of course, to learn to walk in the present marvelous world, to understand and respect it, to love it and try to improve it. That is the lesson we learn from the holy men and women of the various religions, who were aware that everything coming from the hands of the creator is essentially good. They loved nature and life, all life, for they knew that as civilization gives us the means of attaining to human power, so nature gives us God.

"Not so with you": Christ told his disciples that the standard of their individual and communal behavior was to be different. If they were to follow the Master, they had to be reborn and then live in the world without being influenced by the world. That is the great Christian paradox, the snare or challenge that is always present in the life of the Church: to be involved in the world without being worldly, without being overcome by the constant danger of worldliness. It was against this temptation that the Fathers and Mothers of the desert spoke out; monastics have always struggled against it. They have showed us in countless ways the necessity of being evangelizers while not succumbing to the mediocre values of the world.

When monastics, with Christ, long for the Father's will to be done in this world as it is in heaven and in Christ, then even the smallest and most ordinary things become holy and magnificent. Then the divine love reveals itself and flowers in God's creation. Then our lives are transformed. This transformation is an epiphany and a coming of God into the world.

Given this perspective, we can point out some of the religious goals and thoughts most pursued and most clearly present in the great representatives of the surprising and moving history of monasticism.

—Death to the world. This goal has always been fundamental in the life and asceticism of the desert; it meant dying in body and in spirit. Monastics wanted their bodies to cease to react "normally" to the needs of the flesh, so that instead they themselves might control thirst, hunger, fatigue, and sleep. "I kill my body because it is killing me" was Dorotheus' answer to Palladius when asked to justify his asceticism. But if he was killing his body, it was in order to form a different body, to reach the state which the ascetical texts call "apatheia" (freedom from emotion or excitement).

—The monastic as another Christ. In the lives and sayings of the Fathers and Mothers and later monastics we find the conviction that they were becoming like Christ in his life and passion. We also see their certainty that they would attain to this conformity in the highest degree by living lives of sacrifice and renunciation.

—Longing for the definitive return of Christ. It is an essential element of Christianity that its followers live in expectation of the Lord's return, awaiting the "appearance" of his Day; this is even more true of monastic life. Those who visited the Fathers and Mothers of the desert confirmed that they had no attachments, no worries, no concern for clothing or food; their sole desire was to wait for the Lord's return. The ancients understood their lives to be but a phase in the great eschatological struggle that had already begun, and each of them felt personally that he was involved in that struggle and was a sharer in the victorious power of Christ.

—The eschatological struggle between good and evil, between Christ and the devil. Those monastics had a very clear awareness that the devil was their great enemy and that it was always present and ready to keep them from a pure and honorable life. They thought of the spiritual life as an invisible war that had been begun triumphantly by Christ in solitude; they felt called to continue it with him and like him. Indeed, they had a very clear awareness that two cities coexisted: the city of good and the city of evil, the city of the angels and the city of the demons; they were also convinced that the whole of reality was permeated by these spirits. The monastic tradition, but especially the Eastern, extensively developed the doctrine of the "angelic life."

—At the origin of life in the desert is the call to a more explicit and radical following of Christ in his rejection and, above all, in his passion. Isidore of Skete, who constantly mortified himself, used to say, "I have no excuse: the Son of God came here for our sake." Poemen, when he came to himself after an ecstasy, said, "My mind was with Mary, the holy Mother of God, as she wept beside the cross of the Savior; I, too, will try always to weep in that way."

—Some flee human beings out of love for God, while others welcome them for the same reason. Hospitality became a monastic characteristic. They fled contact with people, withdrew into the desert, and surrounded their cells with walls, but they practiced hospitality and gave it a privileged place. They were able to break with traditional ways and customs so that their visitors might feel welcome and at home. It was Christ who came and greeted the monastics, and it was Christ whom they received and feted. The monastics managed to turn the coming of a guest into a true festivity.

Monastic life elicited other testimonies, beginning especially in the 5th century: to the beauty that radiated out into the environment, to the order of the monastics' lives, and above all to the liturgy. Here culture, too, had its natural setting, for culture's realm runs from the ability to give a meaning to one's experience, to the preservation of spaces for memory and beauty, and even sublimity.

All these characteristics have distinguished monastics of different origins down to our day; they have marked their personal lives and the charisms of their different Orders. Monastics collaborated decisively in the evangelization of Europe; they played a fundamental role in the rescue of classical culture and in the expansion of agriculture. These are works that still remain as eloquent testimonies to an activity that always combined prayer and labor.

As a matter of fact, the monastic-world relationship does not run in only one direction. It is not only the world and Christians that benefit from the prayers and asceticism of monastics. The latter, in their turn, need to know what the world is if they are to complete their realistic vision of human life. Moreover, they must act in turn on this world and commit themselves to causes that promote and bring about a better human race. The vows have their full meaning only if they are understood as a commitment to the service of others, as a fervent concern for truth and for our neighbor, all our neighbors.

An illustrated historical atlas of monasticism bears witness to the twofold Christian paradox: on the one hand, "being in the world without being worldly," while the very monastics who have most fully embodied that statement also show us the other side of the paradox, namely, that monasticism has changed the world and even its natural and cultural landscape. Without centuries of monasticism the world in which we live would be a different place.

ATLAS

1. *Painting representing a holy hermit. Church of the Redeemer of Calendžiha, in Mingreliya, Georgia. The Eastern Christian tradition, of which Georgia has been a part from the early centuries, has kept a strong presence of the eremitical experience in its monasticism.*

2. *Detail of a Gothic miniature, ca. 1350. Royal Library of Brussels, Belgium. Here an abbot is represented; the abbey is a typical form of the Western monastic community.*

1. ANCIENT EASTERN MONASTICISM

HINDUISM, BUDDHISM, AND JAINISM

1. Atman in Search of Brahman: Indian Monasticism

India represents the historical prologue and prototype of the religious spirit among the nations and has, down the centuries, preserved an admirable respect for and an exceptional dedication to whatever has embodied the life and manifestation of this spirit. For thousands of years on this vast subcontinent we see peoples concerned with the beyond and with the religious dimension of life. In fact, India is often thought of as the land of contemplation, that is, of the method and frame of mind that unites a human being with the absolute, with God; it is so thought of because its Hindu ascetics and solitaries have sought earnestly and perseveringly for that liberating encounter. The most common method of achieving it has been meditation.

According to the Upanishads, the individual principle (atman) and the cosmic principle or essence of the universe (Brahman) are utterly one. True happiness consists in the definitive union of the atman with the Brahman. The fundamental obstacle to the attainment of this unity is the difficulty the atman has in recognizing its own nature as it really is: it lacks personal experience of the truth that the individual "I" is not an independent reality but a participation in Brahman or absolute being, with which it desires to unite itself to the point of becoming identical with it.

A virtuous life and asceticism promote this understanding and resultant union. How is this understanding to be achieved? By withdrawing (this holds for both women and men) to the "wilderness," living an austere life, and devoting oneself to meditation. Due to their reputation and methods, holy solitaries usually attract groups of disciples who try to imitate their manner of life.

Until the 6th century groups and schools of a monastic kind multiplied and developed very radical forms both in their ascetical methods and in their withdrawal from the world, for example, the renunciation of temporal possessions that reached an extreme in the naked monks, "clothed in air," who practiced the most radical way of showing unqualified detachment and utter aloneness. All these methods seemed to be the surest way of reaching happiness and freedom.

An age-old Hindu tradition sees the normal life of a religious man as having four successive stages: celibate student, father of a family, hermit, and monk. This final stage is one of complete renunciation, preparation for death, and concentration on religion.

All this represented a very free kind of monasticism, a pluriform kind that lacked any type of organization and, for practical purposes, knew nothing of a common life. Monks were obliged to observe five main vows and many other secondary ones. These main ones were: not to harm any living thing, to be sincere, not to steal, not to lose self-control, and to be generous. The secondary vows obliged them to keep their composure, to obey the guru, to be kind and clean, and to eat only simple foods.

2. Buddhist Community Organization

Buddhist monasticism has been characterized from its beginnings by its community organization and, in addition, has distinguished

3. Design copied from a statue found in Sanchi, India. It represents a Brahmanic hermit. The habit is made from tree bark; only one shoulder is covered while the robe is a sort of kilt. The hair is tied and styled to form a sort of hat.

4. Drawing representing a Sanyasi Hindu, copied from a picture found in a cliff monastery of Ajanta in India. For a long time, Hindu monks did not wear the habits made of strips of bark like those used by hermits of earlier periods. With the rise of Buddhist monasticism, the Hindus also wore fabrics of ocher or reddish ocher. On account of this, it is difficult to distinguish Buddhist from Hindu monastics. In the picture one sees a cloth going around the sides and then thrown over the shoulders.

3

5. At Ellora in India, there are Buddhist, Hindu, and Jainist temples and monasteries. The most celebrated Hindu monument is the Kailāsa, pictured here, an example of the monastic custom of excavating monasteries from the rock. In this case, an enormous block of stone is carved and sculpted to represent a mountain, the paradise of Siva. This sanctuary, to which pilgrims came in great numbers, was run by the monks. The pilgrims, having

4

crossed the threshold (lower left on the photo), passed through the three stories of the sanctuary: the roof of the second is a blooming lotus flower while the third, the highest, culminates with a lingam, Siva's emblem. Thus from ascent to ascent the pilgrim gained access to Siva's mountain.

5

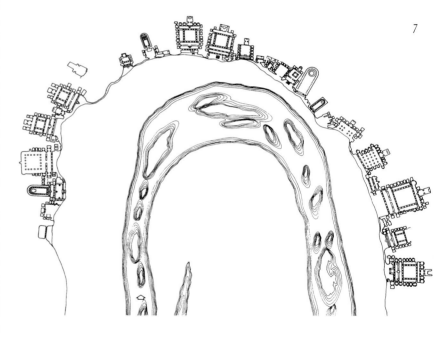

itself from Hinduism by eliminating the castes that play such a large part in that culture and by scorning its constant speculations. Buddhist communities follow a rule of life that emphasizes the practice of poverty. The Buddhist monk is detached from the world, desires to die to everything, seeks with determination a personal interiorization, and practices celibacy. According to Buddhist teaching, there is only one real problem that truly merits our attention, liberation from the pain produced by desires and passions. This deliverance is an individual goal and requires an individual effort; each human being must struggle against his or her own feelings and succeed in extinguishing them for the purpose of escaping from *sansara,* the cycle of lives and deaths which is the cause of so much suffering and constant disquiet.

Buddhism reached Tibet by way of India and underwent an extraordinary expansion there. We find that within a short time it had spread to Indochina, China, and Japan. In Tibet its followers cultivated a ritual, meditative practice, that is, a series of semi-liturgical rites, accompanied by a profound meditation on a mandala or graphic visualization of the universe. The practice of meditation was the core and main achievement of the program and showed its power and influence by allowing the practitioners to focus on themselves and on liberation from their passions. These monks practiced an unqualified submission and surrender to the guru or teacher. This classic form of instruction had many traits similar to those we find in the lives of the eremitical or itinerant religious teachers so common throughout the entire history of India. Beginning in the 8th century there was a shift from small "parochial" monasteries—each of which served for the teaching and devotion of a village or group of villages—to large centers for study and seclusion, very like colleges or even universities.

3. Jainist Radicalism

Jainism derives its name from the Sanskrit verb *ji,* meaning "to conquer." The reference is to the ascetical battle which Jainist

6–7. View and general plan of the cave of Ajanta in India. It consists of an extraordinary ensemble of sanctuaries (chapels) and Buddhist monasteries which surround a small valley on three sides. The monasteries have a quadrangular plan; the rooms are delimited by a colonnade and surrounded by small individual cells also excavated from the rock. The chapels have an apsidal or an elongated rectangular plan. In the early centuries of our era, the monasteries and the places of pilgrimage were helped by the patronage of the sovereigns of the Gupta period (3rd century C.E.) who supported the arts of sculpture and painting.

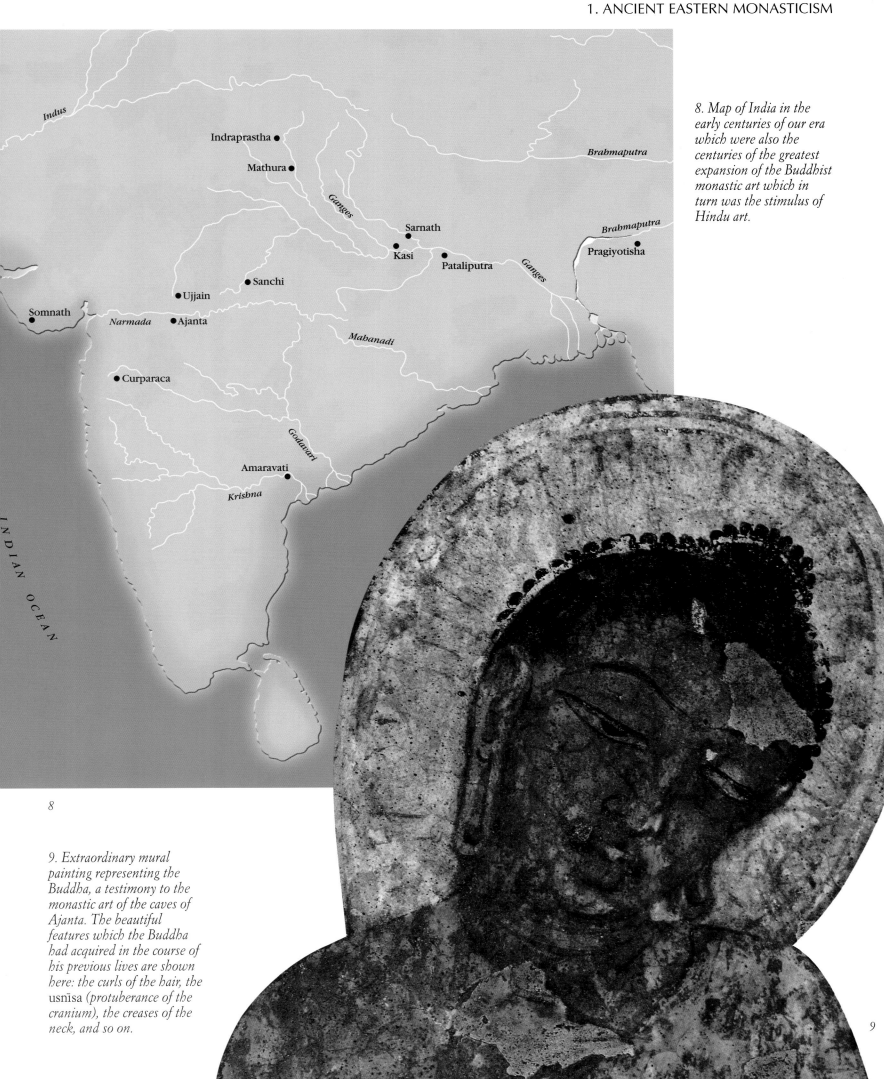

8. *Map of India in the early centuries of our era which were also the centuries of the greatest expansion of the Buddhist monastic art which in turn was the stimulus of Hindu art.*

8

9. *Extraordinary mural painting representing the Buddha, a testimony to the monastic art of the caves of Ajanta. The beautiful features which the Buddha had acquired in the course of his previous lives are shown here: the curls of the hair, the* usnīsa *(protuberance of the cranium), the creases of the neck, and so on.*

9

10

11

10–11. The cave at Ellora, that is to say, the complex excavated from the rock and known as Indrasabhā (Assembly of Indra, the divinity common to Hinduism and Jainism), dating back to the 9th and 10th centuries. It is a most beautiful cave, the fruit of Jainist monasticism, with its meeting rooms established on several levels, with their carved figures, with the decorations on their balconies in which Jainist figures alternate with animals: elephants and lions. The staircase one sees on figure 11 leads to the high-placed sanctuary of figure 10. This sanctuary is built on the model of the Hindu Kailāsa illustrated in figure 5.

monks must carry on against the bodily senses and passions in order to purify the soul of everything that keeps it tied to a bodily existence and, in this way, to attain to omniscience and purity of soul. Jainism is one of the three oldest traditions of India and has its own specific monasticism.

The more perfect monks go naked and spend long hours motionless in the *kayotsarga* position: arms hanging at the sides, hands a little open, and gaze fixed on the end of the nose. They have an unqualified respect for all life, an attitude that imposes many prohibitions in the areas of food, profession, and sex. They never lie, preserve an unbroken sexual continence, and own absolutely nothing. They do not react to heat or the insects that torment limbs weakened by a cruel asceticism.

12

Their lives are completely organized; they give blind obedience to superiors who direct and channel their severe austerities according to their spiritual state and their ability to understand the meaning of their practices. Their rule of life includes meditation, prayer, study, poverty, asceticism, and the practice of one daily meal, which is limited to food that fits into the palm of the hand.

The renunciation practiced by Hindu, Buddhist, and Jainist monks is inspired by the conviction that the world and their individual persons are a mere but unfortunate illusion.

As is well known, due to Alexander the Great not a few of the ways and customs proper to the East made their way into the West. It was at that point that the manner of life of the monks of India gained popularity in Europe, chiefly through Greek literature.

12. This masterpiece of sculpture is in one of the meeting halls of the Jainist monastery in figures 10 and 11. It shows Yaksa Mātānga on his elephant under a mango tree; he displays the marks of opulence: a prominent belly and a real mount.

2. MEDITERRANEAN ROOTS OF A WAY OF LIFE

13. One of the few representations of Serapis (200–180 B.C.E.). Painted on wood, it is part of a triptych of unknown provenance, but probably from the funerary sites found in al-Fayyum, Egypt. J. Paul Getty Museum, Los Angeles, California.

1. The "Cloistered Monks" of Serapis: Egyptian Monasticism

Egypt is par excellence the country of deserts. In its isolated and silent great temples, priests lived a laborious, simple, silent life. In contrast to the cities with their noise, their empty agitated activity, and their licentiousness, this withdrawal represented a search for what is essential and for the calm presence of the spirit. These men were searching for God in silence and solitude.

The methods followed differed, of course, depending on place and circumstances. One well-known group was the cloistered monks in the temples of Serapis; they were not priests of the god but sought the seclusion of his temples in order to know him and obtain an oracle or to obtain a healing for themselves or for others for whom they prayed and from whom they received a wage. Their goal was not personal perfection or a closer union with God, but rather the acquisition of a concrete, useful gift. In fact, apart from strict seclusion in the temple, their practice had little in common with the outward manifestations of monasticism, Eastern or Western, contrary to the view of some authors who at the beginning of the 20th century claimed that the Pachomian monks were following the example of the monks of Serapis.

2. Philosophical Monasticism

In the Greek world, and especially in the world of the philosophers, we find forms of ascetical and communal life that remind us of elements traditional in every kind of monasticism. Pythagoras inaugurated one kind of ascetical community and gave it a rule of life that included strict regulations on silence, abstinence, and a daily examination of conscience; these methods and practices were meant to foster a more rational kind of person, one more conscious of his own capacities. To that end, the novices kept perpetual silence, in the awareness that excessive talk was the root of countless personal and social ills.

These individuals were seeking self-mastery and a greater interior purification. There is no doubt that devotion to philosophy and speculation brought with it special requirements. Dio Chrysostom wrote, "Education and philosophy obviously call for a great deal of solitude and withdrawal." Emperor Marcus Aurelius, a thinker rich in ideas, was unable, because of his office, to withdraw as much as he would have liked into solitude; therefore, as far as possible, he "used to withdraw into himself." The life of Apollonius of Tyana, a Pythagorean, describes him as spurning wine, meat, and woolen garments; he dressed in linen and walked barefoot, wore his hair long, and kept his eyes down; he professed perpetual chastity. The Pythagoreans were of the opinion that all human beings constituted a single great family, because all were, in the strict sense, children of God.

Empedocles started a movement whose controlling practice was vegetarianism; this was not so much an ascetical practice as a way of promoting "metempsychosis."

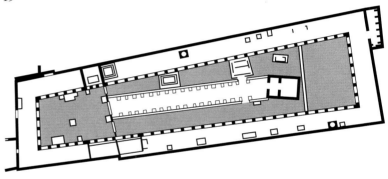

14. Reconstruction of the plan of the Serapeum on the island of Delos, Greece (3rd–2nd centuries B.C.E.).

Plato's spirituality was nourished by scorn for the things of this world. Seneca spoke frequently of work and the struggle against one's passions. In his writings he saw a deep religious meaning in withdrawal from the world, in solitude, and in mastery of one's sensual nature. The Neoplatonists sought an encounter with the One, the supreme God who is the source and goal of all things. To this end, they led a very austere kind of life; they often did not marry, did not eat flesh, slept little, and chastised their bodies.

3. The Heralds of the Kingdom of Light: "Manichaean Monasticism"

In Manichaeism, to know oneself is to contemplate one's soul as participating in the nature of God. Knowledge constitutes the only way to salvation. In order to attain to this knowledge, it is necessary to overcome the ignorance and lack of self-consciousness found

15

15. Bust representing Pythagoras. Capitoline Museum of Rome.

16

16. Mosaic from the 1st century C.E., from Pompei. National Archeological Museum of Naples. Once interpreted as a representation of the seven sages, it is now considered a depiction of Plato's school and is explained thus: the first person could be Heracleides Ponticus engaged in making a discourse, then comes Speusippus, Plato's nephew and successor, then Plato pointing to the celestial globe. The last figure on the right, after three successors of Plato, could be Aristotle in a dialectical attitude with regard to the others. The mosaic remains a splendid metaphor of the human community dedicated to philosophizing.

17

in those who are controlled by their flesh, by fornication, procreation, possessions, and the desire for food and drink. Those unable to overcome these passions and limitations are condemned to be reborn, over and over again, into bodies that are ever weaker and more defiled.

Only a few decide, successfully, to travel the narrow path of the ascetical life, the only path by which it is possible to rise above the radically evil life of this world. For this reason the community was divided into the perfect and the imperfect, the elect and the hearers, those who fulfill the precepts of morality and those who do not. It was by means of this division that Manichaean theory came to grips with the opposition and resultant domination of contradictory principles: spirit and matter, good and evil, light and darkness. Only the children of the light received an authentic revelation. They were the ones who had embraced a strict rule, often in a community. Their essential practices were prayer and fasting. Those who grasped the truth were considered to be perfect.

17. Stylized representation of Mani, taken from a Chinese picture.

17

3. OLD TESTAMENT MONASTICISM

18

18. *Hypothetical itinerary of the Exodus. Engraving on wood by H. Bünting, 1582, National and University Library of Jerusalem.*

19. *View of the Negev desert in Israel. In the center, one sees the oasis of Ain Hudra. The Negev desert, which the Bible refers to, is interspersed with imposing mountainous regions.*

1. Prophetism and Radicalism

It was in the desert that the Israelites became a people. Throughout their history they looked back to the forty years spent in the isolation of Sinai as the time when they were forged into a single people. The Lord was with them and took care of them, and they, though they murmured and fell into idolatry, were purified to the point where they became a new people. In the time to come, the wilderness would have a special fascination for the great men of Israel, from Elijah to Jesus.

After the wilderness, Jerusalem provided another element of the monastic life, namely, exile. All those who heard in their hearts the call given to Abraham applied it to Jerusalem more than to anything else: "Go from your country and your kindred and your father's house to the land that I will show you" (Gen 12:1). This verse is cited at least a dozen times in the biographies of the monks of Judah, and it can readily be applied to every one of them.

Jeremiah describes thus the command given by Jonadab son of Rechab to his descendants, "You shall never drink wine, neither you nor your children; nor shall you ever build a house, or sow seed; nor shall you plant a vineyard, or even own one; but you shall live in tents all your days, that you may live many days in the land where you reside" (Jer 35:6-7). Among the Israelites there were always examples of the spirit of fidelity and radical consecration to God, a spirit that led to a strict asceticism in face of the weakness and wrongdoing that were so much a part of Israelite history.

The so-called "prophetic communities," which existed as early as the time of Samuel, were conspicuous in the time of Elijah and continued in existence down to the time of the prophet Amos. These were independent, itinerant groups; they had a prophet as their leader, they lived a life of poverty, supported by their own labor or by public charity; some of them were celibates. They could be considered a living proof of the grace and nearness of God: "I raised up some of your children to be prophets and some of your youths to be nazirites" (Amos 2:11).

The religious group known as the Rechabites represented a protest against the religious corruption of the chosen people. Their purpose was to revitalize the purest religious ideals of radical

fidelity to the covenant of the Lord. They were seeking a spiritual defense against contamination from the Canaanites among whom the people of Israel had settled.

The Hasids were a very radical and pietist religious movement made up of priests, scribes, and the simple folk among the people (1 Macc 7:12ff.). They were distinguishable from the rest of the Jewish people by their characteristic love of the Law and their complete rejection of the omnipresent and corrupting pagan culture, which was an abiding temptation for many Israelites. At times, these various groups sprang into existence from a determination to revive the radicalism of Israel's early times. Not a few Jews who loved the law and righteousness fled to the wilderness and settled there with their children and flocks.

These great prophets and their disciples often provided an example which Christian monks could follow. Their lives spent in solitude, prayer, and a constant effort to make the reign of God a reality; their trust in the future liberator of the Israelite people; their consciousness of the continuous presence of God; and the intimacy which some prophets—Enoch, Noah, Abraham—enjoyed with God: all these qualities impressed Christian ascetics of every period, who saw in them the ideal of perfection.

2. Essenes and Therapeutae

The Essenes (135–104 B.C.E. to 68–70 C.E.) likewise turned to the past, to the ideal days in the wilderness and the radical observance of the Law and other traditions of the people. They lived in lively hope of an eschatological and messianic future, for only from the Messiah could they expect the definitive victory of the Lord over Belial. They were convinced that they were living in the final time, those last stages that were preceding the apocalyptic struggle. Several contemporary sources speak of the Essenes, but we have acquired a better knowledge of their organization from the papyri discovered over the last forty years at Qumran, in the wilderness of Judah, where the most important monastery of the sect probably existed.

The point most characteristic about the organization of the Essenes was their division into two well-defined groups. One group lived in a strict community whose members were obliged to obedience, the sharing of possessions, and continence; the second group consisted of families which lived in the wilderness in complete spiritual communion with the first group, on which they also depended in the organization of their material life.

The Essenes spent the day in prayer and work, both intellectual and physical (crafts and farming). They also had a scriptorium for the copying of manuscripts. During the night they held liturgical gatherings similar to those in the synagogue on the Sabbath but with this difference, that they took a meal which had a religious and eschatological significance, at which they shared bread and wine.

The goal of this austere religious movement is set down in the Community Rule: ". . . to live [according to] the Book of the Community Rule, that they may seek God with a whole heart and soul, and do what is good and right before Him as He commanded by the hand of Moses and all His servants the prophets" (trans. Vermes).

The ascetics of Qumran had a profoundly ascetic and mystical sense of things; they valued prayer and cultivated a very respectful and devout attitude toward the divinity. They kept on seeking interior enlightenment and a sapiential and experiential knowledge of things divine.

20

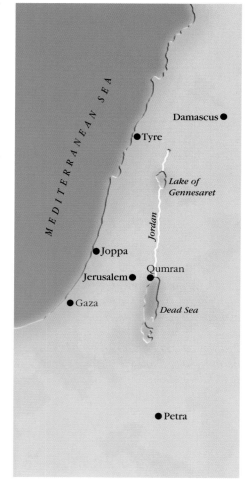

20. One of the caves of Qumran in the desert of Palestine near the Dead Sea. The Dead Sea Scrolls were found in one of the caves; among them was the rule of the Essenes, a Jewish monastic community.

21. Palestine. The site of the caves of Qumran is indicated as well as the sites of the principal cities of the area referred to during the period of the Essenes.

21

22

23

22. *Overview of some of the caves of Qumran. The high position along the rocky crests made the site appropriate for hermitages.*

23. *Mar Saba, Israel. Rock-hewn habitations for hermits, used also in the period following that of the Old Testament.*

A similar attitude was to be seen in the Therapeutae, a Jewish Diaspora sect, who lived in Egypt around Lake Maeotis and were dedicated to a primarily contemplative life. Their main purpose was to heal their passions. They lived in individual cells with two rooms, one of which was reserved exclusively for contemplation. The reading of sacred Scripture and of some books peculiar to the sect fed and gave a focus to their meditation and loving submission to the Law. They renounced private property, practiced celibacy, and lived ascetically in every area of life. Despite a predominantly individualistic and isolated life, community activities were not lacking. On Saturday they held a meeting that included readings, singing, and an address by the eldest and ended with a meal taken in common and consisting of bread, salt, hyssop, and water. Every seven weeks, a more solemn assembly was held that included choral singing which went on through the night.

The Therapeutae admitted women to their solemn Saturday meeting, especially those who were virgins and elderly; the women were, however, separated from the men by a fairly high wall.

1. MONASTICISM AND THE NEW TESTAMENT

AN ABSENT PHENOMENON IN EARLY CHRISTIANITY

24. Baptism of Christ in the Jordan. The Baptist is characterized by the unkempt hair of a hermit. Miniature from the Menologion *of Basil II, ca. 985. Vatican Apostolic Library, Rome.*

25. Christ tempted by the devil in the desert. One sees the cities from above, contrasted with the life of penance and fast led in the desert. Painting by Duccio da Buonisegna. Frick Collection, New York.

26. View of the Jordan, in Israel.

27. Present-day view of the Mount of Temptation, where, according to the New Testament, the devil took Christ.

The earliest monastic writers of the 4th century assumed that their way of life was based solidly on the teachings of both Old and New Testaments. They were convinced that the Bible is always the primary monastic rule. St. Basil the Great described monastic life in terms of fulfilling the commandments, as did St. Benedict, who depicts the life of the monk as a journey using the Gospel for a guide (Prol. 21). But Jesus said not a word about monasticism. Nor were the essential practices of the monastic life a feature of the religion of the people of Israel as presented in the Old Testament. The Acts of the Apostles describes communities of fervent Christians gathered for prayers, the breaking of bread, mutual support, and good works, but these were ordinary people in normal situations. How then could the Bible be the basis for monastic life? It was so in three principal ways: the teachings of Jesus, the hints of ascetical practice found in other New Testament writings, and the example of the prophets and the followers of Jesus.

28

28. Representation of Pentecost in an Armenian miniature in a collection of hymns from 1591. Armenian Museum of France, Paris. The apostles gathered together at the descent of the Holy Spirit will be the symbol of every successive monastic community.

The marks of monastic life are some degree of separation from normal society, special dedication to prayer, a choice to remain celibate for religious reasons, and a reduced dependence on the material comforts of food and possessions. All of these elements are found to some extent in the teaching and life of Jesus, and later became the basis for the Christian ascetic life that developed into monasticism. Jesus himself left home ("the Son of Man has nowhere to lay his head," Matt 8:20) to preach the reign of God, and placed love of God above all ties of human kinship (Matt 10:37; 19:29; cf. Luke 14:26). He spent time in deserted places in prayer and ascetic discipline, most obviously during his time of temptation in the desert near the Jordan River (Matt 4:1-11 and pars.) but also at intervals throughout his ministry. He never married, and noted that some remain unmarried ("eunuchs") for the sake of the kingdom of God (Matt 19:21). Jesus was taught by his cousin John, another celibate preacher, whose renunciation of normal society was even more radical than Jesus' since he chose to live in the wilderness.

Like all good Jews, Jesus fasted on certain days (Matt 6:16-18) and expected that his disciples would continue to do so after he had left them (Matt 9:14-15). He advised at least one person to sell his possessions, give the money to the poor, and follow him (Matt 19:21; cf. Luke 12:33). He compared the reign of God to a pearl of great price worth sacrificing all of one's other possessions to obtain (Matt 13:44). He told his apostles to travel light, carrying only a minimum of personal items with them (Matt 10:9-10). To follow him meant bearing the Cross of self-denial and possibly of martyrdom (Matt 10:38-39). The atmosphere of expectation that Jesus would soon return in glory, heightened by the reality of persecution, gave such radical recommendations a sense of both rightness and urgency.

Even in the New Testament, one can detect an asceticizing tendency that would influence later groups. Luke's Gospel is notably rigorous in its handling of material shared with Matthew and Mark. For example, Matthew's Jesus tells his followers not to accumulate earthly treasures (Matt 6:19), while Luke's version has Jesus telling them to sell what they already have (Luke 12:33). Matthew's Jesus is concerned lest his followers love family more than him (Matt 10:37), while Luke turns that teaching into a dramatic renunciation requiring that one hate family in order to become free for total discipleship (Luke 14:26). This more radical view of Christian obligations would fuel later ascetic and monastic movements.

Paul's letters are the earliest Christian writings we possess. His belief in the imminent return of Christ suggested the advantages of celibacy (1 Cor 7:25ff.). His urgent exhortations to discipline the self for the sake of the "race" set before us (1 Cor 9:24-27), to take off the old self and put on the new in baptism (Rom 6:6), and his comparison of Christian suffering to the redemptive suffering of Jesus (e.g., 2 Cor 4:11) all provided a theological basis for ascetic Christianity. In the later writings of the New Testament there are

29

*29. Painting of the heavenly banquet in the catacombs
of Sts. Peter and Marcellinus in Rome. Iconography
of the heavenly banquet is frequently found in the
catacombs; it recalls the "Eucharistic Banquet" and
symbolizes the community united in the name
of Christ, the paradigm of every Christian
monastic community.*

signs of a growing approval of dedicated virginity (Rev 14:1-5) and a corresponding disapproval of remarriage by widows (1 Tim 3:2 and 12). These traces of early ascetic attitudes pointed the way toward later developments in theology and practice.

Groups of ascetic Christians on the fringe of orthodoxy (and sometimes beyond it), like the Encratites associated with Tatian (active in the late 2nd century), edited the mainstream Scriptures to support their way of life. Tatian created a gospel harmony known as the *Diatessaron* that displayed an ascetic bias. Apocryphal writings like the *Acts of Judas Thomas* and the *Acts of Paul and Thecla* imitated the biblical genre but were much more explicit than canonical texts in their emphasis on virginity and dispossession.

By the time monasticism was developing in the 4th century, its adherents looked not only to Jesus but also to the prophets who preceded him for examples of total self-offering to God. Monasticism boomed in the Holy Land, and communities were established in places associated with Jesus, John the Baptist, and other key biblical figures. Before John was Elijah, who also knew desert and mountain, lived simply, and challenged conventional concessions to material and religious comfort. The author of the Letter to the Hebrews powerfully evokes biblical characters who

courageously left home and family in response to God's call, even "wandered in deserts and mountains, and in caves and holes in the ground" (Heb 11:38), and this text became a favorite in monastic circles. St. Anthony the Great was known to use the life of Elijah as a mirror for gaining self-knowledge (*Life of Anthony* 7). For some writers, Moses' encounters with God at Sinai became a paradigm for mystical ascent to the divine. All of these heroic figures provided inspiration for later Christian imitation.

As monastic groups began to reflect on their vocation, the idealized Christian community of Jerusalem as depicted in Acts 2 and 4 became a powerful exemplar. The apostolic emphasis on shared goods and common prayer perfectly described the fundamental orientation of cenobitic life, in which the formation of community is central. The followers of Pachomius in 4th-century Egypt even called their movement the Koinonia, borrowing the term used for the Jerusalem community in Acts 2:42. St. Augustine evoked the same model in the opening lines of his monastic rule, the *Praeceptum,* and John Cassian saw monasticism as the natural continuation of the apostolic spirit lost in the broader church. None of these monks was writing history. The biblical ideal they meditated upon, however, was incarnate in the monasticism they experienced and fostered.

30. The prophet Elijah. Detail from an icon of the Transfiguration, from the school of Theophanes the Greek, ca. 1403. Tretyakov Gallery, Moscow.
The figure of the hermit Elijah in the desert is prominently represented in both the New Testament and the early Christian community. Byzantine art will develop an image of Elijah in which the image of John the Baptist is mirrored.

31. St. John the Baptist. Icon from 1502, part of a Deesis in which, as is the classic rule, the Baptist is placed at the left of Christ while the Mother of God occupies the right. It is attributed to the school of Dionisii of Gluschitskii. Tretyakov Gallery, Moscow.
The Baptist, though covered with a cloak, keeps his camel's hair clothing and symbolizes eremitical life in the desert.

30

31

2. THE LONG GESTATION

THE SPIRIT OF THE FIRST COMMUNITY

1. *The Spirit of the First Community*

St. Paul, the *Didache,* St. Irenaeus of Lyons, and Tertullian all clearly attest in their writings that the way of life adopted by the first community in Jerusalem was a model set before all the faithful, and it played a part in Christian catechesis during the first two centuries of our era.

In the Acts of the Apostles we find a description of the ideal community: "All who believed were together and had all things in common; they would sell their possessions and goods and distribute the proceeds to all, as any had need" (Acts 2:44-45). They "were of one heart and soul" (Acts 4:32). But the words are in fact an echo of the words of Jesus: "Sell all that you have and give to the poor . . . and follow me!" (cf. Mark 10:21 and pars.). These words were a real incentive to Christian religious life, while in their spirit they were also a model for every sincere Christian.

In the *Letter to Diognetus* we find another description of the Christian community that emphasizes some aspects of this ideal community: "Christians live in the flesh but not according to the flesh; they dwell on earth, but they live in heaven. . . .They love all and yet are persecuted by all. They are unknown and nevertheless they are condemned; they are executed and in this way brought into life. They are poor but they enrich many; they lack everything and yet they lack nothing. . . .They do good, but are punished as evildoers; when condemned to death, they rejoice as if they were destined to life. To put it briefly: what the soul is for the body, Christians are for the world." Do we not hear an echo here of many characteristics of monastic history?

St. Jerome traced the following genealogical tree of monasticism: "As for us, we regard as the leaders of our profession the Pauls, the Anthonys, the Julians, the Hilarions, and the Macariuses. If we turn to the authority of the Scriptures, our leader is Elijah, our guides are the sons of the prophets who dwelt in the fields and the wilderness and pitched their tents by the streams of the Jordan. Here, too, belong the sons of Rechab, who drank no wine or intoxicating liquor, dwelt in tents, and were praised by God through Jeremiah."

2. *First Attempts*

During the first decades of Christianity there were not lacking radical groups which thought that Christianity required an absolute surrender to the demands of the gospel. Thus the apocryphal Acts of the Apostles claimed that the reception of baptism obliged Christians not only to celibacy but also to the state of poor, itinerant ascetics. Thus were born the Sons of the Covenant, of whom Sts. Ephrem in Edessa and Aphraates in Persia would speak later on and who in some churches constituted the last link with premonastic asceticism in the long chain of radical following.

The inhospitable and harsh deserts were regarded as the most suitable dwellings and were sought out as the best places in which to face trials, temptation, and the pitiless struggle with the enemies of God and humanity. It was in the wilderness that Abraham, Jacob, Moses, and Elijah prepared themselves. It was to the wil-

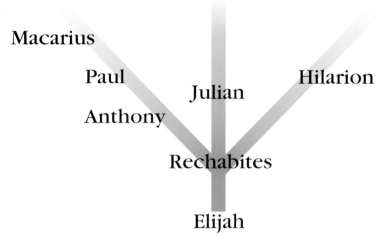

32. First genealogical tree of monasticism drawn by St. Jerome. From the Old Testament, with Elijah and the sons of Rechab, sprouted the first branches of Christian monasticism.

Macarius

Paul   Hilarion

Julian

Anthony

Rechabites

Elijah

32

derness that Jesus Christ withdrew, as the teacher and guide of all who from the very outset tried to follow in his steps. In short, the wilderness was the place of supreme experience, of the testing that led one beyond oneself to an encounter with angels or beasts and even with the devil or God. During one of the most decisive encounters of St. Anthony with legions of demons, Christ himself said that he was an onlooker and, ultimately, the crown and reward of a saint who overcame in the testing.

The first Christian communities included some heirs of the Jewish pietists who lived austerely (abstinence from wine and from some foods, such as meat) and as virgins. The following of Christ demanded of these Christians the abandonment of everything they

33

had and everyone they loved. Rufinus of Aquileia wrote: "There are two kinds of martyrdom: one of the soul, the other of the body; one outward, the other hidden. The outward martyrdom takes place when persons give their bodies to be slain out of love for God; the hidden one when for love of God they root out their vices."

Little by little, the early communities came to contain virgins, the continent, and ascetics, that is, individuals who rejected marriage, procreation, possessions, and the amenities of life. Moreover, in some early texts we find that a life dedicated to the personal experience of God is required if one is to try to reach perfection. The *Didache,* an important manual of moral instruction in the early Church, sets forth for the catechumens of that day a difficult ideal

33. The desert remains the model of the asceticism of the early Christians and of the first monastic forms, eremitical and communal. Shown here is a view of the desert of Paran in the Negev, Israel; in the background is the sacred mountain of Har Karkom which some archaeologists, such as Emmanuel Anati, have believed to be Mount Sinai.

expressed in the opposition between "the way of life" and "the way of death."

3. Once Again the Dilemma:
Are Only Some Christians "New Human Beings"?

From the very beginnings of Christianity, then, we see the invitation to a life of purity, generosity, and commitment that is focused exclusively on the Lord. In fact, however, it was not possible for all to accept this arduous call, with the result that we find the gradual rise of two ways of understanding Christian life and its demands. A ministry as prophet and ascetic will be the task of few, although we find these few in every age and every place. We know of the existence of early communities of this kind in Syria, and of movements of poor persons in other places.

Christian monasticism, then, is a phenomenon that is clearly anticipated in other religions and in Israel, while its fundamental points of reference are to be found in the Gospels and the first Christian community.

These similarities are grounded in the common nature of human beings, who have comparable religious experiences and who respond in very similar ways to deep aspirations and demanding ideals. But the most obvious predecessor of Christian monasticism is the Lord Jesus, who is the exemplar of close union with the Father and of commitment to his sisters and brothers; who was capable of completely disinterested activity, of generosity and abandonment; and who is the unsurpassable way to the encounter of each individual with God. Thus understood, the monastic is the prototype of the "new human being," who aspires to live completely in the image of the dead and risen Jesus Christ. A monk is as it were dead to the transitory things of the world and to earthly concerns and lives in the presence of the Holy Spirit and its gifts, the first of which is love, followed by joy, chastity, obedience, and all the other manifestations of generous surrender to God the Father.

34. Abraham prepares himself for his mission as ancestor of the people of Israel in the desert; his asceticism and his obedience made him willing to sacrifice his son Isaac, but he was stopped by God, who provided a ram in exchange for his son. This is what is represented in this scene of the sacrifice on a painting in the catacombs of the Latin Way in Rome.

35. Moses also prepares himself in the desert for his mission as deliverer of the people of Israel from Egypt. He is represented striking his staff against the rock so that water will gush forth during the Israelites' wanderings through the wilderness. The whole people had to pass through the experience of the desert. Painting from the catacombs of St. Callixtus in Rome.

36. In this painting from the catacombs of the Latin Way in Rome one sees Jesus at the well with the Samaritan woman. Jesus' offering of the living water which gives salvation is the model of every monastic vocation which does not preoccupy itself with the transitory things of this world in order to concentrate on that which leads to eternal life.

37. One of the early baptismal fonts which still remain is this one in the basilica on Mount Nebo in Jordan. Baptism is the point of departure for every Christian life and an indispensable reminder for every monastic decision.

3. ORIGEN, A MONK BEFORE MONASTICISM

1. An Apostolic Life Between Two Eras

Origen, the great Alexandrian theologian, was not a monk, but not a few historians have, with good reason, regarded him as the precursor of monasticism and even as father of the religious life.

In fact, we find in his life and writings the principal elements that have distinguished the monastic life from others. Evagrius of Pontus, Cassian, Sts. Basil, Gregory of Nazianzus, and Gregory of Nyssa, that is, some of the greatest witnesses in the history of monasticism, were truly his disciples in the spiritual life. To a special degree, the monks of Egypt were fervent practitioners of the spirituality of Origen, a fact that led to not a few conflicts in later centuries.

Origen was born around 185; his father suffered martyrdom during the persecution of Severus (202), and he himself underwent dreadful tortures during the persecution of Decius (249–51); as a result of these sufferings he died in 252–53. This personal and family history left its mark on his life and his religious spirit, leading him to confess his faith boldly and devote his life to the good of the Christian community. Throughout his days he led an authentic ascetical life; his fasts were frequent and prolonged, with the result that he gave a strong stimulus to the practice of fast and abstinence among Christians. He slept little, and always on the ground, and he esteemed and practiced poverty in the fullest sense of the term. On one occasion, he sold what he most valued, his books, in order to give the proceeds to the poor. According to him, ascetics lived the apostolic life, meaning by this a life of perfection.

2. "Moral" Apartness, Continual Prayer

When Origen emphasized in his teaching a withdrawal from the world, he made it clear that the separation was moral, not spatial: "We must go out of Egypt, we must abandon the world if we want to follow the Lord. I mean that we must abandon it not as a place but as a way of thinking, not by fleeing it on the road but by advancing in faith." Later on, however, when social conditions had changed, a spatial separation would become one of the essential characteristics of monasticism. Himself a man of continual prayer, his work *On Prayer* was the first commentary, in the proper sense, on Christian prayer generally and on the Our Father in particular. In Origen's understanding of it, prayer was essentially a participation in the life of God.

In this man's life and works we find some themes that are keys to his thought and to what would later on become monastic life: the importance assigned to continual prayer, which is necessarily connected with a virtuous life; the importance in the ascetical life of reading, primarily of the Scriptures, and of meditation; the necessary reciprocal relationship between prayer and pastoral activity; asceticism as a substitute for martyrdom; the dynamic concept of the spiritual life as a continual progress and a wonderful but difficult ascent to a personal encounter with God. The practice of these principles led in Origen himself to a profound

38. *Martyrdom is the model for early monasticism; it is detachment from the world, even at the cost of one's life, in order to proclaim the coming of Christ. The icon from the 17th century reproduced here represents the forty martyrs who froze to death on the lake of Sebaste in Turkey. They were Christian Roman legionaries who in 320 refused to abandon the faith as Emperor Licinius demanded and were therefore condemned to death by being left naked on a frozen lake. Christ received them into heaven, where their souls are represented by the crowns of martyrdom.*

39. *This map shows the cities associated with the names of the saints who became disciples of Origen's spiritual life and thus prepared for the monastic spirituality to come.*

40–41. *Paintings of two holy monks in the church of St. Mercurius, Old Cairo, Egypt.*

38

grasp of the mystery of the incarnation and of the transformation which the Logos accomplishes in the human soul. Piety, mysticism, and monasticism owe much to Origen's religious experience and written works.

At the heart of his theological works was his devotion to the study of the Bible and his effort to understand it and profit by it in attaining to an authentic faith and a true piety. The proper understanding of the sacred Scriptures was, in his view, "the supreme art and the supreme science." Daily reading of the Scriptures was the center of his own religious life and, due to his influence, would become the religious heart of monasticism.

Basing himself on the solid ground of his exegetical labors, Origen emphasized a spirituality of the Exodus. In his eyes, the exodus of the Jewish people provided a grand allegory of the ceaseless progress of the Christian from conversion to baptism, from baptism to death, and from death to heaven. "The Lord rejoices for your sake when he sees you living in the world in tents, when he sees that you have no intention or firm purpose of embracing the world, that you do not desire what is earthly or consider the shadow which this life is to be your permanent possession, but rather that you hasten, like one who is passing through, toward the true homeland of paradise from which you came, and that you say to yourself, 'I am a pilgrim, like all my ancestors before me.'"

Origen often compares preparation for baptism to the biblical story of the Exodus. He often takes the crossing of the wilderness

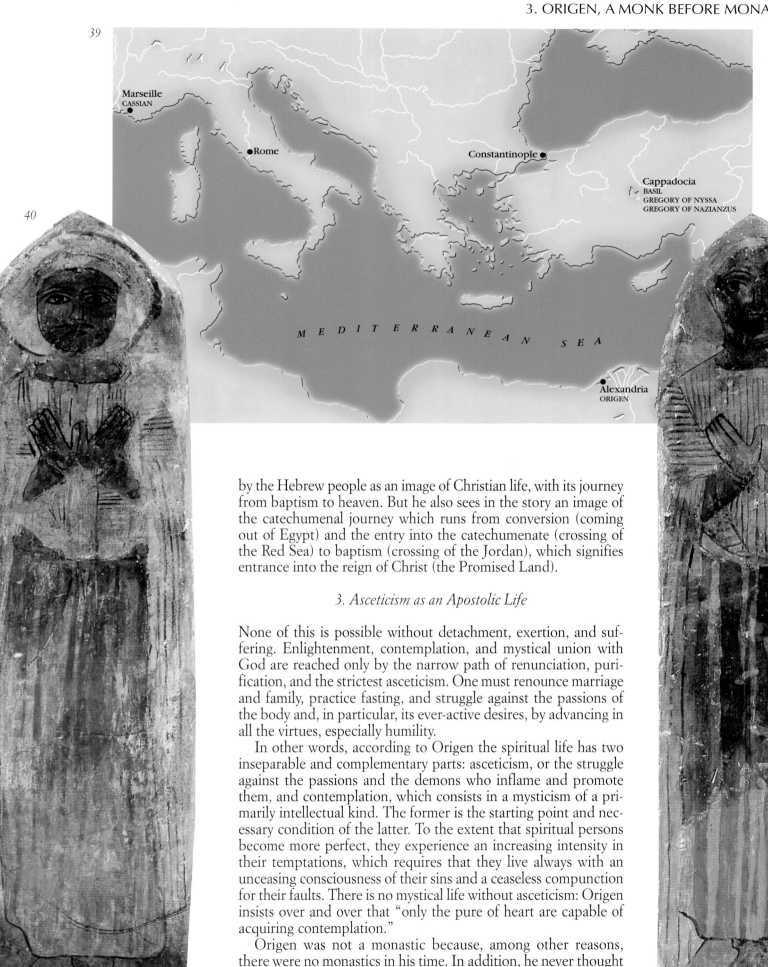

by the Hebrew people as an image of Christian life, with its journey from baptism to heaven. But he also sees in the story an image of the catechumenal journey which runs from conversion (coming out of Egypt) and the entry into the catechumenate (crossing of the Red Sea) to baptism (crossing of the Jordan), which signifies entrance into the reign of Christ (the Promised Land).

3. Asceticism as an Apostolic Life

None of this is possible without detachment, exertion, and suffering. Enlightenment, contemplation, and mystical union with God are reached only by the narrow path of renunciation, purification, and the strictest asceticism. One must renounce marriage and family, practice fasting, and struggle against the passions of the body and, in particular, its ever-active desires, by advancing in all the virtues, especially humility.

In other words, according to Origen the spiritual life has two inseparable and complementary parts: asceticism, or the struggle against the passions and the demons who inflame and promote them, and contemplation, which consists in a mysticism of a primarily intellectual kind. The former is the starting point and necessary condition of the latter. To the extent that spiritual persons become more perfect, they experience an increasing intensity in their temptations, which requires that they live always with an unceasing consciousness of their sins and a ceaseless compunction for their faults. There is no mystical life without asceticism: Origen insists over and over that "only the pure of heart are capable of acquiring contemplation."

Origen was not a monastic because, among other reasons, there were no monastics in his time. In addition, he never thought it necessary to abandon society in order to live a full Christian life. Nevertheless, in his writings and his practices we find the fundamental principles and the spirit that would, years later, shape the institution we know as monasticism.

4. PRE-MONASTIC ASCETICISM

The ascetic life and teachings of Jesus as presented in the New Testament found ready imitators in early Christianity. The total dedication proposed by the Gospels as the Christian ideal was interpreted by many as a call to the renunciation of ordinary social practices and expectations. These choices were individual, lived in the midst of Christian communities and within extended families that provided material support. The first disciples were mostly women. Some widows remained single, some young women did not marry. The role of widows and virgins in the life of the local churches became more evident, and their freedom for prayer, fasting, and works of service was a genuine contribution to the larger community of faith. Some men and women experimented with spiritual (celibate) marriage to create their own domestic arena for prayer and ascetic practice. A series of condemnations of this practice, labeled by bishops and synods as *syneisaktism* (literally, "insinuating" women into the home), suggests that it was attractive to many as a way to navigate competing demands of society and religious vocation.

It is difficult for us today to appreciate how complex the early Christian landscape was before time and experience established more fixed patterns for ascetic life. Gradually, however, asceticism gained a place in the larger church as a viable, respected, and even venerated way of Christian life. Some ascetics may have sought companionship in community, but the model was domestic rather than institutional. Asceticism within marriage was probably the most common form for men, as indeed for women, so that one could first fulfill social expectations. Married couples decided after the birth of children to refrain from intercourse, or to live more simply for the sake of almsgiving. This is the pattern suggested by the Egyptian catechist Clement of Alexandria (d. ca. 212), himself married and a father, but attracted to asceticism as a way to express the deepening of Christian faith with age and experience.

42. This paleo-Christian mosaic on a tomb wall in Tunisia represents a husband and wife. He, a scribe, is shown in a solemn pose; she in the attitude of an orant. The candle, the doves, the roosters, and the roses contribute to create an atmosphere full of religiosity. What will be the rule for monastics was an ideal for all other Christians.

43. Painting in a cupola in Bagawat, oasis of al-Kharga, Egypt. One sees the story of St. Thecla, with the saint exposed to the flames of martyrdom. Thecla, who according to legend was converted by St. Paul and miraculously snatched away from death to be baptized later in the same arena where she became a martyr, is the figure of the noble virgin. Thecla remains a prototypical figure for monasticism and because of that is often present in monastic art, such as that in the church at Bagawat.

44. Painting of a holy woman in the monastery of St. Moses the Ethiopian in Nebk, Syria.

42

43

In the Syriac-speaking churches of Mesopotamia, asceticism seems always to have been central. It may have been the case in those churches at one time that celibacy was required of those who sought total initiation through baptism. The unmarried, virginal, baptized were known as ihidaye, or "single ones," also known as *bnai* and *bnat qyama,* "sons and daughters of the covenant." The married who adopted a celibate way of life in preparation for baptism were the *qaddishe,* "holy ones." Later the term *ihidaye* was transferred to monastics, where it took on the additional note of "solitary."

This identification of asceticism with baptismal Christianity per se was unusual. For the most part, asceticism was a stance within the Church chosen by some as their form of Christian discipleship. As time passed, the practice of asceticism gained both adherents and a developing theology, often expressed in stories about holy women and men who chose a new kind of witness to Christ. Some

of these were apocryphal "Acts" of various apostles, such as the *Acts of Paul and Thecla,* about a young girl's resistance to marriage after hearing Paul preach, or the *Acts of Judas Thomas,* in which the apostle travels to India to teach an ascetic understanding of Christianity. Such writings complemented accounts of martyrdom, showing a way of Christian self-dedication that was freely chosen and available even during times of peace. In the 3rd century Origen (d. 254), brilliant exegete of Alexandria and then of Palestinian Caesarea, developed a theology in which asceticism, especially sexual, anticipated the angelic condition for which human beings were destined after the educative struggles of this life. His understanding was not new, but the thoroughness of his incorporation of asceticism into Christian spirituality was decisive. By the time of the 4th-century *Macarian Homilies,* some degree of ascetic practice was assumed for truly devout Christians in whatever circumstance of life.

44

EMPIRE
95-96
249-251
257-260
303-306
313 *Edict of Milan*

BRITAIN

London

LOWER
GERMANY

●Cologne

Seine

BELGIUM

Paris
250-253
LYON

●Strasburg

Rhine

●Augsburg

UPPER
GERMANY

●Vienna

RHAETIA   NORICUM

GAUL
177-179

AQUITAINE

Loire

Rhine

Bordeaux●

●Lyon

Drava

UPPER
AND
LOWER
PANNONIA

Milan●

Sava

Rhône

Toulouse
250-253

Arles

Po

155-156
162-165
184-186
234-237
306-310

ILLYRIA

●Belgrade

DALMATIA

UPPER
MOESIA

TARRACONENSIS

Duero

NARBONENSIS

Narbonne

Marseille

151-155
162-165
177-180
184-186
204-206
234-237
250-253
254

ITALY

SPAIN
306-310

Ebro

LUSITANIA

Tagus

Toledo

Tarragona

Valencia●

Cordova ●

BAETICA

Majorca

*Balearic
Islands*

Corsica

Sardinia

●Rome

61-62 *Imprisonment of Paul*
110 *martyrdom of St. Ignatius,
bishop of Antioch*
165 *martyrdom of Justin*
250-253

Taranto

MACEDONIA

Thessalonica

EPIRUS

GREECE
155-156
162-165
184-186
234-237
250-253
306-310

●Cartagena

Tangier●

M A U R E T A N I A

Cagliari

AFRICA

Sicily

Syracuse

●Carthage

180-182
198-207
213
250-253
254
257-260

ACHAEA

Athens

Crete

A   F   R   I   C   A

N U M I D I A

●Cyrene

CYRENAICA

45. Historical map of the principal persecutions endured by Christians.

45

Nonetheless, the ascetic option often required great courage, for it was a rejection of normal expectation, particularly for women. Ascetic teachings were frequently regarded as suspect by bishops and leading Christian laity. Asceticism was seen as a threat to home and family, to the importance of Christian marriage, to the goodness of God's gifts of food and drink. Individuals and groups emerged who certainly were elitist, and judgmental toward those who married and lived as part of conventional society. Movements such as the "Encratites" (meaning "abstainers"), led by the Syrian teacher Tatian (late 2nd century), were controversial and suspect. Similarly negative about human embodiment were the Manichaeans. They were not Christians, but their founder, Mani, evidently had a Christian background and they appealed to people like the young Augustine. Among the various kinds of Gnostic groups some were marked by an emphasis on asceticism, as were the prophetic and charismatic Montanists with whom the great

theologian Tertullian (d. ca. 225) became involved toward the end of his life. The orthodox and ecclesially-oriented ascetics had to prove the authenticity of their Christian witness.

The markers of asceticism developed over time. Women who elected lifelong virginity began to wear the veil as a sign of their dedication, thereby adopting the head-wear normally reserved to married women. The bishop did the veiling within the liturgy, and the virgins often had a special place to stand in church in recognition of their being a distinctive "order" in the community. Such a strong statement of ascetic freedom from conventional expectation was controversial. The great bishop Ambrose of Milan introduced the ceremony of veiling upon his accession and was bitterly opposed by leading citizens who found the custom subversive of parental control of daughters.

The move to independent, structured ascetic communities ("monasteries") was not a big step, though it required financial

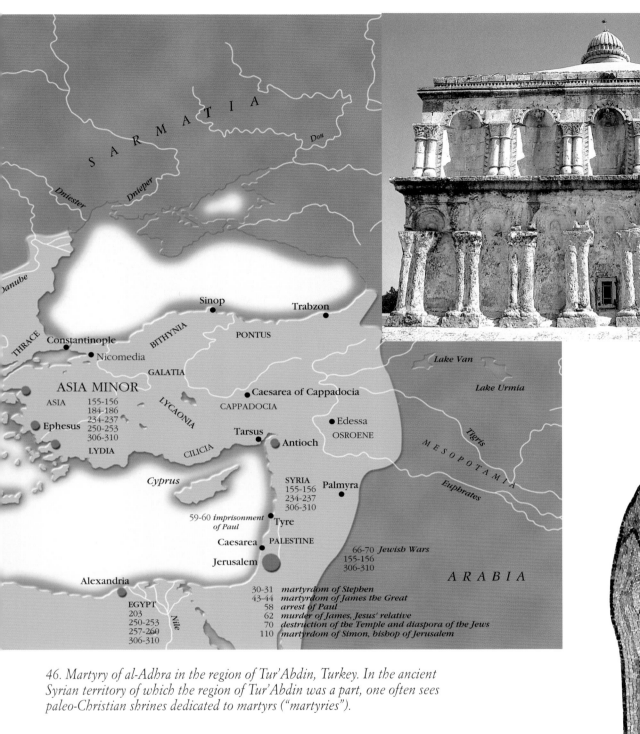

46

47

46. *Martyry of al-Adhra in the region of Tur'Abdin, Turkey. In the ancient Syrian territory of which the region of Tur'Abdin was a part, one often sees paleo-Christian shrines dedicated to martyrs ("martyries").*

support. Often wealthy widows provided the space and the funding for nascent ascetical communities. We know that in late 3rd-century Egypt Anthony the Great could place his sister in the care of "well-known and faithful virgins" who seemed to have some kind of community life.

The evidence for ascetic men is less plentiful. In the 2nd century Justin Martyr noted that "many men and women now in their sixties and seventies, who have been disciples of Christ since their childhood, have preserved their purity: and I am proud that I could point to such people in every nation" (*First Apology*, 15.6). There were the celibate "Sons of the Covenant" in the Syriac churches, and a special link between celibacy and priesthood became more common during the early Christian period. Male asceticism becomes prominent with the earliest monastic texts such as the Life of Anthony.

47. *This representation of St. Ambrose, in the paleo-Christian sanctuary of St. Victor in the Heaven of Gold, today incorporated into the basilica of St. Ambrose in Milan, is one of the oldest we have. Ambrose is to be regarded as a promoter of premonastic asceticism, especially with regard to women.*

1. THE MONASTICISM OF THE DESERT

ANSWERS AND CONSTANTS

The edict granting religious freedom in 313, followed by a rapid and massive conversion of the empire to Christianity, led inevitably to a widespread falloff in the religious spirit and to a relaxation of the ascetical and religious demands made on Christians. But, despite the seeming success and general acceptance of Christianity, many Christians continued to remember St. Paul's exhortations to his communities that they not misuse the things of this world but rather use the world as though they were not using it. And, according to the Lord, Christians should wait for the coming of the Spouse with lamps lit and loins girt—an attitude difficult to maintain in a world seemingly Christianized but too settled and mediocre.

In this perspective, we can better interpret and understand the lives of the desert Fathers as the instinctive reaction of a deep Christian sense against a treacherous reconciliation with the world, which the conversion of the empire might seem to justify. There is no doubt that the more or less conscious desire to prove in an eye-catching way the incompatibility between Christianity and the world and to demonstrate their rejection of the creeping worldliness of Christians was one of the reasons for the multiplication of those Christians who decided to abandon Roman society and live in solitude. In the view of the latter, monastics alone could live the Christian life fully; it could not be lived fully in a corrupt world. In short, they decided to protest, silently yet loudly, against the laxity of Christian life.

According to other historians, monastics were trying to continue, in a different way, the behavior of those Christians who had not hesitated to confront wild beasts in order to defend the integrity of the gospel. Many of the first Christians who lived in isolation and solitude (the anchorites) had fled to the mountains and the deserts because of persecution, but, once accustomed to this new way of life, they decided to remain in those places even after the Peace of Constantine; now, however, they were fleeing new dangers and attacks on the faith, attacks that were less bloody but no less insidious.

The essential realization produced by every experience of solitude, of the desert, of monastic life, is the realization of the existence of evil at the very heart of the world and in the depths of every human being, and of the consequent necessity of fighting against it "through prayer and fasting." Those women and men were conscious that they were fallen human beings and that the world had fallen with them. They and the world had been enslaved by the prince of darkness when they fell into error and sin. Sin made it impossible for them to find once again the way of return to God. Those individuals who fled to the desert in order to satisfy the demands of their faith gradually developed the idea that a Christian life lived in generous self-surrender was a confession of faith, a bloodless martyrdom. In 311 St. Anthony went to Alexandria during the persecution of Maximinus in order to bear witness to his faith. His biographer writes: "Once the persecution ceased in which blessed bishop Peter suffered martyrdom, Anthony withdrew again to his retreat, where, because of the daily effort of

48 & 50. Here two images are compared: that of the great paleochristian basilica of St. Lawrence in Milan, the fruit of a Christianity which had become the dominant religion of the empire, with the risk of losing the early spirit, and that of the monastery dedicated to St. Anthony near the Red Sea in the Egyptian desert where Coptic spirituality has sought to keep alive the asceticism of early Christianity.

48

conscience, he was a martyr every day and daily fought the battle of faith."

Some of these women and men wanted to do battle with the demon in its traditional dwelling place, that is, the desert. There are many testimonies from people who claimed that the desert, which was initially heavily populated by the forces of evil, had been conquered, inch by inch, by the holiness of life of so many people. We must not forget the experience of Jesus in the wilderness of Judah.

For others, this way of life became a substitute for martyrdom. In their view, monastic life, like martyrdom, could take the place of baptism; it forgave all sins and conformed a person completely to Christ. In other words, they were convinced that their special sacrament was their solitary life itself. As Cassian wrote with reference to cenobites, "The patience and strict fidelity with which they devoutly persevered in the profession which they had one day embraced and which never gave any satisfaction to their desires changed them continually into human beings crucified to the

49. *Amphitheater of the three Gauls in Lyon, where many Christian martyrs, among them St. Blandine, gave their ultimate testimony.*

51. *Map showing some places of early monasticism in Egypt, among them the monasteries dedicated to St. Anthony and St. Paul of Thebes.*

MEDITERRANEAN SEA

Alexandria

DELTA OF THE NILE

Cairo

SINAI

Nile

Madinat al-Fayyum

EASTERN DESERT

Monastery of St. Anthony

Monastery of St. Paul

RED SEA

world and into living martyrs." One of the ideas most often repeated at this period was that monastics were to be regarded as the people of the cross. As Basil of Caesarea puts it, "To practice and dispose oneself for dying out of love for Christ, to mortify one's members here on earth, to remain standing in battle array in order to meet all the dangers that can come upon one in the name of Christ, and not to become attached to the present life—this is what it means to carry the cross."

The majority followed this way in a free and generous response to the call of God. Arsenius pleaded with the Lord: "Lead me on the way of salvation." At once he received this answer: "Arsenius, flee other human beings and you will be safe." Following the example of Jesus, these individuals wanted to devote themselves to prayer and penance, while distancing themselves from the world and others in the solitude of the desert. Monks were regarded as the true women and men of God, as charismatics able to heal the sick, console the afflicted, and engender children in the spiritual life.

53. Icon painted in 1723, from Trabzon in Turkey. It shows the monk Zosima who brought communion to St. Mary the Egyptian, considered to be the precursor of women's monasticism. Private collection, Paris.

52

52. Through the centuries Coptic art has kept the iconography of the founders of Egyptian monasticism. In this panel from the 18th century, we see a splendid image of St. Paul of Thebes, considered to be the initiator of Egyptian anchoritism along with St. Anthony the abbot. Museum of Coptic Art in Old Cairo. Anchoritism characterizes the monastic way of life, the "separation" from secular life, and, therefore, the retreat into solitude in the desert.

53

At first sight, the goal of those lives seems purely individual and personal, reducible to the desire to purify and sanctify themselves; it was to this end that they seemed to order all their actions. Nevertheless, from the very outset, their horizon and field of action were much broader, and their ambition extended to the entire field that is the Church. In the words of Eusebius of Caesarea, those who separated themselves from the world and devoted themselves to the exclusive service of God, acted "as representatives of the entire human race."

To the people of that world, the lives of those individuals, despite their remoteness and marginalization, were like "lamps that gave light to all the world." Their way of life and their radical rejection of the world confirmed the markedly eschatological character of their example. To the Christians of their time they became "incarnations of the very eternity" toward which they were journeying and to which they aspired. Their striking rejection of earthly values such as marriage, riches, honors, and comforts might indeed have had its origin in heresies or in radical interpretations that were not in accord with the authentic spirit of the gospel. Generally, however, it represented much more the presence of the Spirit in the midst of humanity and the purifying and saving nearness of what is definitive.

55

54. *Cave of St. Anthony behind the monastery near the Red Sea in Egypt. Tradition recognizes it as the place of the saint's hermitage. The devil, the tempter, is taken from a Spanish miniature in a commentary on the book of Revelation (11th century).*

55. *Image of St. Anthony which is the counterpart of the image of St. Paul of Thebes (fig. 52). On the painted panel, Anthony has the traditional attributes of his iconography: the monastic habit, the beard, and the staff serving as a support. Museum of Old Cairo.*

54

2. COPTIC HERMITS

56. Aerial view of some remains of hermitages at Qusur al-Izayla, part of the celebrated anchoritic complex called Kellia (the Cells), Egypt.

56

In Egypt, the desert was within the reach of all; it was easy to withdraw and hide oneself on the edge of villages or among the ancient tombs that could serve as rudimentary living quarters and where a nearby river or a spring readily ensured a supply of water. Such was the course taken by the first hermits, those Christians who decided to separate themselves from other people and to live alone in order better to come in contact with God and devote their lives to him without limitations. Later on, they went further apart and penetrated into the depths of the desert. Monastic life began in Nitria in the first decades of the 4th century and spread rapidly throughout Egypt, Syria, Palestine, and Asia Minor.

The recruits usually came from the lower classes of Coptic society. The majority of them were peasants with little education and often unable either to read or to write. This explains the distrust they often showed toward theological speculation. They were laypersons and had no desire to receive sacred orders, because this ordinarily meant leaving their solitude and devoting themselves to pastoral work.

Very few of them lived in complete solitude, like the recluses who shut themselves up in caves or inaccessible refuges, often for decades, while public charity provided them with absolutely necessary provisions, passing these through a hole in the wall. The majority lived independently, but some sought out others. In a community that was in fact like a cooperative of solitaries, the

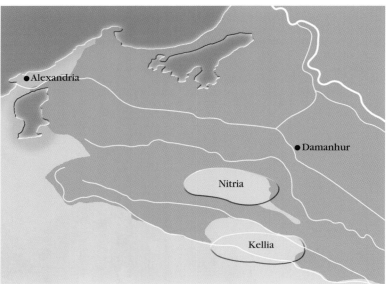

57

57. The map shows the two great early anchoritic sites, Nitria and Kellia, located west of the Nile and south of Alexandria. It is here that we see the beginnings of the Coptic monastic tradition.

58. *Detail of a hermitage at Qusur al-Izayla, part of Kellia.
One can clearly see the niches used by the hermits.*

58

59. *A niche painted with a cross. Coptic eremitical art
is rich in these colored, quasi-aniconic crosses.*

60. *Typology of the different niches.*

59

61

60

61. *Isometric reconstruction of a hermitage in Kellia.*

62. The present-day walls surrounding the monastery of al-Baramus in Wadi al-Natrun. It was the first place to which St. Macarius retired.

hermits did not have to worry about sustenance or how they would receive the sacraments, with the result that they had a total personal freedom.

At the center of a colony there was a church, served by one or more priests who were also hermits. They gathered on Saturdays and Sundays to celebrate the Eucharist and take communion under both species. Some colonies had guest houses for the often very numerous outsiders who came even from distant Christian communities in order that one of the Fathers or Mothers might solve their problems or give them directives for their lives. Hospitality was, from the very outset, a monastic virtue. The hermit Apollo taught: "It is necessary to greet with respect those who visit us, because it is not they whom you are greeting but God. As the scripture says, when you see your sister or brother, you see the Lord your God." It was not always easy to practice this hospitality, because the many visitors who came from Europe and the East interrupted the necessary solitude and recollection of the monastics and caused an unrest that compelled many solitaries to flee to more hidden places.

Those called to solitude looked for a model, some elder famous for her or his austerity and holiness in order that she or he might teach them how to conduct themselves in a hermitage, how to fight against the frequent temptations of the devil, how to make progress in the virtues. It was this spiritual model who passed on to the disciples the maxims and standards of monasticism and trained and directed them that they might better advance in the ascetical life they had undertaken. It was in this way that colonies of hermits arose and became established, hermits who were the more numer-

ous, the more extraordinary and charismatic the teacher was. Some famous colonies were those that grew up around Ammon and Macarius. It was precisely because of these disciples and admirers that these teachers of the spiritual life often felt the need of constantly finding a better hiding place; but then the disciples came in even greater numbers to their new places of residence.

In the hermit's life prayer had a privileged place. St. Epiphanius said, "True monastics must keep prayer and psalmody in their hearts without ceasing." Prayer was either individual or communal, the latter in the nocturnal offices and during the gatherings on the weekend; in either case, it was always the core of the hermit's life. We know, and the hermits knew, that there is in fact only one prayer, which is always personal, a personal contact with the Lord, expressed either in the secret place of the heart and in the chamber or together with the sisters or brothers. All aspired to a constant, intimate, and loving relationship with God, for they knew what this meant for their spiritual life. Evagrius of Pontus taught his disciples that "to keep the remembrance of God alive in the soul one must be free of the vices and persevere in reading, in one's occupation, and in ceaseless prayers night and day."

In reality, this life was made up of continual prayer, labor, and the reading of sacred Scripture. Along with prayer, manual work filled the day of the Egyptian hermit. These individuals were always trying to bring prayer and work into harmony, and to this end they looked for kinds of work that were compatible with prayer: the weaving of baskets, ropes, and mats out of the reeds and palm leaves that were readily available in the vicinity. The products were sold in the villages, and the hermits could live on

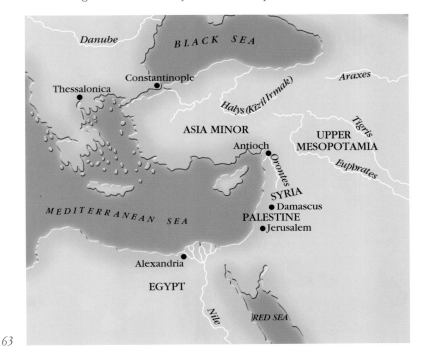

63. *Egypt, Palestine, Syria, upper Mesopotamia, and Asia Minor were the regions in which early monasticism spread.*

63

the payment for the work. Some hermits copied manuscripts, an activity at which the uneducated sometimes looked askance. Others helped the peasants during the harvests in exchange for the grain they needed for their subsistence and for the alms they would give generously to the poor.

They ate once a day and often took nothing for several days in a row. Their menu consisted of bread, salt, and water (this was the permanent diet of, for example, St. Anthony) or only of fruit or some green vegetables. Generally speaking, they abstained from all cooked dishes. While they ate separately, they usually ate at the same time: at three in the afternoon or at sundown. Only on Saturdays and Sundays did they partake, as a community, of an agape after the Eucharist. This was an exceptional meal, and in his old age Anthony would add to his ration of food some olives, some dry green vegetables, and some oil.

On those same days, there were the so-called "collations," that is, conferences on spiritual subjects, discussions of theological subjects, or explanations of some concrete topic, these being conducted by one of the more venerated Fathers. There was thus a real, ongoing formation that was not simply theoretical but also, and above all, based on life and experience.

The best known, most venerated, and most followed of the Coptic hermits was undoubtedly Anthony, who took it as his way of life to give as much time as possible to the soul and only the necessary minimum to the body. His life was written by St. Athanasius, the great patriarch of Alexandria, and became a real manual of life for those who felt the call of the desert and of solitude.

64

64. *St. Athanasius, detail from a wall painting in the monastery of St. Moses the Egyptian in Nebk, Syria. Athanasius, one of the Fathers of the Church, spread the knowledge of monasticism in the West by writing the biography of St. Anthony.*

3. THE CENOBITES

65. Present-day view of the monastery of St. Gabriel in the region of al-Fayyum, Egypt. Cenobitical monasticism involves the creation of complex monasteries, true and distinct settlements with different functions, under the authority of a superior.

65

There has been a great deal of debate over which came first: hermits or cenobites. In fact, there seem to be precedents and data for defending both positions.

In the desert, Coptic hermits appear to have been succeeded by cenobitic hermits. This was due to an effort to regulate anarchy among hermits by bringing the latter together in monasteries where they would live a common life under the authority of a superior. Thus cenobitic life came into existence at almost the same time in various places, although up to the present day the information we have is almost exclusively about the monastery established under the leadership of Pachomius, around 323, at Tabennisi in upper Egypt.

With Pachomius we no longer see a simple grouping of ascetics around a charismatic figure, but rather a community of brothers: "If someone comes to the gate of the monastery with a desire to renounce the world and become one of the brothers . . . let him be closely joined to the brothers." This union was, moreover, not something purely spiritual but extended to practical everyday life. For this reason Pachomius is regarded as founder and father of Christian cenobitic monasticism.

Having taken the Scriptures as his guide and teacher of life, Pachomius expected that the community would live as did the first community in Jerusalem: "being of one heart and one soul." The brothers helped one another as did Christ, who made himself the servant of all. "The love of God," he said, "consists of each one suffering for others." "When Pachomius saw brothers gathering around him, he established the following rule: 'Each brother must be self-sufficient in material necessities, both for his own food and for satisfying outsiders to whom he gives hospitality, since they will eat together.' The monks gave their earnings to Pachomius that he

66. Bulgarian icon representing St. Pachomius, regarded as the founder of cenobitism.

might manage them; this they did freely and spontaneously so he might take care of all their needs, for they regarded him as a reliable man; after God, he was their father."

Later on, all the activities of cenobitic life came to be regulated in minute detail: occupations, work, clothing, diet. A complete life in common excluded an autonomy for the members, who were to live in docile obedience to the superior and without any private property or personal use of possessions and things, which in this new form of life belonged to the entire community. A monastic could not give or lend or receive or destroy or change anything. This meant the disappearance of the autonomy and independence that had been the mark of hermits. The cenobitic monastery thus became an organized body in which each member had a particular, concrete role governed by the needs of the community, even though this role might also differ according to each one's gift.

The disciples of Pachomius preserved the memory of his words, "In our generation in Egypt I see three persons who are moved by God to the benefit of all who hear them: Bishop Athanasius, a champion unto death for the Christian faith; the holy abbot Anthony, a perfect model of the eremitical life; and this community which is the model for all who desire to unite their souls in the Lord in order to care for them until they attain to perfection."

There was no novitiate and no vows except for the promise to observe all the rules of the monastery and to obey all superiors. Pachomius founded several monasteries, but all depended on the same superior in every respect; in other words, there was a single large monastery with several residences. In all these residences the brothers helped and served one another. This ideal of service was the basis of Pachomian cenobitic life.

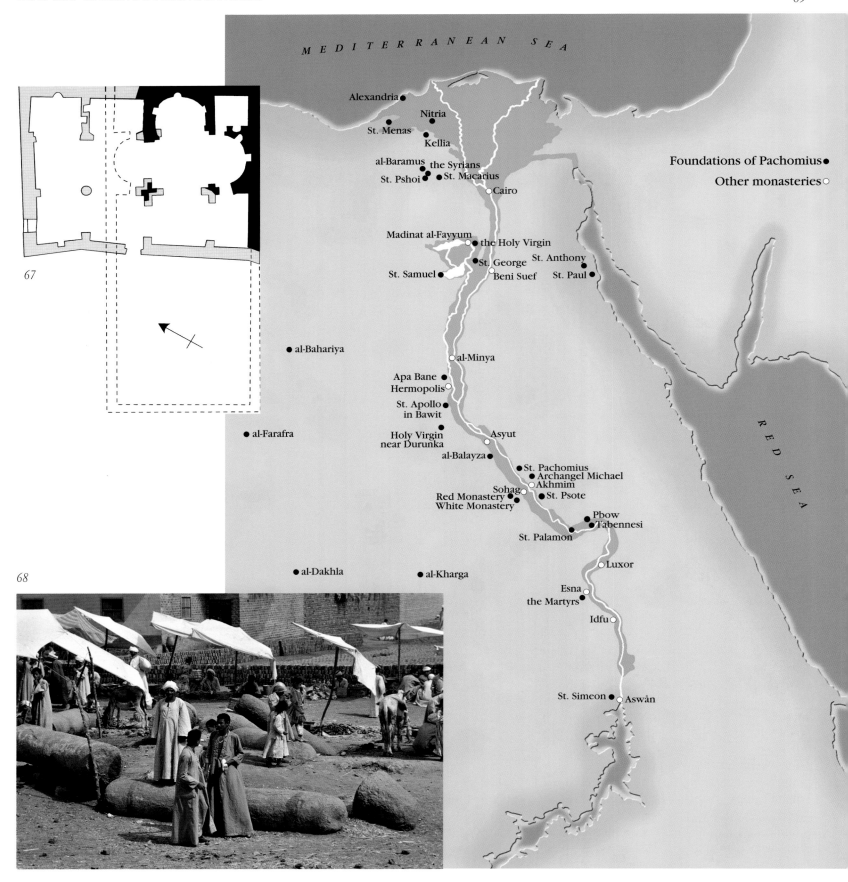

67

68

Foundations of Pachomius ●
Other monasteries ○

67. *Plan of the church of the monastery of St. Pachomius near Akhmin, Egypt. In black, the original structure dating from the 6th century. In grey, the later structure. The hatching indicates the parts of the original structure which have disappeared.*

68. *Remains of the columns of the basilica of the monastery of Pbow in Egypt; it was one of the principal Pachomian foundations.*

69. *Map of the expansion of Coptic monasticism.*

70

The general layout of the monastery recalled the military camps which Pachomius had known in his days as a soldier. It was surrounded by a wall and contained a vestibule, a guest house, a building for liturgical assemblies, a refectory with a kitchen, a bakery, a hospital, and a series of houses in each of which from twenty to fifty monks lived.

It seems, at least, that the sacrifices and austerities practiced in earlier times were moderated. In fact, the manner of life was adapted to a large community that was necessarily made up of people of differing temperaments who might be more or less inclined to austerities, more or less hard on themselves. A minimum was imposed and a good deal of room was left for individual promptings, provided always that these did not detract from community life. One of the rules called for "a hood made of tanned goat skin, and nothing was to be eaten except when this was worn," the purpose being to avoid envious imitation. All those admitted to the monastery had to learn to read and write and also to commit to memory many bits of sacred scripture.

Pachomius had begun his own life as a hermit under the direction of the famous Palamon, a man to whom were attributed such astonishing acts as melting with his tears a brick on which he knelt to pray. In contrast, Pachomius brought a degree of humanism to a way of life that was often excessively radical; at the same time, he was able to move beyond some of the limitations of the excessively autonomous way of life of hermits and to impose the not always easily borne requirements of a common life. Some of his counsels display a profound Christian wisdom that is of universal validity; for example, his exhortation to the monks that they rid themselves of the dangerous tendency to meddle in the business of their brothers and that, instead, they concern themselves much more with the direction in which their own souls were moving. The mutual respect of the monks for one another, this being an external manifestation of love, had to be one of the foundations of concord within the monastery; it was the golden rule of community life.

During Pachomius' life, monasteries of women that followed his rule also arose and were directed by monks whom he and his successors appointed. In fact, Pachomius established eight monasteries, two of them for women. We do not have much information on the subject, but we do know that there were other monasteries governed according to other traditions, although, generally speaking, they were influenced in some degree by the standards which Pachomius established.

In Palestine, St. Hilarion founded the first community in 329. Then, due partly to the religious attractiveness and importance of the Holy Land, monasteries gradually multiplied, especially in places more closely connected with the life of Jesus.

The transformation of the heroic monasticism of the desert into an urban monasticism under rule changed it from a means into a method, from a sometimes eccentric but always extraordinary and spontaneous way of life into a form of life that was austere but acceptable and imitable and marked in good measure by the desire of the members to help and support one another.

4. THE GREAT SYRIAN TRADITION

71

71. *Syriac art is particularly linked with the figure of St. Ephrem. In this miniature from the 12th century, we have a splendid although damaged image of this father of Syrian anchoritism. Library of the Syrian Orthodox Patriarchate in Damascus.*

72

72. *On the left, we see St. Simeon the Stylite, the most renowned among the monks devoted to this type of ascesis on a pillar, and on the right, St. Simeon of the Admirable Mountain, also a stylite. The icon shows how a world of pilgrims, devout and in need, came to the foot of the columns. Monastery of Our Lady of Balamand, Lebanon.*

1. The Call for a Demanding Way of Life

Once the first Christian communities had been established in the provinces of Syria, Phoenicia, Mesopotamia, and Edessa, a type of Christianity developed that was very demanding; it called for a sometimes extremely rigorous manner of life, and it accepted virginity and poverty as characteristic attitudes and states of life.

Some historians point to the influence of Persia and India on the teaching and practices of Syrian monasticism, which was marked by an extreme individualism. Nor may we forget the possible influence of the sect known as the Essenes, although we have hardly any evidence to confirm such an influence. These influences would explain the extremely and often extravagantly radical character of not a few rigorist practices found in this area. St. Gregory of Nazianzus writes with astonishment of the manner

of life of the Syrian monks: they used to fast for twenty days in a row, wore iron shackles, slept on the bare ground, and remained standing motionless in prayer as it rained or snowed and they were lashed by the wind. The "standers," for example, made it their rule to remain always on their feet, without speaking or raising their eyes, without lying down to sleep. Some of the Syrian monks lived like the beasts of the fields, eating grass like them and perching on rocks or in trees like birds. The most bewildering of the hermits who populated the solitudes of Syria were the "madmen," madmen for Christ, who pretended to be mentally deficient. All of these varied types had an insatiable thirst for mortifications. At the same time, they prayed unceasingly and meditated on the Scriptures.

Theodoret of Cyrrhus says of the hermits who populated the deserts and mountains of these regions in the second half of the

73. *Among the ruins of the paleochristian church of Qalat Siman (dedicated to St. Simeon) in Syria is the base of the pillar on which the stylite lived.*

4th century, "They embrace the solitary life, endeavor never to speak except of God, and do not allow themselves the least bit of human comfort." Some dwelt in huts, others in grottoes and caves. Not a few dispensed with any kind of housing: they lived in the open air without any protection from the elements, sometimes in freezing cold, at other times in broiling sun; some remained standing, others surrounded themselves with a wall because they did not want to communicate with anyone; others sought refuge in the tops of trees; still others, without any protection, remained exposed to the gaze of all. St. John Chrysostom was famous for other reasons, but we ought not forget that he began his religious life as a hermit near Antioch. In any case, we are here far removed from other monastic traditions. Recall the teaching of the well-known hermit Poemen, "We are told to kill not our bodies but our passions." The Syrian tradition, however, agreed rather with the reply of Dorotheus to Palladius, "My body is killing me, so I kill my body."

2. St. Ephrem and the Stylites

St. Ephrem (306–371) was one of the best known Syrian hermits, an author of important books, and a defender of the ascetical and eremitical life, which he compared to a martyrdom. He preached an unqualified eremitism, one devoted to ceaseless prayer and the most demanding austerity. He stressed the importance of study, which, in his view, promoted purity of heart.

The manner of life of the stylites was the most astonishing way of living out an absolute renunciation. There were many of these men in Syria and Mesopotamia. They dwelt on the top of a pillar and there remained impassive, not stirring for years on end so that,

74

75

74–75. *Cross and resurrection are the themes of Syrian art; there are no crosses without the resurrection. The evangelistary of Rabbula, dating from 586, unites on the same page Christ on the cross and Christ risen. Laurentian Library of Florence. There is a different depiction in Syriac codex 344: the glorious cross has at its center, surrounded by angels, Christ risen and rendering judgment. Bibliothèque Nationale, Paris.*

76. *Syria and Mesopotamia at the time of the monastic expansion.*

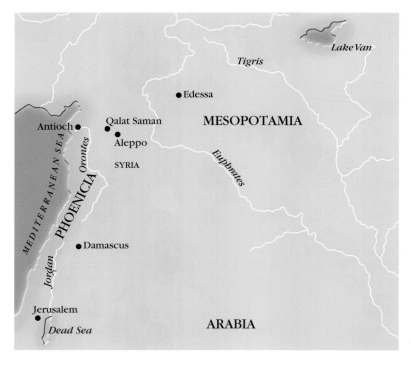

76

though living in this world, they remained distant from it, being halfway between heaven and earth. Simeon Stylites lived in this way for over forty years. "The famous Simeon," Theodoret of Cyrrhus writes, "a great wonder within the inhabited world, is known to all the subjects of the Roman empire; but he is no less famous among the Persians, Indians, and Ethiopians. His fame has spread even to the Scythian nomads." Simeon remained standing on top of his pillar day and night, summer and winter. When he prayed, he constantly made deep bows. He gave good advice to those who remained at the foot of the pillar, preached to them twice a day, combated pagans and heretics, and stirred up the religious fervor of religious and civil authorities.

Simeon began his experience of religious life in a monastery, but after ten years he was dismissed because his fellow monks could not endure comparing their manner of life with the extreme penances of Simeon. This dismissal drove him to live alone and to choose a pillar as the extreme of solitude and a way of escaping the demonstrations of veneration from his admirers.

The people regarded him as a saint; they came in throngs from all parts of the empire and looked on him as a messenger sent by God for the consolation of the Christian people. The astonishing spread of stylitism was due in good measure to the influence of St. Simeon the Great.

Recluses, who lived in windowless houses, tombs, or towers and were often immured, constituted another category of Syrian hermits, who often lived immured. The furniture of these indivi-

77. *Wall painting in the monastery of St. Moses the Ethiopian in Nebk, Syria. In this detail of the Last Judgment, one sees St. Peter opening the door of paradise to male and female monastics.*

duals who scorned perishable things was marked by an evangelical simplicity: "Voluntary poverty," Evagrius Scholasticus wrote, "consists in possessing nothing more than a cloak, a tunic, a Bible, and a cell."

3. Community Life and Individual Cross

In this individualistic and abnormal environment it was very difficult to establish the cenobitic life, which seems in its beginnings to have consisted chiefly of congregations of hermits around a venerated holy elder. By the end of the 4th century community life was becoming the norm, but not without inner tensions, since stability and the economic progress of the monasteries seemed to mean a movement away from the idea of poverty and unqualified asceticism found among the hermits. For this reason, various monasteries gradually established restrictions meant to prevent laxity. One difficulty in the way of establishing Syrian monasteries was the lack of authentic monastic rules and norms for life in common. We do have the examples and ways of life of the more famous abbots and monks, which served as models and points of reference, but there was no strict obligation to follow them.

That situation was, of course, of no help in regulating the life of communities that were becoming increasingly large and complex. In fact, Syrian monasteries were basically schools for solitaries and for training those who would become great ascetics; or else they were residences for recluses, in which real monks were served by second-class monks; some devoted themselves to prayer and asceticism, others worked to ensure the proper running of the monastery. Teacher and disciples gathered in the evening for common prayer and for a meal. The remainder of the time they spent in solitary meditation, with no rule binding them except the example and advice of the teacher.

Despite the numerous oddities of these monks there is no doubt that they were great Christians whose inspiration was the theology of the cross, a death to self in order to be more open to God, with whom they sought a constant communion. In their view, the great enemy was the body, and they therefore sought, constantly and in imaginative ways, to reduce it to nothingness. Christ crucified was always their great model.

5. ASIA MINOR, CAPPADOCIA

According to St. Jerome, it was St. Hilarion, a disciple of St. Anthony, who brought the Egyptian monastic model to the Syro-Palestinian area. In fact, the presence of monasticism in Asia Minor is well documented during the period following upon the Council of Nicea (325). This period saw the spread of the movement begun by Eustathius of Sebaste who took over the motifs of a kind of radicalism that had much in common with Gnostic ideology; this radicalism reached so far as to condemn marriage, Masses celebrated by married priests, and every form of wealth. The Council of Grange (340) directly attacked this radicalism in canons condemning an extremism that favored sexual continence and an extreme pauperism, attitudes that had managed to attract a good number of ascetics. In his youth Basil himself maintained good relations with Eustathius, until the two men disagreed for doctrinal reasons.

Cappadocia was evangelized at a very early period; it may be that Paul himself proclaimed the gospel there. The country produced many martyrs and sent out some missionaries who played a part in the conversion of Armenia.

Sts. Basil, Gregory of Nazianzus, and Gregory of Nyssa were from this area and are therefore known as "the Cappadocians." Religious life developed to an exceptional degree in the area, mainly due to the impulse given by Basil, who began to codify the principles of asceticism.

Basil was born in Caesarea of Cappadocia and chose monastic life after solid studies in rhetoric at the best schools of the age. He visited a variety of ascetical experiments in various areas of the East before withdrawing to live in solitude not far from his native place, on one of his own properties (357/58). There he also began an experiment in community life with some of his friends, among them Gregory of Nazianzus; their fundamental focus was on prayer and study.

During these years he deepened his knowledge of the mysticism of Origen; one result was an anthology of passages from Origen to which Basil gave the name *Philocalia*. This work promoted an exceptional spread of the Alexandrian theologian's ideas in monastic circles.

Basil made his visit to the Egyptian monasteries shortly before the death of Anthony (356). The experience gained on these journeys made him realize the necessity of eliminating the disadvantages of the monastic anarchism so common in many places and of incorporating monasteries into the organization of the Church itself. He came to the conclusion that a monastic life led in a community was better than the life of the hermit: "Love does not seek itself; but the solitary life far removed from all other people has but a single goal, to serve the purposes of the individual in question. Yet this is clearly contrary to the law of love. . . . We have been called and have but the one hope of our calling; we are a single body and members of one another."

Due to Basil, cenobitic life underwent an unprecedented organizational growth in which monasticism was freed from its initial eremitical stamp. Basil rejected the majority view that reduced a monastery to a gathering of solitaries, and developed instead the

78

78. St. Basil the Great in an icon from the 18th century painted by John of Jerusalem. Church of St. Nicholas, Tripoli, Lebanon.

sense of community. In order to overcome individualism, the Rule of Basil emphasized the prerogatives of the superior, into whose hands monastics surrendered their freedom, practicing obedience and following the inspiration of the Spirit. The superior was responsible for the common discipline which had its spiritual foundations in prayer, work, service to the Church, and charitable activity (hospitals, orphanages, schools for children, the feeding of the poor, and so on).

In this perspective, which aimed at a complete communion through daily activity, there was no room for personal initiatives: all were to follow the same pattern of fasts, penances, and ascetical disciplines.

Basil completed his legislation with a penetrating spiritual theology in which we glimpse the practice of the evangelical counsels (chastity, poverty, obedience) as the foundational ideal of monastic reality. In his Rules we also find a strong emphasis on the need of approaching and helping the poor, the needy, and the sick, in whom the monk is always to see Christ.

79. St. Gregory of Nyssa in a medieval mosaic in the apse of the great cathedral Santa Sophia, Kiev, Ukraine.

80. St. Gregory of Nazianzus, also called St. Gregory the Theologian.
This icon is the counterpart of that of St. Basil (fig. 78) and is the work of the same artist and placed in the same medieval church.

80

79

Basil's brother, Gregory of Nyssa, reflected deeply on the first of the three counsels, which is the point of departure on the journey toward the attainment of Christian perfection. He did so in his work *On Virginity (De virginitate),* which is an authentic masterpiece and an authentic endorsement of Basil's Rules. In Gregory's view, virginity is "a door leading to a very holy life." Its power is such that "it persuades God to share the life of human beings, gives wings to the human desire to rise up to things heavenly, and is a bond of union between human nature and God, bringing these two extremes, so disparate in their nature, into harmony." Gregory views the entire divine plan, the entire chain that brings salvation, in the light of virginity. That chain extends from the three Persons of the Trinity and the angelic powers of heaven to humanity as its final link. He calls Christ "the archetypal virgin."

Gregory of Nazianzus was the third of the Cappadocians. He was born in 329 and met Basil at the university of Athens; it was a friendship that stamped his entire life. He spent only a short time as a monk with Basil, but this allowed him to collaborate in the redaction of Basil's monastic Rules. He became the bishop of a

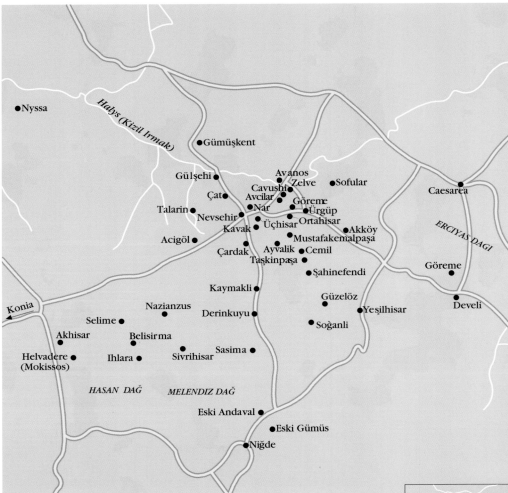

81

83

82

small diocese and there energetically defended the complete humanity of Christ and the absolute equality of the three Persons of the Trinity. His entire life was a continual flight from the world in order to enter anew into himself; his desire for withdrawal and solitude never left him.

The contribution of the Cappadocian Fathers to the advance of theology, the solution of the problem of "Hellenism and Christianity," the restoration of peace in the Church, and the expansion of monasticism would have a lasting influence in the Church.

The legislation of Basil had a great influence even on the monastic traditions of the West. Rufinus of Aquileia translated his Rules before the end of the 4th century; later on, John Cassian and

81. Small map of Cappadocia and map of the Middle East showing Cappadocia surrounding Caesarea in the center of Asia Minor (today part of Turkey). On the small map of Cappadocia, along with the various monastic centers we also find the native places of the great Cappadocian Fathers, Caesarea, Nazianzus and Nyssa.

82. View of one of the valleys with the hermitages and cenobitic monasteries inhabited throughout the centuries in Cappadocia.

83. Presentation of the Lord in the Temple, a wall painting from a church carved from the rock; it shows the damage wrought by pagans while trying to remove the "force" from the image.

84

86

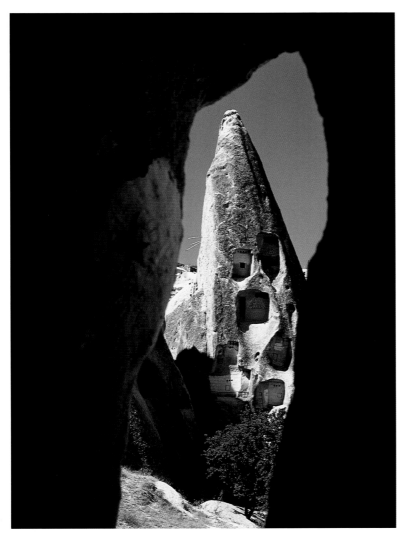

85

84–86. Interior of a monastic church with a basilical plan, excavated from the rock, and its exterior together with the entrances of cells along the rocky walls. The wall paintings tend to be aniconic.

Benedict were familiar with them. Gregory of Tours also mentions them, and they appeared once again in the 9th century in the great *Concordia Regularum* of Benedict of Aniane.

Among the successors of the Cappadocians we should remember Nilus of Ancyra (d. 430), whose teaching on asceticism had an enormous impact on the monasteries of Asia Minor. In his works we find a defense of poverty and work in response to some unbalanced theories that saw an opposition between work and prayer.

1. Two Tireless Propagandists

STS. CASSIAN AND JEROME

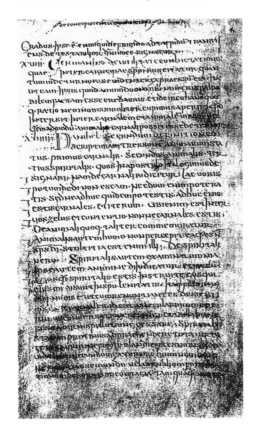

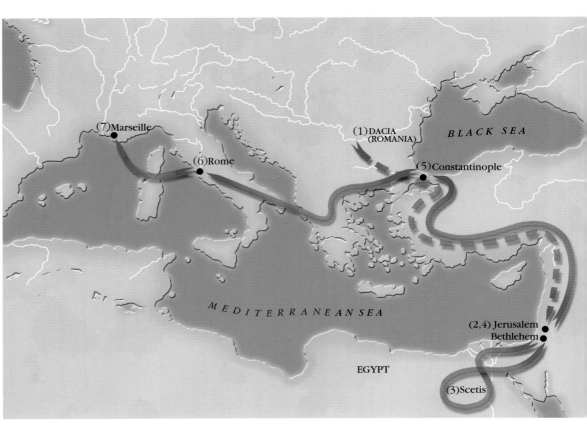

87

88

1. From Africa to Rome

Western monasticism was born and spread first in Africa, but a few decades later it reached Rome. When St. Athanasius, the great patriarch of Alexandria, visited Rome and Trier, he spoke of the value of monastics to Christianity. Later on, his *Life of St. Anthony* was much read and its hero taken as a model. Not a few monastics visited the tombs of Sts. Peter and Paul and became enthusiastic about their example and their words. Nevertheless, European monasticism owes its beginnings, fundamentally, to two individuals whose outlook was very different but whose enthusiasm was equal: Cassian and Jerome.

In not a few places communities were coming into existence that lived the cenobitic life in one or other fashion, but without rules or established common customs. The persons in these communities were Christians who in this way lived out the teachings and practices of the Church and especially its liturgy. In fact, some of these monasteries were founded alongside cathedrals or principal churches in order to take care of and maintain their liturgical rites.

Popular opinion regarding monastics gradually changed: from being misunderstood and looked down on they came to be admired and welcomed. In this change, the example of respected persons such as Melania the Elder or Rufinus, the reading of the life of St. Martin by Sulpicius Severus, and, above all, the writings of Cassian, all played an influential role.

Monasteries proliferated in Italy, as did the examples given by outstanding monastics. Some bishops, St. Ambrose for example, founded urban monasteries that collaborated effectively with him in his pastoral labors. Others, such as Sts. Paulinus of Nola and

87. Page from a codex going back to the 8th century which contains the fourth conference of Cassian. Apostolic Vatican Library (Vat. Lat. 5766).

88. The itinerary of St. Cassian. From Dacia (present-day Romania), he went on a pilgrimage to the Holy Land, probably passing through Constantinople. Having become a monk in Bethlehem, Palestine, he went among the monks of Egypt. After having returned to Constantinople, he became a deacon and was sent as an envoy to Rome. We then find him in Marseille, in the south of France, from where he gave an extraordinary impetus to Western monasticism.

89. Miniature from a manuscript copy of the conferences of Cassian, written in 420. Municipal Library of Valenciennes, France. Cassian is represented on the right as looking at the copyist monks who offer the manuscript to Abbot Amand (7th century).

89

91

90

90. An 1801 print representing, as it appeared at the time, the crypt of the church of the monastery of St. Victor, near Marseille, founded by Cassian. Library of the unicipality of Aix-en-Provence, France.

91. The remains of the columns from the Merovingian period in the crypt of St. Victor.

92

92. Miniature of St. Jerome represented as the translator of the Psalms, a part of his immense work in disseminating the Scriptures. St. Gall Abbey in Switzerland (Cod. Sang. 22).

Eusebius of Vercelli, were able to combine their episcopal duties, their ascetical vocation, their spiritual direction of monastics, and their lives of intense prayer.

2. Contemplation and Action in St. Cassian

Cassian was born probably in what is now Romania, around 360, of a well-to-do family. He mastered Latin and Greek and received his monastic vocation while still a child. He went as a pilgrim to Palestine, entered a monastery at Bethlehem around 378, and some years later traveled to the Egyptian desert, where he settled in the colony of ascetics at Skete and had St. Paphnutius as his spiritual guide. Before 404, St. John Chrysostom ordained him a deacon in Constantinople and sent him to Rome with some messages. Around 415 he was in Marseille, where he focused his efforts on reforming existing monasteries and establishing new ones. Thus he founded two monasteries, one of men (St. Victor) and another of women, and taught all of them the authentic tradition and its meaning. His bilingualism facilitated his effort to be a bridge between East and West. He was in fact an itinerant monk, but the experience of the various forms of eremitism and cenobitism that he had acquired in the East enabled him to propose a model more suited to the Western mentality.

At the request of bishops and ascetics who recognized his authority in the field, this well-educated man with his deep experience of the cenobitic life wrote two works that had a decisive influence on the formation of European monasticism: *The*

Institutes and *The Conferences.* In these he sets down what must be done in a monastery in order to achieve a purification of the soul. The habit, the Divine Office, and penances are all described simply and with unction. The author also teaches how to combat effectively the eight principal vices: gluttony, lust, avarice, anger, sadness, sloth, vanity, and pride. His works are a manual for the perfect monastic. *The Conferences,* for their part, amount to a summa of monastic spirituality. To Cassian's mind, monastics represent the presence, in the Church, of both the fervor of the first community and the Church's eschatological fulfillment. And, in fact, the search for the reign of God and the eschatological character of this reign were central to his theology.

Cassian says that without manual labor spiritual practices become ineffective. He emphasizes the need of suitably integrating contemplation and action; this goal would be a permanent aspiration throughout the history of monastic life. At the same time, however, according to Cassian the supreme aim of a monastic is charity, and the sole means of reaching it is the renunciation of everything incompatible with this charity.

The whole of Cassian's teaching on monasticism is reducible to this equation: charity = purity of heart = pure prayer. Monastics abandon the world in order to seek the reign of God, which consists in union with God through contemplation. While Evagrius distinguishes between the reign of God and the reign of Christ, Cassian maintains that monastics enter fully into the reign of God when through purity of heart they receive illumination from the Holy Spirit, who is the Spirit of Christ.

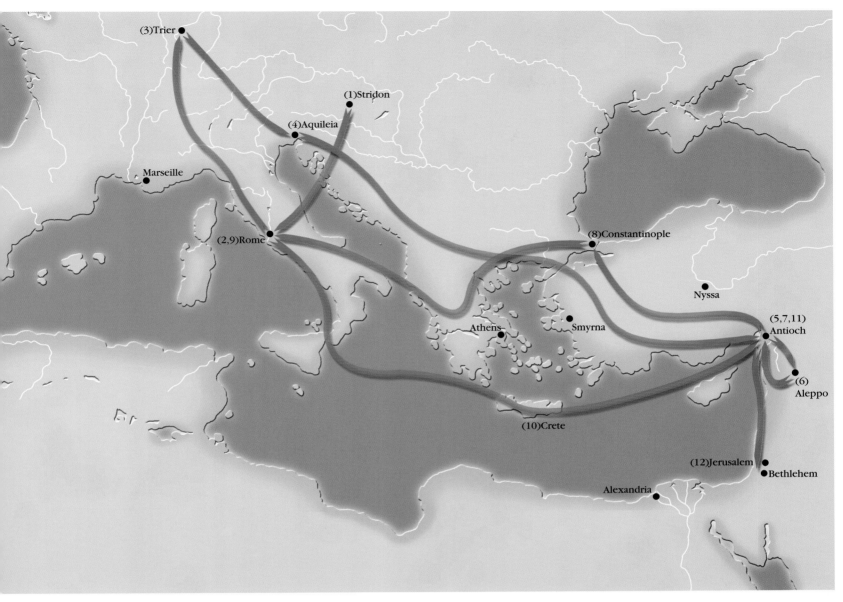

93. The itinerary of St. Jerome. Starting from Strido in Pannonia, now eastern Austria/Hungary, when he was still a youth, he went to Rome, then to Trier in Germany. From there, passing through Aquileia, he went as far as Syria in order to experience eremitical life and to devote himself to biblical studies. By way of Constantinople, he returned to Rome, now a master in sacred Scripture, and from there again traveled to Syria with a stop in Crete. Afterwards he went to Palestine, where he lived the monastic life and composed his principal works.

3. St. Jerome and the "Second Baptism"

St. Jerome (ca. 344–419/20), for his part, chose a busier life and has his place in history because of his knowledge of the Scriptures and his authoritative Latin translation, the Vulgate. In his day, however, he was also well known for his innate polemical disposition and for the bitter controversies he carried on with individuals and institutions. Because of his way of life and what he wrote in its favor, he is also regarded as an exceptional defender and spreader of monasticism.

When very young, he left his possessions behind and became a hermit in the desert of Chalcis (Syria). In the solitude of his hermitage he combated his memories, his fantasies, and his tremendous temptations. He studied Hebrew and became an expert in biblical studies: "Love the knowledge of the Scriptures and do not love the vices of the flesh."

He returned to Rome and there became the spiritual father of well-known aristocratic women and an applauded teacher of sacred Scripture. When Pope Damasus, his patron, died, Jerome traveled to the Holy Land with Paula, one of his most devoted disciples. She established monasteries in Bethlehem, one for herself and her companions and another for Jerome and his monks; she also built a hospice for pilgrims. It was in Bethlehem that Jerome wrote a good many of his numerous works.

In Jerome's view, monastic profession was a second baptism. Monastics had to follow, naked, the naked cross by ridding themselves of all possessions and attachments. The complete gift of self had as its basic focus a chastity preserved by fasting and vigils and the sacrifice of one's own will through obedience.

The Divine Office and the Eucharistic Liturgy are a dialogue of the soul with God, a dialogue nourished by the Bible. The Bible is the alpha and the omega of monastic formation, which is promoted by a taste for and practice of silence and by love of one's cell. According to Jerome, obedience, humility, and, above all, charity are the basic virtues of the monk's holy and even "angelic" life.

2. MONASTICISM IN GAUL

ST. MARTIN OF TOURS AND THE ISLE OF LÉRINS

94. Miniature from the 12th century. Municipal Library of Tours in France. Inside the capital letter D, the miracle of St. Martin is illustrated: with the sign of the cross he avoids being crushed by a tree being felled by peasants who want to put the one God to the test. The tree was near a pagan temple, and Martin wanted to cut it down, so the worshipers at the temple challenged him, "We will fell it ourselves and we will see if your God will save you." The miracle convinced the peasants of the goodness of St. Martin's God.

The most famous monk of 4th-century Gaul, the region more or less that of modern-day France, was Martin (316–397). He was a young man of privilege and a soldier before discovering Christianity and a call to the monastic life. His model of monasticism was that of loose community centered on a holy man. By the end of his life, however, a very different kind of monasticism was emerging in the far south of Gaul on the small island of Lérins.

1. St. Martin: A Monastic Model

Martin's biographer, Sulpicius Severus (ca. 360–ca. 430), knew the famous monk in the final years of his life. He tells us in his *Life of Martin* (ca. 394–397) and *Dialogues* (405) that Martin was born into a military family in Pannonia (eastern Austria/Hungary) and raised in northern Italy, near Milan. As a young soldier he had his now famous dream of Christ clothed in a garment Martin had shared earlier that day with a cold beggar. The dream prompted him to seek baptism. It is unclear how long Martin remained in the army as a Christian, perhaps as long as 20 years. When he ended his military career he attached himself to Hilary, the ascetic bishop of Poitiers in western Gaul. This arrangement was short-lived, for Hilary was soon exiled for his opposition to the Arian view of Christ. Martin then went to northern Italy and lived some time as a hermit.

By 360 it was safe to return to Poitiers, and Martin settled nearby in a place known as Ligugé. There he lived the eremitic life he had learned in Italy. Soon he attracted both disciples and fame, and in 371 was named bishop of Tours. As bishop he established a country retreat at Marmoutier, where a monastic community formed with an emphasis on obedience to Martin as their spiritual father, shared ownership of goods, common prayer, and meals. The younger monks worked as scribes while the seniors devoted themselves entirely to prayer. Martin served as both bishop of Tours and spiritual leader of the community at Marmoutier. Famous for his severe asceticism and astounding miracles, Martin "displayed a kind of heavenly happiness in his countenance, seeming to have passed the ordinary limits of human nature" (*Life,* ch. 27).

Martin left more an example of holiness than a model for monastic community. The cult of the saint spread widely, but his loosely structured form of monasticism centered on a spiritual master was difficult to duplicate. Rule-based monasticism would prove much more successful in the West.

2. A Famous Monastery: Lérins

So while the sanctity of Martin had great influence, the pattern of life and the written monastic rules of the southern island monastery at Lérins were of greater significance in the development of Latin monasticism. The island itself is small, only about 1.5 km in length and less than 1 km wide. It was there, however,

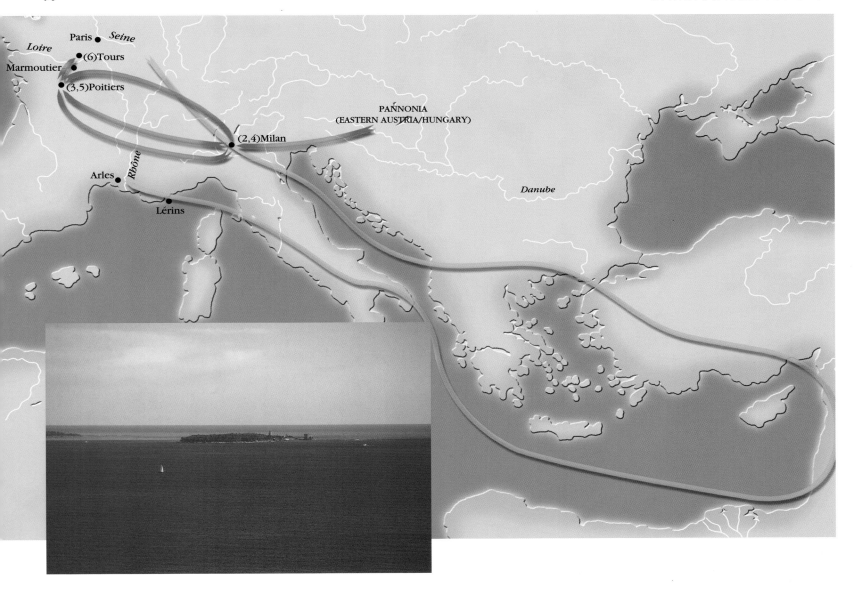

Paris
Seine
Loire
(6)Tours
Marmoutier
(3,5)Poitiers
Arles
Rhône
Lérins
(2,4)Milan
PANNONIA
(EASTERN AUSTRIA/HUNGARY)
Danube

97

95. *Renowned statue on the facade of the Romanesque cathedral of Lucca in Tuscany. St. Martin on horseback cuts his mantle in two in order to give half of it to a poor man.*

96. The red arrow indicates the itinerary of St. Martin. *Martin was born in Pannonia, which comprised today's eastern Austria and Hungary, and spent his youth in Milan in northern Italy. He went to Poitiers because of his friendship with the bishop; then, having returned to northern Italy, he lived there as a hermit; afterwards, he instituted a monastic community in Marmoutier after having followed the eremitical life near Poitiers. At the same time, he became bishop of Tours. The yellow arrow indicates the itinerary of Honoratus. Honoratus was a native of Gaul who traveled a great deal in the Middle East where he became acquainted with Palestinian and Egyptian monasticism. Then, going from Italy to the south of France and to the island of Lérins opposite Cannes, he formed among the hermits there a cenobitical community with one* regula *(rule). Caesarius, the bishop of Arles, was a prominent heir and disciple of his.*

97. *The island of St. Honoratus, a part of the small group called the Islands of Lérins, can be seen from Cannes, on the Côte d'Azur.*

that some hermits had settled who came together to create a cenobitic community under the leadership of St. Honoratus (d. 430). They chose to do so under a written charter, and the various revisions of that first Lerinian rule (the Rule of the Four Fathers) entered the literary stream that would eventually produce the Rule of Benedict more than a century later.

Honoratus was a well-born Gaul who became an ascetic and traveled widely in the Christian East, learning about the various monastic traditions of the Holy Land and Egypt before returning to Gaul by way of Italy. He settled at Lérins at the end of the 4th century, and helped to bring the hermits of the island into a community led by a single superior (called at this early stage *is qui praeest,* "he who is in charge"). The members of the community were to obey the superior and observe the common "rule" of the monastery. Thus was born of the Latin genre of *regula* (rule), that remains the principal means of monastic formation in the West to this day. Although the format of the *regula* was distinctively Latin, the orientation of Lerinian monasticism was decidedly toward the East. Honoratus' pattern for the community shows the strong influence of the Egyptian monasticism he had seen firsthand. There was a daily fast until mid-afternoon; the day was punctuated by communal liturgical prayer; the first three hours of each day were given over to personal prayer and reading (described simply as *vacare Deo,* "to be free for God"); the other hours were devoted to manual labor. Written policies, many of them also based on Egyptian practice, legislated how postulants, guests, visiting monks, and clerics were to be received. The rule shows a concern for liturgical order, sensitivity to individual weakness, mutual service, and correction of faults.

Honoratus became a major figure in both monasticism and the church in Gaul. The early 5th-century writer John Cassian dedicated the second installment of his *Conferences* to Honoratus, describing him as head of an "enormous" monastery at Lérins. After Honoratus became bishop of Arles in 426/27, he was succeeded as superior at Lérins by Maximus. A revised version of the rule, the Second Rule of the Fathers, is thought to date from this time of transition. This text shows the influence of Augustine's emphasis on monastic charity and roots the community's life in the biblical ideal of the Jerusalem Christians described in Acts 2 and 4. The superior is now called *praepositus,* and he is to be both obeyed and loved. The Rule itself stands out more strongly as the unifying axis for the community, and there is heightened concern for liturgical decorum. At this point in its history Lérins experiences a flowering of literary activity and further placement of monks in nearby episcopal sees.

The importance of Lérins lay largely in its contributions to the leadership of the church in Gaul. Monks were drafted from the island to serve as bishops, carrying the rules and customs with them as they fostered monastic life in their dioceses. One of the most important Lerinian exports was St. Caesarius, later bishop of Arles, who spent the last decade of the 5th century at Lérins before being sent to Arles to recuperate from overly-severe asceticism. Within a couple of years he became bishop and an active legislator for both female and male monasticism. His most important monastic text, the Rule for Virgins, preserves many of the liturgical customs of Lérins otherwise lost to us. With Caesarius we arrive at the era of Benedict.

98

99

98–99. View of the inside walls and general view of the exterior of the monastery of Lérins which Abbot Adalbert took care to fortify in the Middle Ages. The monastery was not attacked by the Visigoths or the Ostrogoths, but in the 9th century the Saracenes razed it to the ground and deported the monks to Spain. Liberated and having returned to Lérins, Adalbert built the enormous fortified tower, the remains of which can still be seen. Here the monks took refuge in case of incursions and assaults; an underground passage allowed communication between the tower and the unfortified monastery.

100

101

102

100. *View of the present-day landscape of the island which, when cultivated by the monks, became a veritable garden rich in plants and plantations.*

101. *Ruins of the chapel dedicated to St. Michael in the north of the island.*

102. *The chapel of St. Peter stands a short distance from the fortified monastery along the southern coast; it was restored in 1964.*

3. AUGUSTINIAN MONASTICISM

ST. AUGUSTINE OF HIPPO

1. St. Augustine (354–430) and Hippo

St. Augustine's conversion to Christianity was accompanied by his decision to live in a community, initially in one that was atypical in kind, consisting as it did of a gathering of friends who were seeking truth, but later on in a community of a more traditional kind. His decision was confirmed by his acquaintance with a monastery near Milan, which was headed by St. Ambrose (339–397), a bishop who prized and promoted monastic life and, above all, the common life of clerics, as established some decades earlier by Eusebius of Vercelli. Augustine's decision was also confirmed by his experience of the Roman monasteries which he visited during his short stay in the imperial capital. Other influences were his reading of the *Life of St. Anthony* and the example of Ponticianus, a monk of African origin, whom Augustine knew in Milan where that monk was serving God in poverty and self-surrender. Ambrose's own life was marked by traits typical of monasticism: abstinence, many fasts, a demanding poverty, persevering prayer, and manual work. The bishop also devoted some of his writings to consecrated virginity among women, and his teaching had a profound influence in subsequent centuries.

In Hippo (391) Augustine organized a first community of friends who in fact were philosophers rather than monks, seeking truth, as they did, in the Platonic manner. Later on, after his ordination as a priest, he founded a monastery of priests and, after being consecrated a bishop, he turned his episcopal residence into a monastery (396) in which the priests working in the diocese lived with him. Moreover, for many years he ordained only such men as were ready to live in community and poverty along with him: "Those who desire to have personal property and to live on their earnings will not be with me nor will they be clerics." The standard followed was that of the apostolic community. The community of priests formed one body with their bishop and his church. All lived from the same altar since all shared in the house and its possessions, which consisted in donations from the faithful. Augustine lived in this clerical community for the thirty-four years of his episcopate.

103. Map of the chief places where St. Augustine spent his life: born in Tagaste in North Africa, he studied in Carthage, in today's Tunisia, and became a philosopher and a Manichean. Then he went to Milan, where, under the influence of St. Ambrose and his own mother, St. Monica, he converted to the authentic Christian faith and received baptism, living in a sort of monastic community with his friends. Having returned to North Africa, he became a priest in Hippo but was able to continue his monastic life. Later on, he was the bishop of Hippo for thirty-five years, until the invasion and persecution against Christians which the Vandals carried out in the region.

104. Plan of the famous Roman city of Hippo showing its first Christian neighborhood.

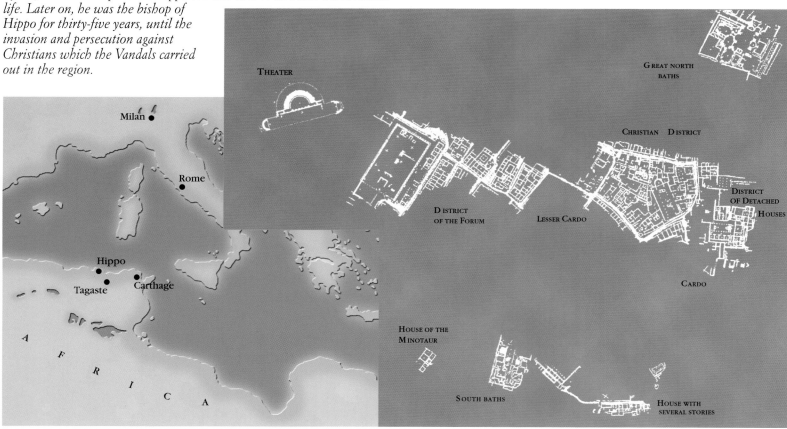

103

104

105

106

105. In a crypt of the paleochristian catacomb of St. Januarius in Naples, we find this extraordinary mosaic representing a black, North African bishop, who has sought refuge in Naples because of the persecution of Christians by the Vandals in North Africa.

106. Present-day view of Carthage, on the coast near Tunis.

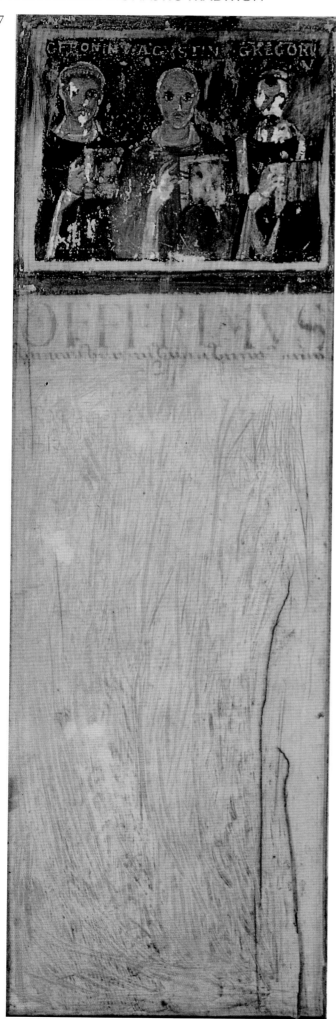

107. Painted paleo-Christian panel of St. Augustine between Sts. Jerome and Gregory. The panel is part of the Diptych of Boethius. Civic Museum of Art and History of Brescia in northern Italy.

Beginning in 425, he accepted an exemption from this Rule for those who were convinced of a vocation to the priesthood but did not feel called to that kind of life. He also founded monasteries of virgins. His sister was head of the one in Hippo.

But the abiding influence of Augustine on the monastic world was due fundamentally to his *Rule for the Servants of God,* which he wrote around 400 for the monks of Hippo. It is not properly a rule in the strict sense but rather a manifestation of the spirit that ought to restrain and guide those living in a monastery.

This great bishop, who was enthusiastic about the monastic life, was imbued with the sublime ideal that had inspired the primitive Church, and it is the search for and implementation of that ideal that explains its precepts. According to Augustine, monks "live in the flesh but not according to the flesh." The contemplative motivation for this heroic way of life is completely new, for Augustine interprets the eremitical life as an extraordinary longing to contemplate God.

2. An Urban Monasticism with Educated Monastics

For Augustine, the cultivation of interiority was absolutely indispensable, that is, the monk's concentration on the depths of his human reality; this interiority was thought of as a fullness of being and life. Self-knowledge opens the human person to the knowledge of God. Prayer and contemplation are the indispensable means of attaining to this knowledge which is, at the same time, union with God.

"A single heart and a single soul" expresses the mystery of the primitive community. Augustine would seek to achieve this goal in the life of his community. Interpersonal relations take on a wholly religious value. The Augustinian community comes together in order to live in a fraternal unanimity and concord: "You are all, therefore, to live in oneness of mind and heart, and to honor in one another the God whose living temples you are." Fraternal charity therefore occupies a central place in Augustinian asceticism. This charity is based on an ongoing and sincere dialogue among the monks and on a community of possessions: "They should especially cultivate charity. Let charity govern their manner of eating, their words, their clothing, the expressions on their faces. We are united with one another in the bonds of the same love; to neglect this is to offend God" (*The Catholic Way of Life* 33, 70).

Augustine speaks about the necessity of prayer and about chastity, but also about diet and the clothing to be worn. He keeps

108. In this painting from the Renaissance, the artist, Vincenzo Foppa, shows St. Augustine with the traditional iconographic episcopal attributes. Civil Museum of the Castello Sforzesco in Milan.

in mind the indispensable requirements for maintaining the physical health of the monks and attending to the needs of the sick; he is also concerned with the use of time and the cultivation of the mind. He is a man who makes demands, but the manner of life he seeks is one that is humane, moderate, and balanced. He looks for a common life that is complete, but he certainly does not see this life as focused on great austerities and fasts but rather, and above all, on service and mutual love. He also requires the monks to gain an intellectual preparation and stimulates them to be able to instruct the minds of other monks.

Underlying these monastic arrangements are the basic commandments: love God and love one's neighbor. Augustinian legislation is thus a prolongation of the divine law. Some references to the Scriptures confirm this bond between the monastic rule and the word of God.

3. Pastoral Service

One of the peculiarities of this kind of monasticism is its devotion to the service of the ecclesial community. Augustine combined the life of a cleric with that of a monk. In his eyes, the apostolate was the necessary consequence of the monk's total commitment to the service of the Church.

Its great originality consists in the complete harmony between study; the most important occupation, which is contemplation; and the apostolate. Because of the decisive influence exerted by this exceptional teacher, a monastery, in addition to being an ascetical arena and a seed-ground or seminary, functioned as a cultural center. Its members concerned themselves, above all else, with the ascetical and scholastic education of the young.

Augustinian monasticism quickly spread throughout North Africa. Many bishops were chosen from these monasteries, and they in turn established monasteries in their dioceses. These houses resisted the violent persecutions of the Vandals and the Berbers. One of Augustine's well-remembered successors was St. Fulgentius of Ruspe, who died in 527 and had encouraged the life of many of these monasteries. In fact, throughout the 6th century, African monasteries were organized according to the principles and methods of the bishop of Hippo.

His Rule was very successful in orders and congregations down the centuries, because it served as a source of inspiration in the composition of other rules and because many religious orders and congregations made it their own.

4. IBERIAN MONASTICISM

110. Miniature from the manuscript De Natura Rerum *by Isidore of Seville, representing the wheel of the seasons and the months. Municipal Library of Laon, France (Ms. 422).*

109. St. Isidore of Seville offers Sister Florentina his De fide catholica . . . contra Judaeis. *Miniature from a French manuscript written ca. 800. Bibliothèque Nationale, Paris (Ms. Lat. 1396).*

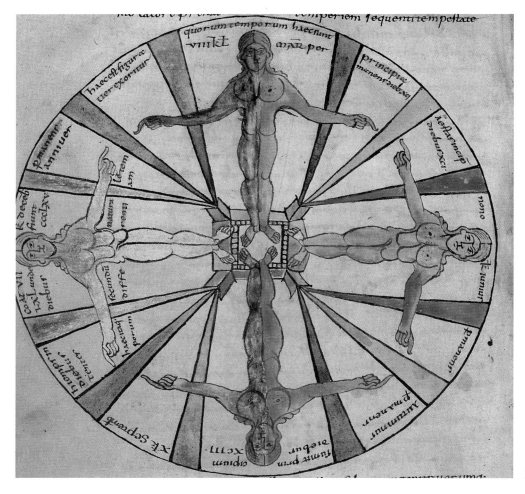

109

110

1. Origins and External Influence

The search for solitude, the practice of asceticism, and the desire for mortification also found their manifestation in the Iberian peninsula. The acts of the Council of Elvira (around 300) tell us of the existence of a rather large number of consecrated virgins. One of the canons severely chastises virgins who did not remain continent, for, in its view, a virgin who sins commits adultery and therefore is unfaithful to Christ, to whom she is married.

Some years later, the Priscillianist movement likewise called attention to the existence of a monastic movement. Priscillian, a stern monk of inflexible conduct and ready to spend day and night in prayer, impressed a strongly ascetical character on his sect; his strict and demanding life and his moral teaching were the reason for the prestige he enjoyed among simple people. But this Priscillianist asceticism also influenced the beginnings of Iberian monasticism, so that some Iberian bishops looked with great

distrust on the incipient monastic movement. This explains why the Council of Saragossa (380) spoke of monastics with suspicion and mistrust.

Another known instance of the monastic life is Egeria, who was probably a Galician nun, fond of traveling, a devout and keen observer. She wrote for the members of her monastery a narrative of her lengthy pilgrimage to Palestine, providing a lively description of the state of Christianity in the Holy Land.

Of the numerous Latin Christians who went on pilgrimage to the Holy Land many stayed on in order to live in the land of Jesus. They often did so in monasteries of Latins, moved by the desire to imitate the Lord's life by walking where he walked and repeating his gestures and actions. Melania the Elder established a monastery for women on the Mount of Olives. At the same place Rufinus of Aquileia founded one for monks where they conducted a school and copied manuscripts. At Bethlehem, Paula, spiritual daughter of Jerome, built two monasteries, one for her and her companions

111–112. Two views of the church dedicated to St. Fructuosus, where the saint is buried, near Braga, Spain. It is an example of the excellence reached by the Christian art of the Goths of Spain. In the picture on the left, one sees the exterior of the east and north wings and the central lantern (thoroughly restored). In the second, one sees the east apse; on the right, one notes the presumed sarcophagus of St. Fructuosus.

111

112

and the other for the saint and those who lived in community with him. It seems that the two groups came together to pray the Divine Office in the basilica of the Nativity.

2. Personalities

Monastic life received an extraordinary stimulus in 6th- and 7th-century Iberia. Sts. Leander, Isidore of Seville, and Fructuosus, all of them tireless and brilliant leaders of the Iberian Church, wrote rules and regulations for women monastics and virgins. They adapted the rules of Pachomius, Cassian, and Augustine for those who did not feel sufficiently strong to follow those rules in all their austerity and completeness. In fact, many monasteries lived in an irregular way, without fixed norms that applied to all the members. The bishops just mentioned, who were regarded at that time as the natural legislators of a life under a rule, decided to provide a rule that was concrete, adapted to the Iberian situation,

and within the reach of all. Isidore, the best known of the Iberian bishops, tried to write and legislate in ways that were simple and intelligible, so that even the most ignorant could understand and practice the precepts of religious life. Fructuosus, for his part, was a Visigoth from a noble Toledan family. He founded many monasteries in Galicia, Portugal, and Andalusia. For them he composed his *Regula monachorum* (around 610), a balanced compendium of other rules and of his own good sense.

St. Martin of Braga founded the monastery of Dumio, of which he was abbot. A man of impressive and attractive personality and bishop of Braga, he was the main driving force of the church in his land and of its development into the national church of the Suevian kingdom. He had a good knowledge of Eastern monasticism and built monasteries; he also devoted his skills to the translation and adaptation of the sayings of the Egyptian Fathers. Isidore was acquainted with a volume of Martin's letters that is now lost, in which he exhorted Isidore to correction, a life of

113

114

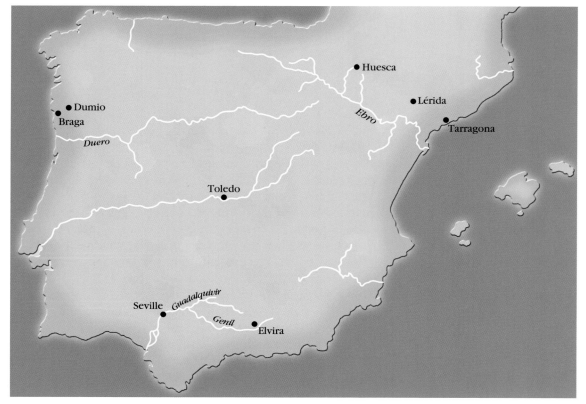

115

113. In the ruins of the Roman amphitheater of Tarragona in Spain, the remains of the church built during the Visigothic and Romanesque periods are clearly recognizable.

114. Remains in the excavations of the Visigothic village and graves in Bovalar near Lérida, Spain.

115. Map of Visigothic Spain showing the principal urban centers of Huesca, Toledo, and Lérida; it was there that councils of fundamental importance for the development of monasticism took place and, through the cooperation between bishops and monastics, for the expansion of Christianity and culture.

116. Miniature of the Codex Aemiliaensis *written ca. 1000. Represented from top to bottom, are the city of Toledo, two churches, a council, two churches and trees. This miniature will pass into history as one of the most symbolic with regard to a council. Library of the Escorial, Spain.*

117. This votive crown is preserved in the treasury of Guarrazar in Toledo; made of rectangular links and semi-precious stones, it is a supreme example of the Visigothic goldsmith's art, demonstrating a mature civilization which from henceforth is one of the centers of European Christianity.

116

117

faith, insistence on prayer, almsgiving, piety, and the practice of the virtues.

3. Contract (pactum) and Rules

Not all the rules in Iberian monasteries had the same character. Fructuosus of Braga, for example, demanded an unreserved, rigorous, and generous determination in order to undertake a monastic life, as well as blind obedience and strict silence, whereas Isidore seems rather to soften the demands of that life. The monastics for whom Isidore legislates support themselves by their own work. They form not only a spiritual but an economic community that is practically self-sufficient. The hardest work is done by the servants of the monastery. Everything that is produced is owned in common; no one can own anything personally or give away anything belonging to the monastery.

A peculiarity of Hispano-Visigothic monasticism was the *pactum,* which gave that monasticism a specific and differentiating character. A *pactum* was a real contract between the monks and the abbot, signed by both parties on the day of monastic profession; it established the duties of both sides, which became mutually conditioning. The contract was often a juridical instrument that communities could use to rid themselves of tyrannical or dissolute abbots.

At the end of the 6th century abbots began to appear in ecclesiastical legislation. Thus the Council of Huesca (598) ordered that abbots and clergy come together with the bishop once a year in order to receive instruction from him. Gradually abbots began to take part in councils. At the eighth Council of Toledo in 653, for example, twelve abbots were present and signed the acts as an integral sector of the Iberian Church.

The bishop, for his part, intervened in the life of the monasteries. The Council of Lerida (546) tells us that religious communities lived under a rule approved by the bishop. Several councils acknowledged the bishop's right to choose and impose the rule which monasteries in his jurisdiction had to follow. But the bishops could not interfere in the administration of a monastery's possessions. Isidore says that the bishop ought to encourage the monks to lead a holy life, correct violations of the rule, and appoint abbots and other officers of the monastery.

Bishops entrusted parishes, especially rural ones, to the pastoral care of monks. The people had a high esteem for these men, and not a few priests asked to become monks.

St. Benedict of Aniane incorporated the rules of Isidore and Fructuosus, as well as the *Regula communis,* into his *Codex Regularum,* thereby allowing Iberian monasticism to make its contribution to the Carolingian monastic reform.

5. IRISH MONASTICISM

1. A Monastic Church

Ireland and Great Britain contained numerous monasteries on their islands and in their mountains, although it is often not possible to count them exactly for lack of reliable sources. From the 6th century on, however, we know for sure of the existence of important centers: Menevia (Mynyw), founded by St. David; Iona, by St. Columcille (Columba); Kilkenny, from which came great missionaries and founders, such as Sts. Brendan, Finnian, and Columban; Clonard, "a real nursery of saints"; and Bangor, in Ulster, an important intellectual center. Some of these places also became important centers of artistic production.

The extreme rigor of the Irish hermits and their location within a systematically limited space surrounded by a stone wall may reflect the influence of eremitical life as lived in the Egyptian desert. The Irish monks were also characterized by their enthusiasm for study, sometimes under the influence of European monks who had fled to the island after the barbarian invasions.

St. Patrick was the apostle who evangelized Ireland. In his eventful youth this Briton was taken as a slave to Ireland, where he learned the language, but then escaped to Gaul and had the opportunity to live for a couple of years at Lérins, the famous

119. *The initial letter from an Irish manuscript from the year 600. It deals with* the Cathach *of St. Colomban. Library of the Royal Academy of Dublin. Monasticism is the principal source of Irish culture when the Middle Ages are about to begin.*

118

119

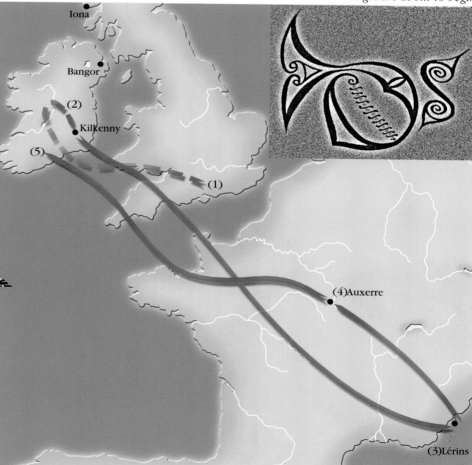

118. *St. Patrick. Drawn from an Irish tombstone from the 15th century.*

120. *Itinerary of St. Patrick. Born in Britannia, in today's England, the last reach of the Roman Empire, and taken to Ireland as a slave, he grew attached to this land and this people. Afterward, he fled in order to live freely and joined the monks of the island of Lérins in the south of France. In Auxerre, in the center of France, he became a bishop and decided to return to Ireland to evangelize it.*

120

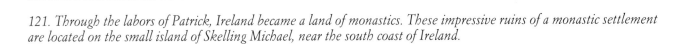

121. *Through the labors of Patrick, Ireland became a land of monastics. These impressive ruins of a monastic settlement are located on the small island of Skelling Michael, near the south coast of Ireland.*

island of monks located off the coast of Provence. He was ordained a bishop at Auxerre and returned to Ireland in order to evangelize it. He died probably in 461.

Patrick must have promoted monasticism, but the greatest expansion of this way of life was surely due to the influence of the monasteries of Whithorn in Scotland and of St. David in Wales. The monks focused their activity on the study of the Scriptures and the Fathers and on the copying of manuscripts, living meanwhile with an intense ascetical and penitential spirit.

The Celtic Church of the 5th and 6th centuries had completely monastic roots. The organization of the church, its finances, and its estates were governed not by bishops, as in the rest of Europe, but by abbots who took on the authority proper to bishops, although the latter continued to perform sacramental functions such as the ordination of priests. Each monastery was completely autonomous and lived according to its own rules and its own ascetical discipline. Ireland was a pastoral land, without cities, and was never under Roman rule. The monastic parish was coextensive with the territory of the clan, whose head was owner of the monastery. The clan regarded itself as responsible for the upkeep and growth of its monastic community, and conversely the monastery served as church and school for the clan.

All this meant that Christian Ireland had its centers in monastic communities rather than in episcopal sees, so that there was no conflict between monastic rights and episcopal rights, as there had been in Gaul.

2. A Special Kind of Monasticism

These monks practiced with exceptional frequency what was known as a *peregrinatio pro Christo,* a kind of voluntary and permanent exile for the love of Christ; it led them to travel through central and northern Europe and turned them into the greatest missionaries of the early centuries. They are not to be confused with the roving clerics and wandering monks who did not submit to any law of stability or to any authority. The exile in question was demanding and painful; it had a definite apostolic purpose and, generally speaking, was accomplished in community. Among the first who took up this practice was Columcille, a member of a reigning family and founder of various monasteries, who died in 597 on the island of Iona after a life filled with adventures and generous personal self-sacrifice.

The Irish monasteries also saw the beginning and development of the practice of (even daily) confession of faults; this was not

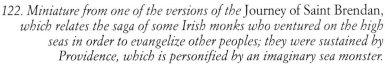

122. *Miniature from one of the versions of the* Journey of Saint Brendan, *which relates the saga of some Irish monks who ventured on the high seas in order to evangelize other peoples; they were sustained by Providence, which is personified by an imaginary sea monster.*

123. *Map from about 1000 showing the multiplication of monasteries in Ireland.*

124. *The so-called "cross of the Scriptures" in the monastic center of Clonmacnoise, Ireland, a true center of study which anticipates the European universities.*

simply regarded as an expression of humility but was also associated with the sacrament of penance. The practice was soon extended to the laity, who approached the abbot or a priest and asked how they could atone for their sins. The penitential books of the Celtic missionaries, containing lists of specific sins, each with its defined penance, played a decisive role in the introduction of private penance. The *regula monachorum* of Columban, which is a real monastic penitential, says that "confession and penance deliver one from death"; it decrees that each monk is to confess even his smallest faults daily and to perform the penance imposed in the established list. The penances generally consisted in fasting on bread and water, reciting psalms, and using the scourge.

3. St. Columban

In 590, Columban (Columbanus) (540–615) and twelve companions left the monastery of Bangor and traveled to the continent in order to evangelize it. By so doing he gave a decisive impulse to the rebirth of the cenobitic life, especially by founding many monasteries, both in Frankish territory (especially the house that would become the famous monastery of Luxeuil) and in Italy

(through the foundation of Bobbio). This holy monk of royal lineage, a lover of study who had a good knowledge of the Scriptures, which he read in Hebrew and Greek, tirelessly traversed central Europe, evangelizing peoples, reforming ecclesiastical structures, and converting kings. He died in 615, at a time when the monastery of Bobbio was beginning to exert its extraordinary cultural influence and become one of the principal centers of spiritual influence in the Italian peninsula. The tireless copying there of manuscripts, both of religious works and of secular literature, played a providential role in the transmission of classical culture to a later time.

The monastic teaching of Columban is to be found in his sermons, all of which were addressed to his monks. In them he speaks about the transitoriness of the world and about God as our refuge. The dignity of the human person consists in its being an image of God. The great duty of Christians is to be "tireless in charity": love of brothers and sisters in the midst of unity and love of God with the desire for heaven.

Columban and his monks spread an original kind of Christianity that differed from the Roman type not in doctrine but in organization, liturgy, and way of life. It was a school of severity, boldness, and Christian heroism.

125–126. *Two examples of the extremely refined art of the Irish monastic miniature. On top, the "Chi-Ro" miniature comes from the Book of Lindisfarne, end of the 7th century. British Library, London. On the bottom, the symbol of St. Mark in the Gospels of Echternach, ca. 710. Bibliothèque Nationale of Paris.*

124

125

126

6. St. Benedict

*128. Gregory the Great collects testimony in order to write the life of
Benedict. Miniature from the manuscript of the* Miracles of
Saint Benedict *by St. Gregory executed by Adravald and
Aimoinus in 1437. Condé Museum, Chantilly, France.*

128

*127. Detail of a wall painting from the 10th century in which
St. Benedict heals a sick person. Church of St. Chrysogonus, Rome.*

The greatest monastic legislator of the Latin West told us nothing
about himself, and none of his companions undertook to write his
biography. We have his Rule, and more than fifty years after his
death, the stylized account of his life and miracles written by
Pope Saint Gregory the Great (as Book II of his *Dialogues,* a work
about Italian saints). This personal modesty, frustrating to the
historian, is nonetheless notable for its representation of the
central theme of Benedict's Rule, humility. Gregory claims to have
learned about Benedict from four of his disciples. Though he
mentions Rule, he never quotes directly from it. The careful
reader can detect affinities and even echoes of Benedict's own
teaching in Gregory's portrait as well as gain some sense of how
Christians in Benedict's time understood monastic sanctity.

The Benedict of Gregory's *Dialogues* possesses all the pres-
cience and miraculous powers expected of a great saint, and the
stories are often clearly modeled on biblical types. Gregory
describes him as someone who "from childhood had the heart of
an old man" (Dial. 2, Prol.). At the same time, Benedict clearly
emerges as someone who grew into wisdom and learned from
experience, often painful. Born around 480 in Nursia (Norcia), a
town northeast of Rome, Benedict was the son of parents wealthy
enough to send him to Rome for his education. Shocked by the
worldliness of the big city and the behavior of his fellow students,
he abandoned his education and withdrew into "the desert" of
the countryside, taking as his sole companion his boyhood nurse.
Staying at a church in the small town of Effide (Affile), Benedict

127

129. *A miracle of Benedict in which the saint recognizes the poisoned bread. Wall painting by Master Conxolus, 12th century. Lower church of the Santo Speco monastery, near Subiaco, in central Italy.*

129

130

130. *Benedict convinces the king of the Ostrogoths, Totila, to check his destructive advance in Italy. Miniature by Jean de Stavelot in a copy of the* Miracles of Saint Benedict. *Condé Museum, Chantilly, France.*

131. *Unlike the other founding fathers of monasticism, Benedict accomplished his entire work, which was to influence the whole story of Western monasticism, in a limited section of Italy. Having left his native Norcia in Umbria, he retired from Affile in the Latium to live as a hermit near Subiaco, where he founded his first monastic community. He then went to Cassino, where he established cenobitical monasticism and wrote the celebrated rule.*

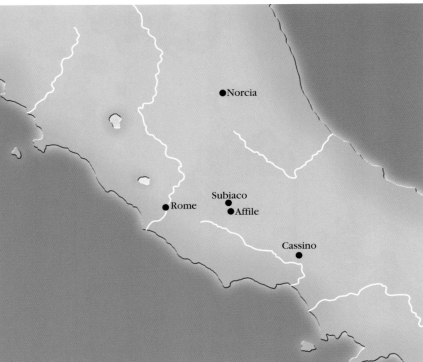

and his servant were welcomed by local luminaries. Benedict attracted considerable attention by miraculously restoring a broken kitchen tool borrowed by his nurse. The item became the focus of veneration and its restorer received the homage of the whole town. In crisis over this unexpected attention, Benedict ran away, leaving behind even his nurse, and found a cave nearby at a place called Subiaco. Someone from a nearby monastery gave him the monastic habit and he lived as a hermit for three years, isolated so totally from other people that he did not even know that Easter had come until a local priest brought him a festive meal.

Hermits attract attention. Soon the members of a nearby monastery prevailed upon him to become their abbot. It was a disastrous situation, for Benedict was intolerant of anything other than perfect observance of the monastic life. Soon his monks rose up against him, and conspired to poison his wine. Spared by God's help (the poisoned vessel shattered when blessed), Benedict returned to his solitude. His failure was clearly a problem for Gregory, who devotes several paragraphs to explaining why it was right for Benedict to walk away (Dial. 2.3). He continued to attract disciples, however, and created a decentralized monastic structure of small monasteries, each with its own spiritual father, under his oversight. He kept with him those whom he felt would benefit from his own example, including his most famous followers, Maur and Placid. They figured in his most famous miracle, when Placid was rescued from drowning by Maur's walking to him across the

131

water in obedience to Benedict's command (Dial. 2.7). The envy of a local priest, culminating in another attempt at poisoning, led Benedict and a small group of his closest disciples to leave Subiaco for the hilltop at Casinum (Montecassino), where they cleared a temple of Apollo with its sacred grove in order to build their monastery (Dial. 2.8).

Montecassino was to be Benedict's most lasting earthly home. Seasoned by his experience of both solitude and community, he established a firmly cenobitic way of life and wrote his Rule. Gregory depicts the monks of Montecassino as very engaged with the world around them, both religious and secular. Sometime in 546 Benedict had an encounter with Totila, king of the Goths, which Gregory alleges to have had an ameliorating effect on Totila's cruelty (Dial. 2.14-15). Warfare was not the only challenge his monks faced; Gregory tells of miraculous survival in times of famine (Dial. 2.21). Benedict and his monks created a place of stability in very difficult times, and it is little wonder that many were attracted to him and his monastery. He was willing to engage those in pastoral need: Gregory records that as soon as he arrived at Casinum, Benedict evangelized the residents of the area with his "continual preaching" (Dial. 2.8).

On a more personal level, as Benedict matured, his capacity and aptitude for close human relationships grew. The trajectory away from human society in his early years gradually curved back into social connection. Gregory describes three examples of Benedict's move into deeper human relationships even as he grew in his prayer life. The first was his bond with his sister, Scholastica.

132

132. On Benedict's order, Maurus saves Placid from drowning. Detail from the Predella of the Coronation of the Virgin by Lorenzo Monaco (1414). Uffizi Gallery, Florence.

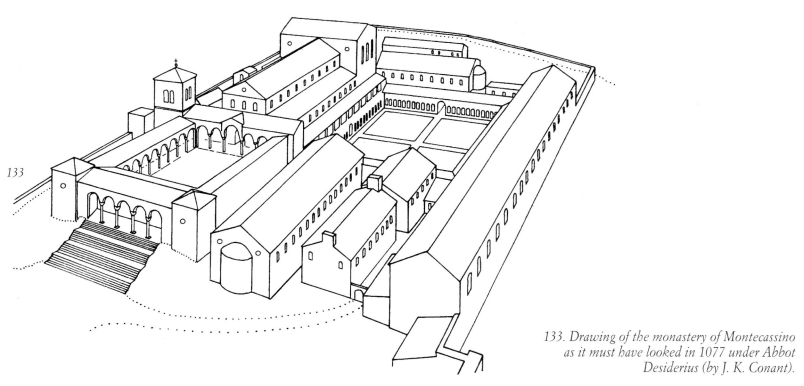

133

133. Drawing of the monastery of Montecassino as it must have looked in 1077 under Abbot Desiderius (by J. K. Conant).

134. Among the abundant iconography devoted to Benedict which the murals of the monastery of Sacro Speco, near Subiaco, have preserved, this image stands out; it represents the saint seeing his sister Scholastica's soul carried into heaven by angels.

134

She appears toward the end of the story of his life, in a vignette of great charm of spiritual depth. The story goes that the two siblings would meet annually for conversation at the foot of Montecassino. Scholastica, like her brother, had entered the monastic life. On what turned out to be their last reunion, Benedict resisted his sister's efforts to prolong their conversation. Benedict arose to go, rather haughtily insistent that he must return to his monastery for the night. Scholastica bowed her head in prayer, and immediately the calm of the night sky became a vicious storm that prevented Benedict from returning home. Horrified at Scholastica's daring and power, Benedict yielded to the proof that hers was, as Gregory notes, the greater love. Three days later he was granted a vision of his sister's soul ascending to heaven in the form of a dove, and proved the depth of what he had learned from her by ordering that her body be placed in the tomb which awaited him (Dial. 2.33-34).

Benedict had a close friend named Servandus, a deacon and abbot of a nearby monastery. They would meet regularly for an exchange of "sweet words of life." During one of his visits, Servandus was awakened in the night by Benedict, crying out his name. He ran up the stairs into Benedict's room and saw an unusual light. The saint explained that God had shown him the entire world gathered into a single ray of light, brilliant even amidst the darkness. As he looked, he saw the soul of his friend Germanus, bishop of Capua, carried off by angels in a sphere of fire (Dial. 2.35). Even his most profound spiritual encounter included friends, as part of the vision and as witness.

Several days before he died, Benedict had his monks open the tomb he would soon share with Scholastica. Growing weaker, on the sixth day he asked to be carried to the monastery's oratory, where he was given Holy Communion. Standing before the altar, his arms held up in prayer by his disciples, he gave up his spirit between the words of his prayer. He died among those he loved most (Dial. 2.37).

After Benedict's death, his monastery would endure less than fifty years. The Gothic conquest under Totila had spared Montecassino, but the Lombard invasions later in the 6th century would not. In 577 the monastery was destroyed and the monks escaped to Rome. They would not return to Montecassino until more than 140 years later. Gregory's *Dialogues* provided one assurance that Benedict's legacy would endure; Benedict's own Rule provided the other, and more important, one.

7. THE HOLY RULE

135

135. *Benedict as he writes his rule. Detail of a pen and ink drawing in the Codex Zweifalten (1138–1147). Würtembergische Landesbibliotek, Stuttgart, Germany.*

136

136. *Benedict explains the Rule to a monk. Miniature from* The Rule of Saint Benedict *in Latin and French, 1437, Liège, Belgium.*

Tradition associates the Benedict of Montecassino of whom Pope Saint Gregory the Great writes in his *Dialogues* with the monastic rule that bears the name of Benedict. Though Gregory does not quote from the Rule in his account of Benedict's life, he refers to it as "a rule for monks remarkable for its discernment and clear in language" (Dial. 2.36). Scholars have been able to trace an early 9th-century copy of the Rule at St. Gall in Switzerland (Sangallensis 914) back to the community at Montecassino (founded by Benedict around 530. The oldest manuscript of the Rule, dating from the early 8th century, was written for monasteries in England and is now in Oxford (MS Hatton 914).

Benedict was a deeply traditional monk who knew earlier monastic writings well. He directs his own readers to the conferences, institutes, and lives of the great monks. He names Basil the Great as a particular authority (RB 73.5), and required his monks to read aloud from a monastic text each night after supper (RB 42.3). The Rule is full of quotations from and allusions to earlier texts, both patristic and monastic. As was customary in his time these borrowings are not indicated and their authors are not cited. His major debt was to a lengthy, idiosyncratic monastic text written shortly before his own. Known as the Rule of the Master, this text was usually thought to have been a later expansion of Benedict's Rule. During the 20th century, however, a series of analyses have demonstrated that the Master was first, and Benedict did a brilliant abbreviation and adaptation of the longer rule to create what is really a new text. One third as long as the Rule of the Master and influenced by other traditions besides the Master's, the Rule of Benedict represents a creative synthesis of the textual materials available to a 6th-century monastic legislator.

A study of the structure of the Rule reveals both Benedict's debts to tradition and his own originality. The Rule consists of seven principal sections: a Prologue, constitutional principles (chs. 1–3), spiritual principles (chs. 4–7), prayer (chs. 8–20), communal organization (chs. 21–67), fraternal relations (chs. 68–72), conclu-

137. Benedict gives the
Rule to monastics. Mural
by Sodoma (1505–1508).
Cloister of the monastery
of Monte Oliveto
Maggiore, Italy.

137

sion (ch. 73). Within this structure are some repetitions and curiosities of arrangement that betray the use of source materials, especially the Rule of the Master.

The Rule opens with a personal invitation: "Listen, my son, to the Master's instructions and attend to them with the ear of your heart. This is advice from a father who loves you: receive it willingly and put it into practice effectively" (Prol. 1–2). These lines, beloved by Benedictines, are adapted from a Latin ascetic text that was itself modeled on biblical Wisdom literature. The Prologue continues with material largely inherited from the Rule of the Master emphasizing the return to God by obedience and fidelity to the commandments. Benedict speaks again in his own voice at the end, when he assures his monks that though the path may be difficult at the beginning it will become smoother with experience, as the "heart expands with the inexpressible delight of love" (Prol. 49).

Because Benedict writes for cenobites, whom he defines as those who "serve under a rule and an abbot" (RB 1.2), he devotes two early chapters to his understanding of the abbot's role as shepherd of the community and the monks' role in providing counsel for major decisions (RB 2–3). Here Benedict innovates over against the Master and others who did not provide for such a consultative process. The abbot's task and the monks' responsibilities toward him and each other are so important that Benedict returns to these themes at the end of the Rule with a distinctive treatment (RB 64 and 68–72).

The basic spirituality of the Rule is contained in a reinterpretation of Christian ethics in monastic terms (RB 4) and a trilogy of chapters on the central themes of obedience, proper use of speech, and humility (RB 5–7). The most important is humility. Benedict presents a "ladder" of twelve steps of humility, an image borrowed from the Master (who in turn had used material from John Cassian) that will bring one from the initial stage of fear of God to the final experience of the love of God that casts out all fear. As in the Prologue, the disciplines of monastic life become more natural with experience, until they are done "out of love for Christ, good habit, and delight in virtue" (RB 7.69).

Benedict prescribes a program of common prayer seven times each day: Vigils, a lengthy service of psalms and readings in the middle of the night; Lauds, a morning prayer at dawn; Prime, Terce, Sext, and None, brief gatherings for prayer at intervals during the day; Vespers, the evening prayer; and Compline, the final prayer of the day (RB 8–17). He asked his monks to pray all 150 psalms in the course of a week (RB 18). His instructions for seasonal adjustment to the variable hours of daylight are keyed to the liturgical cycle, which itself turns on the annual celebration of Easter. He also writes of the monk's inner disposition at both common and personal prayer, insisting on awareness of God's presence and purity of intention (RB 19–20).

Benedict was experienced in the exigencies of the common life (RB 21–67). He provides for an array of monastic officials, prescribes for common meals, and establishes a process for addressing faults and reconciling the estranged. He also shows sensitivity toward the special needs of the young, the old, the sick, and the guest. His approach is in sharp contrast with that of the Master, who was suspicious of those who did not conform totally. Here Benedict shows both his own pastoral experience and the influence of Augustine, whose monastic rule (the *Praeceptum*) Benedict knew and quoted. Notable, too, is Benedict's unusually severe attitude toward two faults: private ownership and complaining, which he refers to as "murmuring." The first strikes at the essence of cenobitic life, interdependence; the second corrodes the bonds of community by undermining constructive efforts.

The last section of the Rule (RB 68–72) returns to the themes of obedience and communication addressed earlier, but in terms not shaped as extensively by the Rule of the Master. Some have suggested that he added these chapters at a later stage of redaction as a kind of final reflection on important themes. They certainly are the fruit of his own experience of community life.

Benedict wrote his Rule for his own monastery. He foresaw that others might use it, and assured them that adjustments could be made in practical matters dependent on climate (RB 40.8, 48.7, 55.1-2) and even on the arrangement of psalmody for common prayer (RB 18.22). The Rule was sometimes combined with others to create a "mixed rule" *(regula mixta),* or when preserved integrally it was supplemented by monastic customaries or constitutions that addressed topics he did not and modified his prescriptions according to local needs. Benedictine reform movements such as the Cistercians (12th century), the Trappists (17th century), and the "Primitive Benedictines" (19th–20th centuries) rallied around strict observance of the Rule, but even they had to make adaptations to circumstance. The significance of Benedict's achievement lies in the spiritual vision that shaped his own adaptation of living tradition.

138

138. Benedict gives the Rule to Abbess Aelika. Frontispiece of a manuscript containing the Rule, from the abbey of Ringelheim, 1025. Staatsbibliotek, Berlin (Preussischer Kulturbesitz ms. Theol. Lat. 199).

139. Benedict holds the Rule. This is perhaps the most important iconography of the Rule, shown here in the celebrated Codex Benedictus. *Apostolic Vatican Library (Vat. Lat. 1202).*

Cum domibus multis plures pariter accipe libros·

8. THE SPREAD OF THE BENEDICTINE RULE

140

140. *Benedict shows the beginning of the Rule: "Listen, my son, to the precepts of the master and incline the ear of your heart." The Renaissance sculpture is painted terra-cotta from the school of Della Robbia and is placed over the door of the monastery of Monte Oliveto Maggiore in Italy.*

For over two centuries after the death of St. Benedict, his Rule was not much known or applied. After the destruction of Monte-cassino by the Lombards (around 577) and the departure of its monks to Rome, we know nothing of Benedictine foundations in Italy, not even of St. Andrew, where St. Gregory the Great lived as a monk.

Except for references by Gregory in his *Dialogues,* the first mention of the Rule appears in a letter of Venerandus, founder and abbot of the monastery of Altaripa in Aquitaine (620–630). St. Columban, when at Luxeuil, knew of the Rule, for he mentions it in his own rule, and it was in his monasteries that it was known and valued and began to exert an influence for the first time.

Throughout the 7th century the Benedictine code is mentioned, along with other rules, as a source of inspiration and of suggestions and regulations useful for community life.

The reception and introduction of the Rule depended a great deal also on the travels of the manuscripts containing it, for in the Middle Ages books did travel. That is, their comings and goings as such were important, since each manuscript carried a message or a particular rule.

The reception also had to do with the geographical location and importance of the monasteries. The numerous small dioceses of southern Italy contained many small urban and suburban monasteries that were under the direct supervision of the bishops. In contrast, the monasteries of the north underwent a more autonomous development that would lead in time to exemption from episcopal control. In addition, the smaller number of dioceses in the north facilitated the appearance of large, powerful monasteries which had an influence far beyond the walls of their cloisters due to their extensive administrative and economic

141   *142*

141. Funerary bas-relief of the Benedictine bishop Agilbert, dating from the 7th century. Crypt of the abbatial church of Jouarre, France.

142. Vows of the first monks (ca. 800) of the abbey of St. Gall, Switzerland. A folio from the Book of professed monks. Monastic vows were taken according to the various rules that were followed; however, the mother rule at St. Gall remained the one given by Benedict.

reach. This in turn had an important social and civilizing impact, because kings granted their favors more readily to monasteries than to episcopal sees. Generally speaking, the large monasteries accepted the Benedictine Rule sooner than did the small ones.

Monasticism in the Iberian peninsula was likewise immersed in the common monastic tradition of the West, of which, of course, the Rule of Benedict had become a part. The rule composed by St. Isidore of Seville, for example, contains many traces of Benedict.

In the 8th century, the Benedictine Rule slowly began to assert itself over other rules. Montecassino, the Holy Mountain, was on the route of pilgrims to the Holy Land and of travelers to the East. One of the pilgrims was Petronax, whom St. Gregory II encouraged to restore monastic life at Montecassino. Some monks from other monasteries joined him, and there were already "some simple men" who had withdrawn to the mountain. In a few

decades, Montecassino became a center which all of Europe watched and whose authentic monastic observance it began to imitate. The life there was officially approved by Pope Zacharias, who, as we know, translated the *Dialogues* of Gregory into Greek; he gave the community, among other books, the autograph of the Benedictine Rule. Montecassino would achieve an importance that was not only religious but also political, for it acted as peacemaker in a society that was in constant internal conflict.

The abbey of Montecassino became a great monastic center that created a Benedictine consciousness. It was from there that Charlemagne obtained a copy of the Rule in 787. The Rule then began to spread slowly but was not yet dominant. Boniface, an Anglo-Saxon pilgrim on the continent, contributed mightily to its spread by imposing on the new monastery of Fulda the regular discipline, observance, and monastic customs that Benedict had established. In addition, in 742 the so-called "Germanic Council" prescribed that henceforth the Rule of Benedict was the standard to be observed by all monastics, men and women.

As a result of these several factors, by the middle of the 8th century the famous abbeys of Luxeuil, St. Gall, Corbie, and others, which owed their existence to Irish, Gallo-Roman, or Frankish monks, all accepted the Rule of Montecassino. As the popular saying had it, "St. Benedict lay down in St. Columban's bed."

St. Benedict of Aniane compared existing rules with that of Benedict, saw the superiority of the latter, and imposed it at the council of abbots which he convened at Aachen in 817. Henceforth, monastic Europe would be fundamentally Benedictine.

Various considerations influenced the decision of Benedict of Aniane. There were political reasons, visible in the resolute support given him by the Frankish kings; there was also the conviction that it was not good for the monasteries to be so autonomous. Other factors were the obvious enthusiasm which Gregory showed in his *Dialogues* for the person and work of Benedict. But especially there were the intrinsic merits of the Benedictine Rule: its clarity, its organized structure, and the moderation of its regulations, which clashed with the rigorism and exaggerations of other rules. Benedict of Nursia had developed these characteristics on his own spiritual journey, a journey in which he had, in a way, recapitulated the history of Eastern monasticism from St. Paul of Thebes by way of Sts. Anthony and Pachomius to St. Basil the Great.

Meanwhile, the name of the builder of Montecassino found a growing place in the calendars, martyrologies, sacramentaries, and other liturgical books, to the point where he became a venerated popular figure. Beginning in the 9th century, the monks of Fleury claimed that, as the result of an obscure history, they possessed the authentic relics of Benedict, and for this reason their monastery became a very active center for the spread of the saint's liturgical cult.

All of this contributed, of course, to the importance and gradual introduction of the Rule of Benedict, but this was a slow process, for monks did not forget or reject en bloc their earlier observances. At the end of the 8th century Ambrose Autpert wrote: "It is necessary always to live according to the Rule of the Fathers, but first and foremost according to that of the holy confessor Benedict. Do not depart from it, either to the right or to the left, and do not add anything to it or take anything from it, for it contains everything needed." In fact, down the centuries the Benedictine Rule has been followed with modifications and additions. Benedict of Aniane himself, in the reform which he inaugurated, used not only the Benedictine Rule but a series of norms and observances that adapted that Rule to different places. The same course would be followed by all the later reforms, such as the Cluniac, and even by some orders, including the Cistercians, who, in addition to returning to the Benedictine Rule, have declarations, constitutions, and additions that complement the Rule.

143. The Benedictine genealogical tree of the saint's "spiritual progeny" grows from Benedict's body. Miniature by Jean de Stavelot in the Vie de Saint Benoît. *Condé Museum, Chantilly, France. Jean de Stavelot was a monk of the abbey of Saint-Laurent in Liège, Belgium, and flourished about 1432–1437. In the "spiritual progeny," we notice several persons whom we have met or shall meet again in this atlas, such as Columban, Anselm, Bede, Odilo, who was abbot of Cluny, and Gregory the Great.*

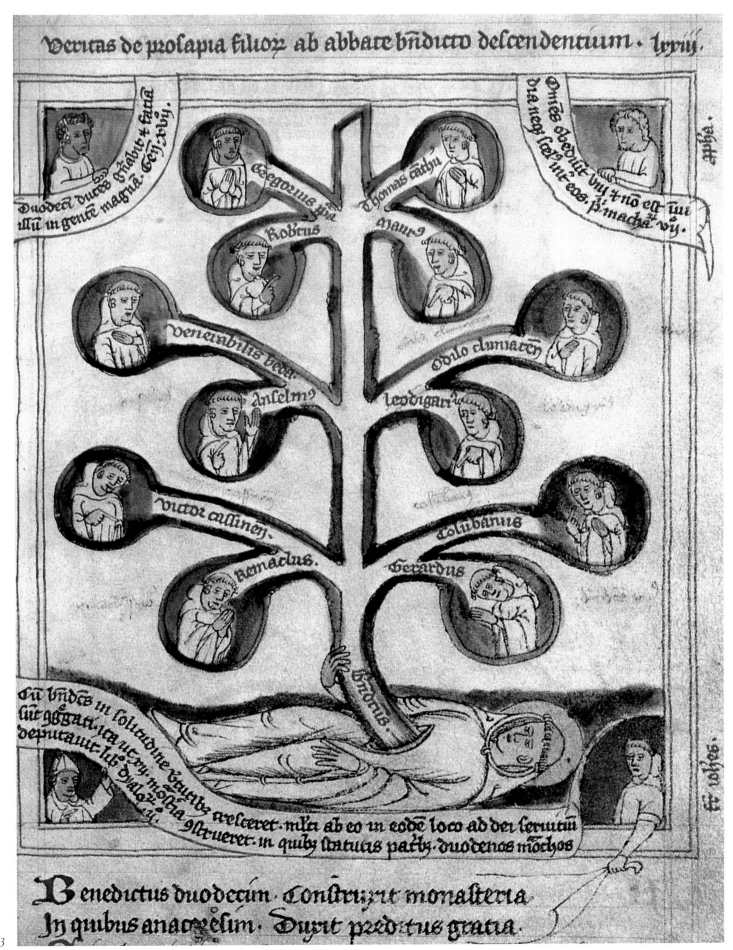

1. ST. BASIL THE GREAT

AND THE TRADITION OF THE EASTERN ORTHODOX CHURCH

144

St. Basil the Great is one of the three Church Fathers from Cappadocia, or the so-called Cappadocian Fathers, and undoubtedly one of the greatest of all time. He was born around 330 in Neocaesarea in Pontus of wealthy and, what is even more important, devout parents who were known as pious Christians. Basil drew upon their faith all his life: "My blessed mother Amelia and my grandmothers Makrina taught me to believe in God and to be a true Christian. That same faith, naturally now even stronger, I still nurture in myself" (Letters 203 and 223). He received his early education from his father, a teacher of rhetoric in Neocaesarea.

Around 345 he left for Caesarea in Cappadocia, where he met Gregory Nazianzen, also one of the three Cappadocian Fathers, who was to become and remain his closest friend for the rest of his life. There he also met Julian the Apostate, who was to become the emperor and his later opponent. Basil then left Caesarea and went to Constantinople. Later, around 352, he left for Athens, then the most renowned Hellenistic center of learning, and continued his education, studying rhetoric, grammar, philosophy, astronomy, geometry, and arithmetic with Imerios and Proeresios, the famous Athenian sophists. In the four years he spent there he received an excellent secular education, which he never underestimated. Gregory the Theologian used to say that only those who wanted others to remain as ignorant as they themselves were looked down upon such an education. While in Athens he met again his friend Gregory, and Julian. Gregory considered the time spent there the best period of their lives.

Basil then left Athens and returned to Caesarea, where he was baptized by Dianus, bishop of the city, and it was there he was ordained a monk. He then traveled to the East in order to learn all about monastic life; he met a great number of monks and learned their customs and rules. It was during these travels that Basil came to realize the greatness of monasticism, but he also discerned a certain lack of regularity in the organization of monastic life; this inspired him to write his Monastic Rules.

Basil was ordained a deacon around 360 and later a priest by Bishop Eusebius. As a priest he contributed greatly to the efforts of the Church to counter Valens' Arianism and Julian's efforts to introduce polytheism. When Eusebius died in the autumn of 370, Basil was elected archbishop of Caesarea in Cappadocia, with the majority of only one vote, that of St. Gregory the Theologian.

His activities as archbishop were multifold. Among other things, he built churches, hospitals, orphanages, and old people's homes on the outskirts of the city, an area which became almost a town in its own right and was known as Basiliade. The work in these institutions was done mainly by monks. As archbishop he finally realized his vision of monastic life in Cappadocia, establishing monasticism as a way of life governed by a rule, although he never denied either the skete community of hermits or the monastic life of the Desert Fathers. That was how he served as an example to future generations of monastics and exerted a notable influence upon most later monastic leaders in Syria, Palestine, Constantinople (St. Theodore the Studite), in the West (St. Benedict of Nursia), as well as on Mt. Athos, and in Slavic churches.

144. St. Basil the Great, represented in the exterior narthex of the church of the Presentation of the Virgin in the Temple (middle of the 17th century) from the Serbian monastery of Chilandari on the peninsula of Mount Athos in Greece.

His ascetic and monastic works consist of the *Moral Rules,* the *Longer* and *Shorter Rules,* two groups of *Epitomes,* and the *Ascetic Regulations.* The monastic rules, the *Longer* and *Shorter Rules,* are the two most significant collections. They were written as answers to monks' questions, and that was how they were preserved, in the form of a dialogue. The *Longer Rules* are comprised of fifty-five chapters and speak of general and basic principles of monastic life: love of God and one's neighbor, the life of reclusion, austerity, etc. The *Shorter Rules,* which comprise 313 regulations, speak of certain issues of everyday monastic life. The community living in common, which Basil presents as the basic form of monastic life, was the renewal of the first Christian community in Jerusalem, considered by Basil as both an authentic "early church" and an eschatological community of the body of Christ. The *Rules* are neither a typikon (a manual of rubrics for religious services) nor regulations which are concerned specifically with monasticism and monasteries, but present principles regarding virtues and duties all Christians have to observe on their arduous way to the reign of God. According to Basil, the basic monastic virtue, and ultimately the most essential Christian virtue, is the love of God and one's neighbor.

Monastic life should not be interpreted as a way of escaping from the world, of despising secular ways and habits, but merely as an attempt to form an eschatological community in our history. The monastic rules of Basil have had a strong impact upon monastic life in the Eastern Orthodox Church for centuries. Their evangelical and ecclesiastical character seemed to have been of fundamental importance, especially in Athonite monasticism, in Constantinople, and in Slavic monasteries. Rufinus' translations of these rules into Latin at the end of the 4th century influenced John Cassian and Benedict of Nursia in the West. Apart from the translation into Latin, there are also translations of these texts into Armenian, Georgian, Arabic, and Old Church Slavonic, as well as many Western languages.

Basil the Great not only contributed to the organization of monastic life but also exerted significant influence upon the liturgical life and practice in the Eastern Orthodox Church, particularly in worship. This Holy Father is rightly called the Great. He died on December 31, 378, at the age of forty-nine and was buried on January 1, 379.

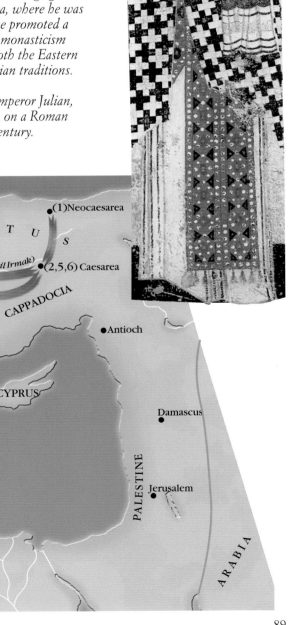

145

145. St. Gregory of Nazianzus in an icon of the school of Pskov, from the beginning of the 15th century. Tretyakov Gallery, Moscow.

146. Itinerary of Basil. Born in Neocaesarea in Pontus, near the Black Sea, he went to Caesarea in Cappadocia when he was very young; there he met Gregory of Nazianzus and Julian the Apostate. He went to Constantinople and then to Athens where he completed his studies. Having returned to Caesarea, he was baptized and afterwards traveled in the East to study monasticism. Having again returned to Caesarea, where he was appointed bishop, he promoted a thorough reform of monasticism which influenced both the Eastern and Western Christian traditions.

147. Effigy of the emperor Julian, called the Apostate, on a Roman coin from the 4th century.

146

BLACK SEA

(3) Constantinople

GREECE

Thessalonica

P O N T U S

(1) Neocaesarea

Halys (Kizil Irmak)

(2,5,6) Caesarea

CAPPADOCIA

Athens

Ephesus

Antioch

147

CYPRUS

Damascus

CRETE

PALESTINE

M E D I T E R R A N E A N   S E A

Jerusalem

ARABIA

Alexandria

E G Y P T

148. *Impressive view of the monastic dwellings excavated from a mountain in Cappadocia. In this region, Basil and the other Cappadocian Fathers gave an impetus without precedent to monasticism which still marks the valleys intersecting one another for kilometer upon kilometer.*

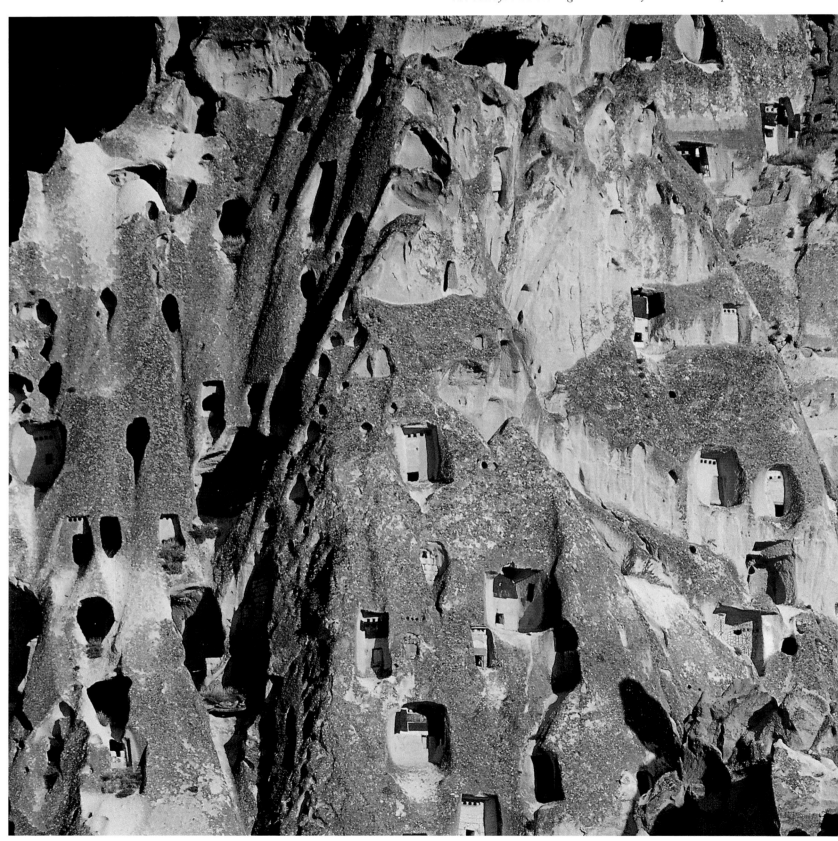

148

149. *Santa Sophia in Constantinople, which became a mosque upon the fall of Byzantium, is the most typical expression of the Constantinople of Justinian, who was indebted to Basil for his contribution to the formation of the Eastern Christian Church.*

150. *The monastery of the Caves near Kiev, Ukraine, in a photograph taken before World War II. Since that war, destruction has not altered the landscape. The Russian Church considers the church of Kiev as the first heir of Constantinople and Basil's work.*

151. General view of the Great Laura of Mount Athos in Greece. Athos with its monasteries was the place where Orthodox spirituality as well as the work of Basil were preserved after the fall of Byzantium, and it is so to this day.

149

150

151

152

153

152. General view of the Santo Speco monastery near Subiaco, Italy. Sacro Speco is one of the symbols of the spirituality of St. Benedict, which was influenced by Basil and which later on was to be a living force in the whole of Western monasticism.

153. View of the present-day monastery of Lérins in the south of France, founded by Cassian, who in his turn was inspired by Basil the Great's monastic vision.

2. St. Sabas and His Rule

154

154. View of the Laura of Calamon in Palestine not far from the place where the river Jordan empties into the Dead Sea. The foundations date back to the 5th century, a crucial period for the development of cenobitic monasticism in Palestine.

St. Sabas (439–532) was one of the greatest representatives of Eastern monasticism. He was a monk and an archimandrite of monasteries in Palestine, the most important of these being the Great Laura, which he founded and which still exists and is known today as Mar Saba.

Sabas was born at Mutalaska in Cappadocia in 439. As a little boy he was given into the care of a nearby monastery which followed the Rule of Basil. In 457, at the age of eighteen, he left Cappadocia and settled in Palestine, leaving there for only a short period in Alexandria in Egypt. His experiences as a cenobite in the Palestinian monasteries of Passarion, Theoctistus, and Euthymius, and his experiences as a hermit in the nearby desert led him to follow his own path, a way of life halfway between the cenobitic and the eremitical. He withdrew first into a cave, then into a tower near the Dead Sea, and finally, in 478, settled in the Kidron valley, between Jerusalem and the Dead Sea in the wilderness of Judah. It was there, on the right bank of the Kidron, that he began in 483 to accept his first disciples and to organize his famous laura, which was later called the "great" or "greatest" *(hē megistē laura),* although even at the time of its greatest prosperity it never had more than 150 monks. If we add the monks in his other foundations, there were as many as 500 living under his di-

rection. Even though he was the head of such a large group of monasteries, he himself was a simple monk. Not until 491 was he ordained a priest.

Sabas structured monastic life as a large set of hermitages (known precisely as a "laura," that is, a collection of individual cells of monks assembled under one leader). Here the monks lived a life that combined eremitism and cenobitism (not unlike the life in the later Skete).

Despite his love of solitude, Sabas did not refuse to enter the struggle for the freedom and the interests, even economic, of the Palestinian Church as represented by the patriarchs of Jerusalem. This commitment led him to make two celebrated journeys to Constantinople and the courts of Anastasius I and Justinian and to engage in real political demonstrations at the head of a throng of monks from the local monasteries.

Between 483 and 531, Sabas founded and organized four lauras; meanwhile, his disciples founded three more: the lauras of Firminus, the Towers, and Neelkeraba. Like the Great Laura, each of these had a central set of buildings (common church or *katholikon,* which could hold over a thousand people, assembly hall, library, refectory, kitchen, a hostel for pilgrims, and so on); around this center of gravity, as it were, a variable number of hermitages

155

155. *The Laura of St. Sabas, Mar Saba, still active today. Founded by the saint in 484 in the desert of Judah in Palestine.*

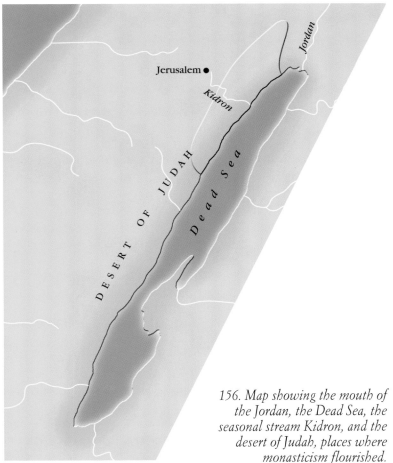

156

156. Map showing the mouth of the Jordan, the Dead Sea, the seasonal stream Kidron, and the desert of Judah, places where monasticism flourished.

were scattered, everything being enclosed within a great stone wall. The founder's disciples gathered every Saturday and Sunday and spent the night in between keeping vigil; this vigil was an original innovation that was thereafter faithfully observed. After the monks had celebrated the Divine Office and the Divine Liturgy together and had received communion, they returned to their cells, bringing with them the Eucharist, water, a store of food, and so on.

In addition to the lauras Sabas established *cenobia* or monasteries, two of them, at Gadara and Emmaus, during the period in which opposition from the monks drove him away for some years from his laura; to these his disciple Severian added a seventh in 514/15.

Beginning in 493, the patriarch of Jerusalem appointed Sabas the head of all the hermits of Palestine; in addition, he was "superintendent" of the ancient monasteries of Euthymius and Theoctistus (St. Theodosius was in charge of all the others).

The way of life which Sabas established there by means of rules, including written rules (the typikon), was firmly based on Chalcedonian orthodoxy. What Sabas succeeded in doing within the framework of the laura was to combine Basilian cenobitism

157. Image of Sabas on a triptych from the 14th century. Monastery of St. Catherine, Sinai.

158. Image of St. Euthymius, one of the fathers of Palestinian monasticism, in the church of the Anarghiri Saints of Kastoria in the north of Greece.

157   158   159

and the eremitical ideal inherited from Egypt. This balance explains the lengthy survival of his principal foundation (the Great Laura) despite the raids, pillaging, destruction, and massacres inflicted first by the Persians during the invasion of 614 and later, on various occasions, by marauders and the Muslims. That same balance explains a phenomenon quite rare in the East: the co-existence in one monastery of Greeks, Syrians, and Georgians. This in turn made possible, among other things, the production of first-rate translations of important texts. In addition, it explains the spread of the "Rule of St. Sabas" through the typikon that bears his name and through the emergence of some major personages from among the "Sabaite" monks (e.g., John Damascene, the hymn writers Cosmas of Maiuma and Stephen, Theodore Abu Qurra, and Leontius of Damascus).

The typikon known as that of St. Sabas or of Jerusalem has been attributed to Sabas, and the attribution is correct to the extent that basic to the work are certain rules set down by him or by St. Euthymius. Later on, however, the rules were updated by others, including Sophronius, John Damascene, and Nicholas Grammaticus.

Beginning in the time of Photius, the use of this typikon spread, largely in Asia Minor; then, beginning in the 11th century

with Simeon of Thessalonica, it became the common rule and liturgical guide in the churches of the Byzantine Rite. There were, however, variations: in Bithynia, for example, the lauras were made up not of individual hermits but of groups of two or three hermits under a single superior. Monastic life on Mt. Athos was likewise modeled on Mar Saba. On the other hand, the Great Laura which Athanasius the Athonite founded there in 963 is not a laura in the sense Sabas gave the term, but is simply a monastery. The practice of giving the name laura to important monasteries was also followed elsewhere later on (in Russia, for example).

Another book attributed to St. Sabas is the *Constitutions of St. Theodosius,* intended for the life of both cenobitic and eremitical monks; this was a set of basic regulations for his own monks, which the saint passed on to his successor, Melitas of Beirut.

Sabas died on December 5, 532, at the age of ninety-three; his body was later taken to Venice where it rested in the church of St. Anthony until November 12, 1965. At that time, as a sign of reconciliation between the two great Christian churches, it was restored to his laura, where it now rests. The veneration of this great founder spread in the West as well; one evidence of this is the fact that toward the middle of the 7th century a monastery on the Aventine in Rome was dedicated to him, probably by Greek monks.

159. Image of St. Mary the Egyptian who greatly influenced monasticism in Palestine and the Middle East. Syrian icon from the 18th century. Monastery of Our Lady of Balamand, Lebanon.

160. One of the principal figures of Eastern monasticism that influenced Byzantine and Orthodox spirituality throughout the centuries was St. John of Damascus. We mention him here because he in his turn could be regarded as the continuator of the work of St. Sabas in the task of bringing the latter's monastic rule, the Typicon, up to date. Wall painting from 1408 in the church of St. Simeon in the monastery of Novgorod, northern Russia.

160

3. MONASTICISM AND ICONOCLASM

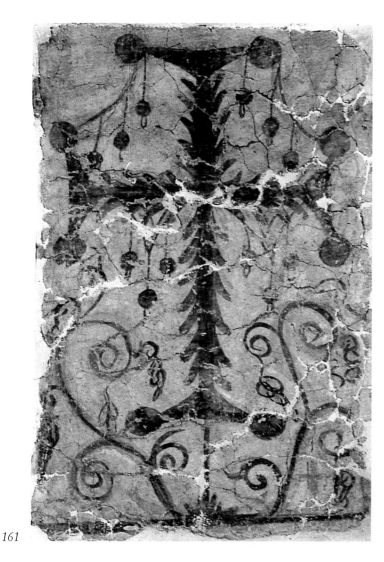

161

We have here a strange, complex, and painful war of all against all that preoccupied and buffeted the Byzantine Empire at least during the 8th century and a good part of the ninth. This was the very time when the Arabs and Bulgarians were sapping the Empire's ability to defend itself, occupying a good part of its lands, and attempting to conquer Constantinople.

The iconoclasts ("destroyers of images") agreed with the prohibition of Exodus and Deuteronomy against representing in images the beings of heaven and earth and with the resultant decision of the Jews and the Arabs that there must be no images made of God. Involved here were the fear of falling into the pagan practice of worshiping idols, the uncertainty and doubts of many Christians on the subject, and also the excessive power and influence of monks in Byzantine society.

The movement began when Emperor Leo III, who was of Syrian origin, violently attacked the veneration of religious images; his motive may have been his own family tradition, or it may have been his desire to ingratiate himself with nearby Arabic peoples. Such images were forbidden by the Mosaic Law and by the Quran, but they played a large part in Christian devotion. In fact, religious images seem to have been central in the life of the Byzantine Empire. The people had multiplied sacred images, placing them not only in churches and monasteries but in private homes and public buildings, on furniture, in windows, on clothing, seals, and pendants, or, in short, in all areas of social life both public and private.

Theologians generally regarded images as a good servant of apologetics and prayer, for, as Patriarch Nicephorus said, "vision leads to faith." But not a few thought that the cult was excessive and often crossed the line into idolatry. Sts. Athanasius of Alexandria, Cyril, John Chrysostom, and Gregory the Theologian were eloquent defenders of images: "The mute painting speaks from the walls and does a great service."

The Second Council of Nicaea (797) issued this decree: "We decree that, like the figure of the honored and life-giving cross, the

162

161. *A so-called cross of the iconoclasts in a hermitage of Kellia (the Cells) in Egypt. The absence of the figure of Christ is compensated for by the union of the symbols of the tree, symbol of life, and the cross, rich in ornaments and already a symbol of resurrection. Coptic monasticism, as we have seen, meditated on the unbreakable connection between the cross and the resurrection.*

162. *This large cross adorned with gems is painted on the ceiling of the chapel of St. Basil near Mustafapaşa in Cappadocia. It is not sure that it dates from the iconoclastic period but it expresses well the predilection for the representation of the cross characteristic of the iconoclasts.*

revered and holy images, whether painted or made of mosaic or of other suitable material, are to be exposed in the holy churches of God, on sacred instruments and vestments, on walls and panels, in houses and by public ways" (*Decrees of the Ecumenical Councils,* ed. N. Tanner, 2:135–36).

Beyond a doubt, there was at work here a fundamental motive, namely, the unquestionable connection between devotion to images and the Arian crisis, for monks and other devout Christians considered the rejection of images to be nothing but an echo of Monophysitism, that is, a new way of rejecting the incarnation of God. As St. John of Damascus wrote, "It is not anything material that I worship, but the one who made matter and became material for my sake, who chose to dwell in matter and who through matter accomplished my salvation."

On the other hand, the majority of monks displayed an excessive devotion to images and supported and shared in the most exaggerated manifestations of these. This was a further reason why Emperor Leo III the Isaurian combated with equal energy both devotion to images and the monks.

There was thus a convergence of theological arguments, deep devotion, and an at least equally deep ignorance of doctrine.

The entire story involved not only a theological disagreement but also, and above all, uncontrolled passions. The emperor and his soldiery committed every kind of terrible act against images, against the simple people, and against the monks. The monks, however, refused to be daunted, but showed a tenacious resistance; for over a century they stirred up the fervor of the people so that the latter never ceased to venerate images but followed the example of their monks more than ever.

Emperor Constantine V decreed the confiscation of monasteries, their transformation into barracks, and the induction of the

164

163

monks into the army. This was the first such direct attack on the monks and the reason why many of them emigrated to southern Italy. In some cases, and due perhaps to the very resistance put up by the monks, the latter became one of the most important foci of Byzantine religious life and acquired public and political influence.

The theologian best known and most influential in the iconoclast controversy was John Damascene, a Palestinian monk, who wrote three defenses of images. Also important was Theodore the Studite, a reformer of monastic life and a fervent defender of images of Christ. Both men developed the theology of images.

In 843 the legitimacy of icons was finally accepted. The result was a feast which the Orthodox have celebrated ever since on the first Sunday of Lent. Monks continued to be the soul of the Byzantine Church and of Byzantine religious life on into its golden age.

163. This miniature, executed in Constantinople around 1000, is one of the oldest extant representations of the Holy Face, a subject that played a major role in the controversy over images. The attacks on the face of Christ, even though they happened later on, show how hostile the iconoclasts were to the attribution to God of a human form. Apostolic Vatican Library, Cod. Ross. Gr. 251.

4. THE STUDITE REFORM AND ST. THEODORE

REFORM OF THE MONASTIC OFFICE OF CONSTANTINOPLE

165

165. A most expressive representation of Theodore the Studite in a mosaic from about 1040. Monastery of Hosios Lukas, Phocis, Greece.

The monastery of Studion, originally the parochial church of the Holy Precursor in Constantinople, was founded by the senator Studius in the 5th century. In the course of time it became the most significant monastery not only in the city but among all the monasteries in the western part of the Byzantine Empire. The whole series of monastic rules from the 11th to the 12th centuries were based on the Studite rule.

St. Theodore the Studite, who died in 826, wrote the typikon (a manual of rubrics for religious services) for the service which was soon to be accepted in the western part of the Byzantine Empire. Owing to Theodore, his monastery became a renowned center of learning, particularly known for its scriptorium. Later the monastery was devastated and then reconstructed by Constantine Paleologus in 1293.

In the process of service reforms undertaken under the influence of the rite of the Holy Sepulchre in Jerusalem, the Studite Typikon accepted poetic works by the best authors belonging to the order of the Sabaites such as Andrew of Crete, Cosmos of Maium, and John of Damascus from the monastery of St. Sabas the Sanctified.

Thus, the Studite Typikon for the rite was influenced by the Jerusalem Typikon. Later the Studite was to influence the Jerusalem, but the latter ultimately ousted it, and the former was not preserved in its original form. The Studite Typikon was partly made known in the middle of the 9th century, and in its somewhat longer form in the eleventh, namely, when Alexius, the patriarch of Constantinople (1025–1043)—who before he was elected patriarch had been a hegumen according to some and an ecclesiarch (sacristan) of the monastery of Studion according to others—presented the Typikon to the monastery of the Dormition of the Holy Virgin, which he had founded in 1034. The Founder's Typikon of this monastery, known also as the Alexius Typikon, was largely a version of the Studite Typikon. Truth to tell, Patriarch Alexius also drew heavily upon a number of other monastic rules and the practice of the Great Church (Santa Sophia) in Constantinople.

The actual difference between the Studite Typikon and that of Jerusalem is a point of special interest. It had been tackled by Nikon of the Black Mountain, an 11th-century monastic writer from Antioch. He was renowned for his work on the substitution of the Studite by the Jerusalem Typikon. According to that of Jerusalem, the rite consists of Vigils, stichera are chanted, while Matins are combined with the service of the first hour (there is no mention of Vigils in the Studite Typikon). All year round the rite consists of Vespers, nihterinon, and Matins; the great doxology is never chanted, and apostycha are read on major holidays.

According to the Studite Typikon, the service takes place seven times a day (see Ps 119:164), starting with Matins. Psalm 5 is read at the first hour (Lauds), Psalm 85 the ninth hour, and Psalm 103 at evening prayer (Vespers). During Matins the life of the saint of the day is read, while the Exaltations of Theodore the Studite are read during Vespers. According to the Studite Typikon, the Divine Liturgy is not celebrated every day.

166. *The church of St. Andrew (870–871) in Peristerai, Greece, is an example of the revival of monasticism at the end of the iconoclastic period. The monks, convinced iconodules, were for the most part forcefully "silenced" and often in the matter of building as well.*

166

Besides the Founder's Typikon by Patriarch Alexius, there are several other founders' rules which were written under the influence of the Studite Typikon, but some akoloutha and all the Menaia are left out. The following typika rank among them: the typikon of Cryptoferrata Monastery and that of Grottaferrata Monastery, both founded by the monk Nilus (d. 1004) about thirty kilometers from Rome; the typikon of the monastery of Nicolo Cassugliano in the eastern part of Calabria, founded in 1099, which was written by the hegumen Nicolas in 1174, who drew upon the godly fathers Sabas and Theodore the Studite; and the typikon of the monastery of the Mother of God Euergetis, founded by the monk Paul (d. 1054) on the outskirts of Constantinople in 1048.

Although the Studite Typikon started being replaced by the one of Jerusalem after the decline of the Latin Empire in 1261, some of its rites, as it has already been pointed out, have been preserved not only in the founders' typika already mentioned but on the pages of the Jerusalem Typikon as well. They can therefore be traced to the first translation of the Jerusalem Typikon into Old Church Slavonic, in the typikon of the Serbian archbishop Nikodim in 1319.

5. STS. CYRIL AND METHODIUS

167

167. A portable icon of Sts. Cyril and Methodius.

The brothers Constantine (called the Philosopher) and Methodius were born in Thessalonica—the second city of the Byzantine empire—into a noble family known to the emperor. Methodius was born in 815 and Constantine in 826. Methodius pursued a career in the administration of a Slavic principality which his biographer does not identify, but there are good reasons to believe that it was Bithynia in Asia Minor. He also wrote juridical treatises which attest to his thorough knowledge of the law. His younger brother followed a different route: he studied in the capital of the empire under the best masters; then he was ordained reader, that is, he was a cleric of low rank, however, a rank necessary to open to him later on the position of secretary of the patriarchal chancery. Uninterested in the duties this position entailed, Constantine soon tended his resignation and withdrew to Kleidion Monastery in the

capital. When he chose to stay in that monastery—six months at the most—there is no doubt that Constantine's intention was not to become a monk there but to be in a peaceful environment in order to concentrate and take decisions about his future. The atmosphere of the monastery provided this opportunity; however, his choice to live there shows how familiar he was with monastic life.

After nearly twenty years as governor of the "Slavic principality," Methodius reappeared but this time as a monk. His biographer relates that "when the opportunity presented itself, he left the principality behind and went to Mt. Olympus in Bithynia where the holy fathers live." There he received a black habit and lived in humble obedience, observing fully the monastic rule and being in charge of the books. A little later, Constantine, who in the meantime had taught philosophy and accomplished an official

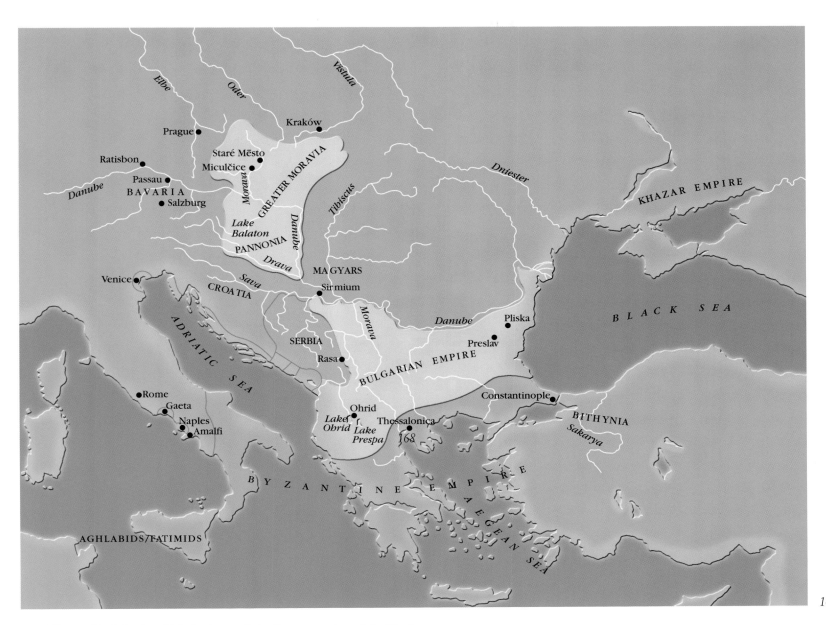

168. The world of Cyril and Methodius and the first expansion of the Slavic church as far as Greater Moravia and in Pannonia; their disciple, Clement, will cause a new monastic expansion in the Bulgarian world, now christianized, in the region of Lake Ohrid.

mission to the Arabs, came to join his brother and, like him, care for the books. It is sure that Methodius had become a monk whereas Constantine did not receive the tonsure, although he continued to function as a reader.

Mt. Olympus was an important monastic center encompassing many monasteries, some of which were illustrious because of their ascetics. Since the 8th century, the region had welcomed almost 200,000 Slavs from Bulgaria who asked the Byzantine emperor for permission to settle there, a permission which was granted. It is known that among the eminent monks of Mt. Olympus, there was Joannice the Great (754–846), who was a Slav. This shows that already the Slavs living in Bithynia were attracted to the monastic ideal.

Constantine and Methodius had come here, the latter to become a monk, and both of them to "care for the books," as their biographers state. This occupation logically suggests that while residing in the monastery of Mt. Olympus, the future apostles to the Slavs, helped by Slavic monks, had begun to prepare the great Slavic mission by working on the translation of the sacred texts into the Bulgarian language. Thus the monastery of Mt. Olympus, where Methodius lived, had become a center of Greco-Slavic literary collaboration, an example that the Greek monasteries of Constantinople, Sinai, and Mt. Athos would follow later on.

While at the monastery, the brothers were entrusted by the emperor with a mission to the Khazars. That mission accomplished, Constantine came back to Constantinople while Methodius

*169. Monastery of St. Naum on Lake Ohrid,
which attests to the spread of the monastic
posterity of Cyril and Methodius.*

169

returned to Mt. Olympus. The emperor and the patriarch wanted Methodius to be ordained to an important bishopric, but he declined the honor. So they appointed him abbot of the monastery of Polychron, which was rich and counted seventy monks. Obviously, this choice was not haphazard; that the patriarch had the right to appoint the abbot of a monastery—a right exclusively reserved for monks—means that this monastery was under his immediate jurisdiction. The direct sources do not tell us what went on during the rule of Abbot Methodius in the monastery of Polychron, but it is highly probable that he was busy with the problems of the Slavic mission which the empire was in the process of preparing. Thus, we are not surprised that it was from Polychron that the emperor ordered Constantine and Methodius to go into the Slavic country of Greater Moravia in order to

respond to the request of its sovereign, Rastislav, who wanted Byzantine missionaries to preach the gospel to his people in the Slavic language.

When leaving for Greater Moravia, where their missionary and literary activity was intense, the brothers were accompanied by confreres, among whom were Slavic monks from Bithynia. After a stay of forty months in Moravia, where they made the Slavic language that of the church, the two brothers set out for Rome. On their way, they passed through Pannonia, and upon the entreaties of its ruler, Prince Kocel, preached in that region also. Finally, still accompanied by their followers, they reached Rome to meet the pope and found hospitality in the Greek monastery of Rome.

There, Constantine, worn out by his labors, fell sick. Feeling death approaching, he asked to be clothed with the monastic habit,

170. In this mural from Assisi, Italy, Benedict, the patron saint of the Western church and the primary source of Western monasticism, is placed between the patron saints of Slavic Christianity and monasticism, Cyril and Methodius.

171. Interior view of the church of St. Clement in Rome, where Cyril was buried.

which was done, and it was only then that he received the name of Cyril. Before dying, he told his brother that he knew how much he liked his monastery in Bithynia; however, he advised him not to go back there but to continue his missionary work. Within eight days he died, a simple monk. Methodius then told the pope, "Our mother asked us to swear that the first one of us to die would be brought back by his brother to his monastery and buried there." These words tell us that Cyril was predestined to die a monk. He was buried in the church of St. Clement in Rome. The brothers' biographies—true literary compositions—have bequeathed to the Slavic people the love of monastic life that burned in the hearts of those who gave them their alphabet and created their liturgical books.

6. A VARIETY OF MONASTIC RULES

172

172. *Image of St. Anthony, the progenitor of Eastern monasticism. Mural of the church of the Anarghiri Saints of Kastoria in Greece.*

173–176. *Four views of the Coptic monasteries which are the witnesses of the great tradition of St. Pachomius.*
From top to bottom: *Deir al-Malak, the monastery of the Archangel Michael, in the region of Naqada and Qamula, north of Luxor.*
In the same region, Deir Mari Buqtur, the monastery of St. Victor, and Deir Anba Pisantius, the monastery of Abbot Pisantius.
The monastery of the Martyrs, Deir al-Shuhada, south of Luxor. Founded on the site of the martyrdom of the Christian community of Esna and its bishop.

177. *The angel's appearance to Pachomius. Wall painting in the monastery of Aghiu Pavlu on Mount Athos in Greece.*

Unlike what we find in Western monasticism, there are in the East no religious "orders" distinguished from one another by their specific charism; there is but one type of monastic life, and every monastery is autonomous. The differentiation of "rules" in the East depended on the several ways of life: from eremitism to the small community of two, three, or more monks (skete), to the laura-group of small communities, to cenobitism, that is, large communities living a common life under the direction of an archimandrite or hegumen (leader of a monastery). At the basis of all of these there is an awareness that monastic spirituality is simply an eschatological radicalization of one's baptismal promises and that it is therefore a model for all Christians.

As a result, the necessity of directing monastic life by means of an appropriate rule was not seen at the beginning, another reason being that the first form of monastic life was the charismatic choice of the individual hermits who began to withdraw into the desert of Egypt in the 3rd and 4th centuries. Their experiences gave rise to "traditions," but these did not yet constitute rules in the juridical sense; they were simply model ways of life.

St. Athanasius (295–373), bishop of Alexandria, was conscious of his responsibility for the monks and felt the need of giving a well-defined direction to the monasticism that was taking form before his eyes. Even then he did not appeal to a legislative document but wrote his *Life of Anthony,* which "was a sufficient basis on which monks could define their asceticism." Thus he did not set down a minimum of practices to be observed but rather set the ideal of perfection before the monks.

The first rule, then, was a charismatic saying, a logion, addressed personally by an elder to his spiritual son and based on his authority. As such, it became part of spiritual direction. This personal logion, which might be taken over by others who also felt its value for their own lives, sprang from oral tradition. In a further step, some sayings became famous and were written down. The sayings thus fixed in writing were then grouped systematically and subsequently incorporated into similar collections (*Apophthegmata*).

At the end of this development there came the "Rule of the Tradition of the Fathers," which, however, had no other purpose than to foster the spiritual advancement of the individual; it did not as yet make any claim to regulate common life. This "rule" was followed by hermits and recluses.

Completely different was the Rule of Pachomius (ca. 290–347), the founder of cenobitic monastic life. This was inspired by the need of fostering peace and recollection in the life of a well-ordered community. But, while the logion of an elder had to do with the content of an individual's spiritual life, the Rule of Pachomius aimed rather at adapting human juridical experiences to spiritual ends and therefore to regulate the external aspects of monastic life. For this reason the monastic Rule of Pachomius can be regarded as a kind of Christian social humanism. The danger lurking in it was that of secularizing common life to some degree.

St. Basil of Caesarea (ca. 330–379) seemed to have this danger in mind when he composed his Rules, for in order to unite the brothers spiritually, he uses the word of God, which is the real Basilian rule. Everything else is regarded as an explanation of that

173

174

175

176

177

178. St. Basil the Great. After the fathers of the desert, the first organizer of Eastern monasticism. Detail of a mural depicting officiating bishops (1208–1209) in the apse of the church of the Mother of God, at the monastery of Studenica in Serbia.

178

word. Basil thinks of monasticism not as an autonomous institution within the Church, but simply as a miniature model of the Church, and one that is available to all.

The development of the Basilian rule can be divided into three stages or steps. The first text, which can be regarded as a "rule" in the proper sense (and was considered such by Basil and his contemporaries), consisted of the *Moral Rules.* Here over 1500 verses from the New Testament were distributed under eighty rules *(horoi),* which were in turn divided into subchapters; they summarize, in a systematic way, what is to be done and avoided. This rule might be described as a rule of life for a committed Christian.

The second stage consisted of the small *Asceticon;* it reflects the practical needs that had emerged in Basil's conversations with monks of the various ascetical brotherhoods, who often asked him to answer their questions. As a result, the work retained the form of a dialogue, of questions and answers. In this *Asceticon* there is a kind of transition: from an ecclesial group of "committed Christians" in the direction of an organized and institutionalized monastic order. The emphasis, however, is still more on the interior life than on externals.

The third stage is represented by the large *Asceticon* which is subdivided into Short Rules *(Regulae brevius tractatae)* and Long Rules *(Regulae fusius tractatae).* The former consist of numerous individual regulations, while the latter are a final systematic summary of the same. The entire *Asceticon* is, for practical purposes, simply a commentary on the *horoi* taken from the Bible. In it Basil sets down particular regulations for a way of life that can now be called monastic.

Drawing his inspiration from Basil, St. Sabas (6th century) combines in his famous typikon elements of the Basilian rule with his

179. The ladder of paradise according to the vision of St. John Climacus. Mural on the north facade of the church of the Resurrection in the monastery of Suceviţsa in today's Romania.
John Climacus, who lived between 570 and 640, wrote the famous Ladder of Paradise *in Greek while he was abbot of the Sinai monastery. This book, which today would be called a best-seller, was translated into Latin, Syriac, Arabic, Aramaic, Armenian, Church Slavonic, and subsequently into various modern languages.*
Ascetical life is interpreted as a ladder which the monastics must ascend, each step corresponding to a virtue which they are called to acquire.

There are thirty steps just as there were thirty years in Christ's hidden life before his public ministry.
The influence of this work on Eastern monasticism, particularly in Slavic countries, was enormous.

180. Bridging the 8th and 9th centuries, Theodore the Studite (759–826), like St. Sabas in the 6th century, reinvigorated monasticism, once the iconoclastic crisis had ended. The wall painting reproduced here comes from the monastery of Chilandari on Mount Athos (1621–1622) and is the work of Georgije Mitrofanović.

own experience of the eremitical life as lived in the Great Laura in Palestine, which he himself had founded and governed.

St. Theodore the Studite (759–826) wanted to reform monastic life in the cenobia of his time. He did so by returning to the Rule of Basil, while adapting it on certain points, for example, the much greater importance which his typikon, known as the *Hypotyposis,* gives to the superior. His work led to a large number of typika, on which, later on, Slavic monasticism was likewise based.

In the Byzantine tradition, the name typikon (from Greek *typos* = rule, regulation) was given to a book of customs, or consuetudinary, that regulated the everyday life of a monastery from the juridical and monastic but chiefly the liturgical viewpoint and served as a perpetual calendar. In general, two kinds of typika are distinguishable. The first originated in a spiritual father, the founder of a monastery, who lived the monastic life and codified it for those who would follow him. In addition to those already named, mention should be made, above all, of the typikon of Nikon of the Black Mountain (d. 1088), as well as his *Pandekta,* a canonical and liturgical compendium.

The second group of typika are known as *ktetorici,* or foundational, because they had their origin in a civil authority (usually a nobleman who built a monastery and formulated the typikon that would regulate the life of those who accepted his gift). Such typika appear from the 10th century on, almost exclusively in the Byzantine Empire.

In addition to typika, which were always individual, there were regulations binding generally. In the Christian East it was often the public authorities who issued monastic legislation. Imperial laws (Justinian) or episcopal synods (especially the Council of Chalcedon) formulated monocanonical regulations for discipline in all of Byzantine monasticism.

7. Monasticism under Islam

181

181. *The splendid remnants of the pavement of the church of St. Stephen (8th century), in Umm al Rasas, Jordan. Among other things, one sees the representation of the principal cities of the time. The church was built when the region had come under the caliphate of Damascus; yet the splendor of the decoration shows that it was possible for the Christian community to live amicably within the Arabo-Islamic culture of the time. A Christian monument of this period rivaled any other building and was fully woven into the cultural fabric of the time. If later on the region fell into decadence, it was due to the transfer of the caliphate from Damascus to Baghdad and the centers of the Roman* Provincia Arabia *were thus cut off from the age-old roads of communication.*

182

182. *The monks also helped in the building of the church of St. Stephen, a proof of which is this panel in the south aisle with the portrait of a benefactor and the fully visible inscription, "Remember, Lord, your servant Kaioum, a monk and priest of Fisga."*

The presence of Christianity in the Middle East, which had been its cradle, and in Africa, of glorious memory for its martyrs, its saints, and its over seven dioceses at the beginning of the 5th century, was, for practical purposes, wiped out by the invasion of Islam's armies and the introduction of its religion.

What catches the eye is the weak resistance of the various populations. This was due in part to African particularism, which rejected the domination of the Byzantines, and in part to the seemingly superficial Christianity of many of the barely romanized native peoples. The telling remark of some Monophysite villages was recorded: "The God of vengeance has sent us the Arabs to rid us of the Romans." They thought the new invader would have greater respect for their religious choices than the Byzantines had had: they were soon disillusioned by events.

The fall of Syria, Palestine, and its symbolic city Jerusalem meant a decisive break in the history of Christianity. On August 20, 635, Damascus surrendered, and Jerusalem in 638. The apathy of the population and the support from Monophysites in not a few instances explain a situation that came about more because of anti-Byzantine nationalism than for strictly religious reasons. Greek civilization, which for a millennium had covered

183. *An arch of the side aisle of the church of San Michele di Cuixá in Catalonia. The edifice was built in the 10th century and the arches clearly show the influence of Islamic art.*

the entire Near East and had given birth to shining throngs of wise persons and thinkers was now swept away and replaced by a new mentality and a new culture. Syria in fact turned Arabic with surprising ease. On the whole, the Christian population showed a resigned submission.

The North African Christian societies of Augustine and Cyprian disappeared completely. Although Christians were initially allowed to retain their religion while paying a special tax of one-fifth of their incomes, this toleration soon ceased and, from the mid-8th century on, they had to choose between apostasy and exile. For in fact, although Muslims held that they should tolerate Christianity and Judaism, the other two religions of the Book, their attitude varied greatly from period to period and according to the group in power.

The coexistence of Christians and Muslims was certainly not as idyllic as some claim; in some places, indeed, the Arabs incorporated Christian communities into their society, and the latter preserved their faith and ecclesiastical organization down the centuries, but they were always in a position of inferiority in relation to the Muslims and, in the majority of cases, saw their

forces gradually lessen until they disappeared.

Visigothic Spain, for its part, collapsed like a castle of cards in 711; and although the long-time Christians coexisted with the invaders, who never had much to do with the native peoples, that part of the peninsula gradually accepted Islam, the religion of the majority. A minority of Christians took refuge in the north, where they were prepared to hold on to their territory and customs and to stand up to the invaders.

In these adverse circumstances, monasticism came to the fore in especially important ways. The coming of the Muslims often meant the destruction of monasteries and the flight of monks to places still Christian. This happened in Sicily, where the majority of monks fled to Calabria, and, often, in Muslim Spain and in not a few places in the East. But in areas of Christendom that were subject and often mistreated, but that still preserved a good deal of their previous internal organization, monasteries were not lacking, nor Christians who continued to live their calling as hermits. These monks, living a life devoted to charity, preaching, the singing of hymns, and teaching, often served Christians as basic points of reference for

184. Ruins of the monastery of Makaravank in Armenia, whose construction began in the 9th century. In certain periods, the monastery was under the authority of the Islamic government.

185. Historical map showing the year of the establishment of Arabo-Islamic governments around the Mediterranean and in northern Mesopotamia and the Caucasus.

184

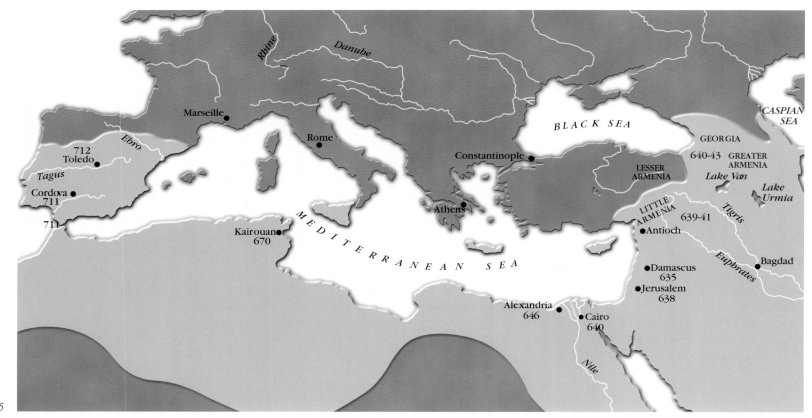

185

186

186. *Monastery of Nekresi in Kahetia, Georgia, founded between the 6th and the 7th centuries (the murals are from the 16th century); for a time it was under the Islamic regime.*

their own devotional lives and the preservation of their identity as Christians. The Maronites came into existence in present-day Lebanon in the region around the monastery governed by St. Maron, and they were able to preserve their faith and their roots. In Armenia and Georgia the people remained faithful not only to Christianity but also to their national identity, thanks above all to the work and example of the monks, who were a constant model and inspiration for the people's lives. In medieval Muslim Cordoba monks were a salutary shock to some communities often grown drowsy and in danger of being assimilated. This brought the monks to martyrdom but also produced a painful but effective awakening.

Monks were obviously not the only witnesses to a living Christianity, because there still existed an ecclesial organization made up of clerics and laypeople, but we often see in the monasteries a concentration and epitome of the Christian spirit and, at the same time, a tenacious defense of the most fundamental traditions of the various national groups.

On the other hand, in a society in which Christians found themselves surrounded and controlled by the culture and ways of life of the Muslim population, efforts were not lacking to relate and accommodate Christianity to Muslim teaching, the aim being to achieve a better coexistence with them. In that situation, two cases in particular became motives for confrontation and bitter controversies. In an islamicized Spain, the adoptionist heresy was renewed, that is, an effort to set aside the complex mystery of the Trinity, which supplied Islam with an abiding denial of the oneness of the Christian God, by asserting that Christ was not true God but only a human being adopted by God. In Byzantium, meanwhile, there arose the rejection of images of the divinity, a rejection like that of the Muslims. The iconoclasts believed that this rejection would make it easier to convince and assimilate believers in Islam. In both cases, there were monks who with great fervor combated these heresies bent on appeasement and who defended traditional teaching.

Even today we find some monasteries in countries that are almost exclusively Muslim. Times have changed a good deal, but circumstances continue to be difficult. In Algeria, a few years back, a monastery of Cistercian monks surrendered their lives and gave a new example of committed fidelity to the Christian ideal.

1. St. Gregory the Great

THE FIRST POPE-MONK

187

188

189

187–189. The world of the monk-pope Gregory the Great is that of one Rome, which is represented on the paleochristian apse of Santa Pudentiana, and was reconquered by the Goths in 553. The city will remain within the orbit of the Byzantine empire, which was represented on the cupola of Santa Sofia until 755. Nevertheless, in this Rome, into which government functionaries, religious, soldiers, and artists converged, Gregory, who had been imbued with Eastern spirituality, will become the promoter of a monasticism which today we recognize as Western.

190

191

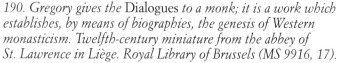

190. Gregory gives the Dialogues *to a monk; it is a work which establishes, by means of biographies, the genesis of Western monasticism. Twelfth-century miniature from the abbey of St. Lawrence in Liège. Royal Library of Brussels (MS 9916, 17).*

191. St. Gregory and the deacon Peter. Miniature from the Moralia *of St. Gregory. Library of Montecassino (MS 73).*

Beginning in 568, the Lombards destroyed a good part of the ecclesiastical and monastic organization in northern Italy. We must not forget that the monasteries were closely tied to the ecclesiastical organization and under the direct control of the bishop and had no direct connections among themselves. As a result, they shared the fate of the ecclesiastical organization of which they were part and suffered the consequences of the invasion. Many monks fled the battlefields and formed new communities in more peaceful spots, often with help from the popes. In Rome, the basilicas and more important churches often relied on monasteries of men and of women.

St. Gregory is one of the most appealing and admired popes in the history of the Western church. He was born into a noble family around 540, received a good education, and at the age of thirty was appointed prefect of the city due to his talents and personality. In order to provide a refuge for the many monks who, after fleeing their houses because of the Lombard persecution, reached Rome confused and without resources, Gregory established six monasteries on his estates in Sicily, and a seventh in his own family home on Monte Caelio, to which he himself then withdrew.

After ordaining Gregory a deacon, Honorius II sent him as his ambassador to the court of Constantinople (579–586); this was a sensitive and important office, and one in which Gregory was aided by the excellent relations he established with the imperial family and with the patriarch of Constantinople. While there, he familiarized himself with the spiritual teaching of the Greek Fathers and made contacts with Eastern monasticism.

In 590 Gregory was elected bishop of Rome and received episcopal ordination. The difficult problem of reconciling the active and contemplative lives would be with him for the remainder of his years. He never abandoned the austere and devout life of a monk and sought always to live a life of prayer while not neglecting the duties of his office.

Gregory can be regarded as the spiritual father of the Middle Ages, and, in fact, monks considered him the teacher of the interior life. We owe to him a splendid set of writings that express the spirituality of monasticism in a most satisfactory and thought-provoking manner. His greatest success was due to the fact that he presented the teachings of the Greek Fathers and of St. Augustine so that they were accessible to the monks of his own time. His *Dialogues* tell the story of outstanding figures in pre-Lombard monasticism and, in a special way, the life of St. Benedict, to which the entire second book of the work is devoted.

Gregory was not a Benedictine nor do his rules and counsels belong properly to the Benedictine tradition, but he had a good knowledge of Benedict. He wrote that saint's biography and reported his teaching, so that it can be said that his own monastic ideals were permeated by the same spirit as those of Benedict.

Gregory thought of a monastery as a serene and safe place in which to take refuge from the turmoil and busy life of the world. In that place people sought to strip themselves of everything worldly, to rise above the sinful human condition, and find delight in the joys of eternity. In a monastery they could devote themselves to contemplation and focus their minds on prayer. Nothing was to disturb the tranquility and peaceful setting that monastic life needed. There was no place for frequent sorties from the monastery nor for the personal administration of possessions located outside it nor for the reception of crowds of guests.

Gregory's election to the papal office snatched him from the monastery but not from his ideals; moreover, his new office gave him a better understanding of the spiritual value of apostolic work. He wrote, "I have no fear for myself, but I have a great fear for those entrusted to me," and he devoted his time and energies to solving the problems of the Western church and spreading the message of Christ.

In this arduous task he made extensive use of monks. He put them in episcopal sees; they helped him directly in his own work of governing; he sent them to England on one of history's best-known missions of evangelization. Although no one has asserted more forcefully than he the difficulty of discharging at the same time the duties of a cleric and those of a monk, Gregory also made it clear that the good of the church, the conversion of pagan peoples, and the salvation of the faithful could require that some monks collaborate as bishops and priests. This seeming inconsistency on Gregory's part is explained by his personal experience: "A contemplation that to a certain point is excessively tranquil and excessively sure of itself prevents a monk from maturing amid the difficulties and troubles of the active life."

This man, who experienced a constant longing for his lost monastic life, was very conscious that "any who, though possessing many virtues, refuse to feed God's flock, should be convinced that they do not love the supreme Shepherd." In his hands, monasticism became the providential instrument for the internal rebuilding of the church and for the evangelization of distant peoples. But despite all this, there is no doubt that his conception of monasticism remained focused on separation from the world and even from ecclesiastical life.

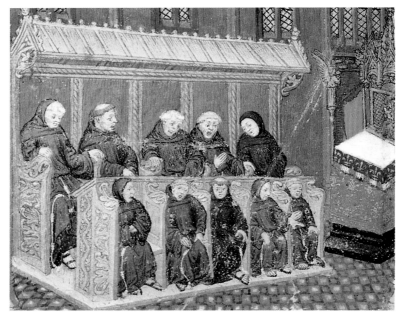

192. Scene from monastic life: monks in their choir stalls. Miniature from the 15th century, from the Psalter of Henry VII. British Library, London.

192

In order to surmount this seeming inconsistency, Gregory did not hesitate to improve the spiritual state of monasteries and the life of monks. He reformed them, when he thought it necessary, by a constant stream of provisions, with the result that he became the pope who had the greatest influence on the monastic law that was coming into existence.

One of his most far-reaching steps was to clarify relations between monasteries and diocesan bishops. The one who governs a monastery is the abbot and not the bishop of the diocese, although the latter retains jurisdiction over it. Although the bishop ordains the new abbot, he does not intervene in his election. The bishop is obliged, then, to be solicitous for monastic observance but not to administer monastic property nor take possession of monasteries nor dispose of their members as he wishes, nor diminish their prerogatives. It can be said, then, that in a way the regulations Gregory issued took the first clear step toward the exemption of religious, a matter that has always produced conflict in the life of the western church.

193

195. *Scene from monastic life: the communal meal. The representation connects it with the miracle of the multiplication of sacks of flour, which is illustrated in the background of the scene.*
Mural by Sodoma (beginning of the 16th century) in the cloister of the monastery of Monte Oliveto Maggiore, Italy.

194

195

193. *Scene from monastic life: at work in the scriptorium, a fundamental occupation of monastics promoted by Gregory the Great.*
The miniature is the work of the celebrated scriptorium of Echternach, ca. 1040. Staatsbibliotek, Bremen, Germany.

194. *Scene from monastic life: seasonal agricultural work near the abbey.*
Miniature from the abbey of Montecassino (Codex CXXXII).

2. THE MIXED RULE

When St. Benedict died, he left behind a written rule and three active monasteries: Montecassino, Subiaco, and Terracina, which coexisted for centuries with a multitude of monasteries of every kind that depended on other traditions and followed other rules. The Rule of Benedict spread only very slowly, and it spread not so much because more Benedictine monasteries were founded as because existing monasteries gradually adopted his Rule as their own.

How, meanwhile, did so many monasteries carry on when they were so autonomous and were not part of a group? They did so with the aid of what has been called a "mixed rule" or "abbot's rule," that is, with rules of every kind and origin that stamped and directed the life of monasteries from the middle of the 5th century to the 9th century. These rules were countless, varied in conception and application, and drawn up in order to organize a particular community or, in some cases, a group of monasteries.

Some thirty such rules have come down to us. Back in the 5th century John Cassian had already remarked that there were as many rules as there were monasteries.

In reality, it was the abbot of each monastery who selected, compiled, and imposed the rules. In their monastic libraries abbots had codices that were often real compilations of monastic rules; here they found a direction for the spiritual and temporal regimen which they imposed on their houses. They chose the norms which they thought most suitable in each concrete case. This amounted to saying that they composed a rule by selecting from a menu.

Some of these rules had little legislative efficacy. Many were rather brief, and the principles set down were incomplete in regard to the demands of community organization; they gave more space to monastic theory or to ethico-religious reflections than to concrete norms of behavior; their tone was often paternal

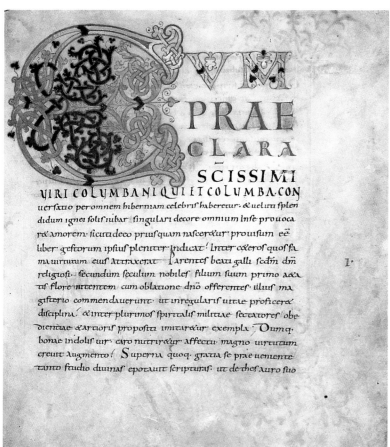

196. *Liturgy is an indispensable component of monastic life; consequently, the liturgical texts are a vivifying instrument. Here one sees Luitherus dedicating his antiphonal to St. Gall, ca. 1135 (Cod. Sang. 375).*

197. *The biographies of holy founders or reformers are a basic help to "understanding" the rule on the plane of religious anthropology, that is to say, to perceive it in their cultural and spiritual motivations. The miniature from St. Gall (Cod. Sang. 562) reproduced here is the beginning of the biography of St. Gall by Walafrid Strabo.*

and familial, and unsuited for disciplinary purposes. In other words, this rich ensemble of rules resembled ascetical suggestions and edifying examples to be imitated rather than binding codes.

This approach to the subject had obvious advantages, but it also had serious drawbacks. It made it easy to adapt the rule to the real existing community at a given moment, but everything depended on the character of the abbot, and we know that not all abbots were first-rate. A mediocre or wretched abbot could easily destroy the spiritual and economic life of his monastery, something that happened with great frequency. Above all, we must bear in mind that these rules did not establish definitive obligations but, rather, were sets of instructions describing the path good monastics ought to follow and the spirit in which they should do it.

To eliminate this drawback, Benedict defined a monastery as a community that lives "under a rule and an abbot"; the abbot too must submit to the rule and follow it in all its parts. It was several centuries before this golden idea of Benedictine monastic life prevailed, although the *pactum* of Spanish monasteries was also based on such a reciprocal obligation.

It is a fact, of course, that abbots were not as autonomous as might seem at first sight since they had to submit to an ensemble of more universal laws that imposed some seemingly definite restrictions on them; these were the imperial laws, the decretals of the popes, and the canons of the various ecumenical councils, especially those of the council of Chalcedon (451), which were very important for monastic life. The fourth canon of Chalcedon decreed that no one could establish a monastery without the authorization of the bishop, that monastics were subject to the diocesan bishop, that they must devote themselves to a life of fasting and prayer and reside in the appointed place, that they must not interfere in ecclesiastical matters, and that they must

198–199. The very arrangement of the monastery reflects the provisions of the Rule. What is reproduced here is the celebrated plan of the abbey of St. Gall (an idealized representation of a Carolingian monastery) executed in the scriptorium of Reichenau ca. 825. Today in St. Gall (Cod. 1092).
1. Church; 2. Scriptorium, with library on upper floor; 3. Sacristy on two levels; 4. Building for the preparation of the hosts and oil; 5. Cloister; 6. Chapter house; 7. Heated room and dormitory; 8. Baths and hygienic facilities; 9. Refectory, with vestiary on upper level; 10. Kitchen; 11. Wine cellar, above: food stores; 12. Parlor; 13. Room of those in charge of the poor; 14. Guesthouse for pilgrims; 15. Brewery and oven for the pilgrim's guesthouse; 16. Porter's room; 17. Quarters for the director of the school; 18. Lodgings for traveling fellow-monks; 19. Brewery and oven for guests; 20. Guesthouse; 21. School for day students; 22. Abbot's quarters; 23. Room for those who have been bled; 24. Physician's quarters; 25. Small herb and spice garden; 26. Hospital;

198

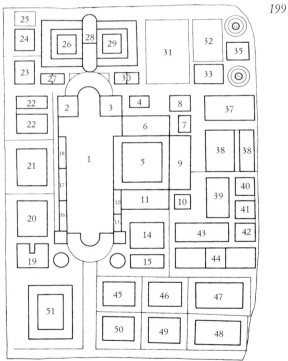

199

27. Kitchen and hot baths for the hospital and room for those who have been bled; 28. Double chapel for the hospital and the novitiate; 29. Novitiate; 30. Novitiate kitchen and baths; 31. Cemetery and orchard; 32. Garden; 33. Gardener's house; 34. Duck yard; 35. Caretaker's house; 36. Chicken yard; 37. Granary; 38. Workshops; 39. Monks' kitchen and brewery; 40. Mill; 41. Wine press; 42. Drying shed; 43. Granary and cooper's workshop; 44. Stable for bulls and horses; 45. Sheepfold; 46. Tower; 47. Goat shed; 48. Cow shed; 49. Stable; 50. Pigsty; 51. Servants' quarters.

200. The foundational texts of monastic life were copied again and again. This miniature of St. Benedict with Abbot Theobald is found in a copy of the Moralia *by St. Gregory. Library of Montecassino (MS 73).*

200

201. Liturgical art is not limited to books or the furnishings of buildings; here we see a Romanesque episcopal crozier from the monastery of Boscherville in Normandy, France, on which we note the Christian reappropriation of Celtic and pre-Christian animal symbols.

201

not leave their monastery unless their bishops requested it. Only too often, unfortunately, these norms were not followed.

Sometimes, the term "mixed rule" was applied to a combination of the Rules of Benedict and St. Columban. The latter, the content of which was more doctrinal and penitential, contained few practical norms, except in the area of penance, a field in which all the regulations were practical. For this reason, but with little justification, these mixed rules were described as penal codes. In everything else but penance, the Benedictine Rule applied, and this was an eminently practical monastic code. For this reason, some scholars claim that Benedict entered the Western monastic world on the arm of Columban. Beginning in the mid-7th century, some French monarchs imposed this mixed rule on some of the most important monasteries of the realm: those, for example, of St.-Denis, St.-Martin of Tours, and St.-Germain of Auxerre.

In the 8th century Louis the Pious and Charlemagne imposed the Benedictine Rule on all the monasteries of the empire, while the Cluniacs made it known, and imposed it, on the Iberian peninsula.

The authors of the several rules regarded as promoters of disorder and anarchy those ascetics who refused to be part of a stable community but lived independently, whether alone or in very small groups, and wandered from place to place. St. Jerome, in a letter of 384, bemoaned the spread of this practice; Cassian condemned it severely, and Benedict harshly rejected it. The complaints of these several men show that monastics were very slow to live according to a rule and that vagabond monks were considered a threat until well into the Middle Ages.

In the eyes of Jerome and Cassian, to be a monastic meant living in a monastery under the government of a superior. For Benedict and other authors of his time, obedience had to be twofold: to the rule and to the abbot or abbess: "cenobites . . . serving under a rule and an abbot" *(genus coenobitarum . . . militans sub regula vel abbate)*. This was a new formula that made the rule an entity distinct from the authority of the abbot and gave it priority, although we must be aware that the ancient concept of a monastic rule was different from ours and did not turn the rule into an overriding legislative instrument. In the eyes of the early legislators, the source of all the prescribed behaviors was the Bible; only through a constant appeal to Scripture could they establish a different kind of society. Rules were not self-contained texts but complements of the one great rule, Scripture. This explains how it was acceptable to read, compare, and mingle different rules.

At this period, double monasteries were founded in Gaul, that is, monasteries housing communities of men and communities of women in the same enclosure. A double monastery was not, of course, a mixed society of men and women. It consisted of two separate communities of men and women, who lived near one another; in some cases they gathered in the same church for liturgical functions and they had a single superior, often an abbess.

3. MONASTICS AND EVANGELIZATION

At first sight, a monastic vocation requires stability, silence, and enclosure. Yet monastics have played a very important role in the history of evangelization.

When St. Gregory the Great decided on the evangelization of the Saxons, he thought of monks as the best instruments for the purpose. For that reason, he sent St. Augustine and his forty companions—monks from Gregory's own Roman monastery of St. Andrew—to the kingdom of Kent; thus was opened one of the most dazzling pages in the history of evangelization. Although these monks were initially not convinced that their voyage was a suitable one, the pope's clarity and decisiveness not only changed their attitude but turned them into effective evangelizers. Gregory's homilies on Ezekiel show his conviction that the contemplative life of monastics is completed through action. The first mass conversion in England took place as early as 597.

On being appointed the first archbishop of Canterbury, Augustine did not delay in establishing a monastery in his see: the first Benedictine monastery outside of Italy. St. Bede the Venerable describes with simplicity the apostolic life of the monk-apostles to England: "When they took over the dwelling given to them, they began to imitate the apostolic life of the primitive Church, giving themselves to regular prayer, vigils, and fasts, preaching the word of life to whomever they could, and scorning as alien to them all the things of this world." Around 610, what would later become the renowned abbey of Westminster was founded in London. Monasteries of men gradually grew in number and became authentic breeding grounds for the apostolate and evangelization.

Irish monks also played a crucial role in the evangelization of Scotland and northern England. They were great travelers and began the missionary and cultural tradition of the *peregrinatio pro Christo,* "traveling (or exile) for Christ," that is, abandoning their monasteries and engaging in endless journeys, full of hardship and suffering, to pagan lands where they would proclaim the good news. Preaching was no less a vocation than the search for solitude. It was an ascetical, difficult, and sacrificial way of life, given the hardships, privations, and dangers of every kind which they inevitably encountered in the countries in which they tried to settle.

It is fitting to remember especially the holy island of Lindisfarne, founded from Iona by St. Aidan and a monastery from which came some of the most important Irish manuscripts, such as the famous Evangeliary from the end of the 7th century. Here again, the monasteries were the main hubs of evangelization.

Irish and English monasteries of women, whose abbesses often had a high social and spiritual rank, were likewise very important in the christianization of England and other continental lands.

St. Columban was an important example of the Irish missionary monk. At the age of 41 he felt called to preach the gospel on the continent. In Burgundy he founded the monastery of Luxeuil on the ruins of a Roman fortress; this community in turn would found many other monasteries. It became a nursery of

202

202. *Computer drawing of an initial letter from the Evangelistary of Bobbio in which the Irish source is obvious.*

Gallo-Frankish missionaries who had a revitalizing influence on their own Frankish church and, together with the Irish missionaries, brought Christianity to the still-pagan Germans who had fallen under the power of the Franks. Years later in Italy, Columban founded the monastery of Bobbio, where he died in 615. The spirit of Columban's monasticism was austere, demanding, and individualist; it thought of the monastic life as a struggle in which the monastic tried to attain to a complete renunciation of self and an absolute submission to a superior.

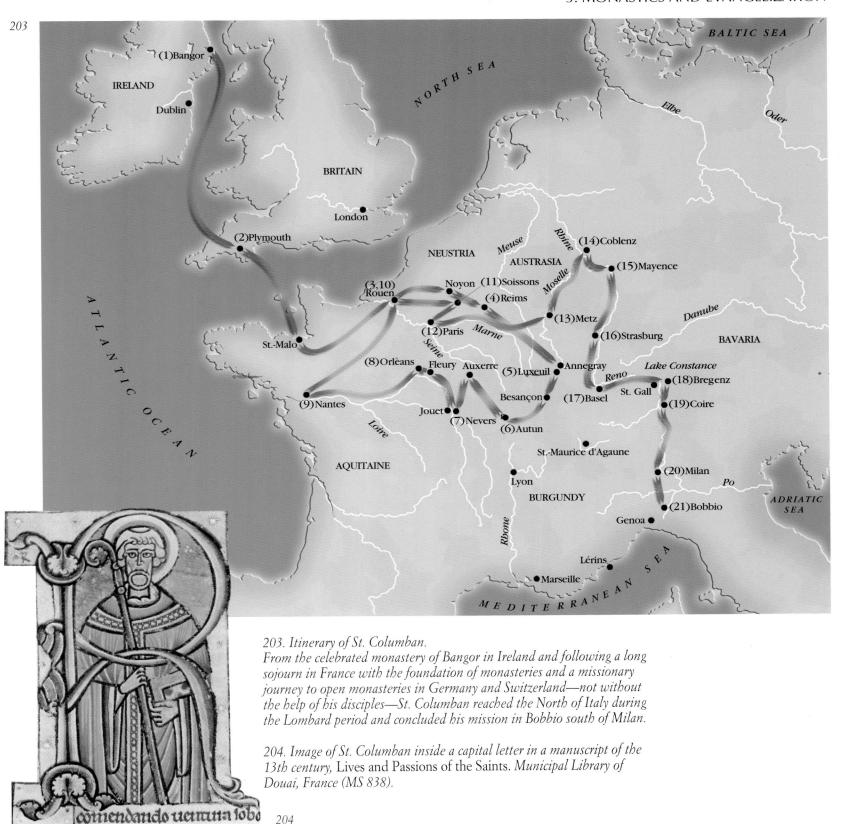

203. Itinerary of St. Columban.
From the celebrated monastery of Bangor in Ireland and following a long sojourn in France with the foundation of monasteries and a missionary journey to open monasteries in Germany and Switzerland—not without the help of his disciples—St. Columban reached the North of Italy during the Lombard period and concluded his mission in Bobbio south of Milan.

204. *Image of St. Columban inside a capital letter in a manuscript of the 13th century,* Lives and Passions of the Saints. *Municipal Library of Douai, France (MS 838).*

204

Columban was accompanied by some outstanding Irish monks, such as St. Gall, who lived as a hermit in the part of Swabia that is now Switzerland, and St. Killian, who evangelized present-day Franconia (Würzburg).

Today's Low Countries, Germany, parts of Poland and Bohemia, Denmark, and Sweden were evangelized in large measure by Anglo-Saxon monks in the Benedictine tradition. St. Willibrord with his eleven companions, Sts. Boniface (Winfrith), one of the great missionaries of history, Pirminius, Anskar, and many other Saxon, Frankish, and Visigothic monks, brought to those lands the faith, culture, and Rule of Benedict. These missionaries took into account the structures familiar to the Germanic peoples and therefore sought mass conversions by winning over the chiefs and kings, often through marriages with Christian princesses. Willibrord is regarded and venerated as the apostle of the Low Countries; Boniface, a man of marvelous and tireless activity, was the apostle of Germany, reformer of Bavaria and Gaul, and archbishop of Mainz.

205

206

206. Tradition states that this Codex Ragyndrudis *is the very one held by the saint at the moment of his martyrdom; the cuts in the page would have been made by the blows of the sword. Treasury of the cathedral of Fulda.*

205. Scenes of the life of St. Boniface. A baptism and the death of the saint in 754, with only his gospel book as protection. Miniature from a missal of Fulda in Germany, dating from the beginning of the 11th century.

These monks preached, baptized, and founded monasteries which became indispensable bases for evangelization. They established the beginnings of an ecclesiastical organization and built cathedrals, as well as monasteries. As a result, around 800, all of western Europe was full of great abbeys: Corbie (657), Echternach (708), which was a true seedbed of missionaries, Reichenau (724), Fulda (744), which from its very foundation was exempt from the authority of any and every diocesan bishop, St. Gall (750), and Corvey (822). Rudolph of Fulda summarized this policy in his life of St. Lioba: "When that blessed man Boniface saw that the Church of God was growing . . . he set up two ways of increasing religion. He began to build monasteries in order that people might be drawn to the Catholic faith not so much by the labors of clerics as by communities of monks and virgins. . . . To Montecassino he sent his disciple, Esturnus, a man noble both by birth and manner of life, in order that there, in the monastery founded by the blessed father Benedict, he might learn regular discipline and monastic life and customs."

In their work these monks not only Christianized but also civilized. Fulda and the majority of monasteries became focal points of religious and ecclesiastical life and centers for the spread of culture. The libraries; the work of copying manuscripts, which rescued and preserved a large part of Greco-Roman culture; the monastics' own writings, which provided reliable chronicles of these times and manifested the original thought of their authors—all these made the monasteries irreplaceable centers for the growth and spread of culture.

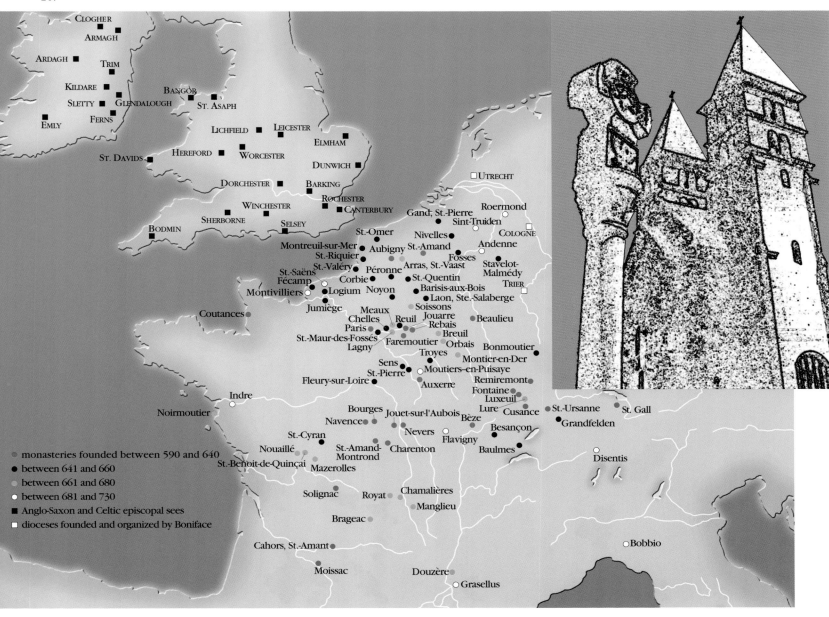

CLOGHER
ARMAGH
ARDAGH
TRIM
KILDARE
BANGOR
SLETTY GLENDALOUGH
ST. ASAPH
FERNS
EMLY

LICHFIELD LEICESTER
ELMHAM
HEREFORD WORCESTER
ST. DAVIDS
DUNWICH
DORCHESTER BARKING
WINCHESTER ROCHESTER
SHERBORNE CANTERBURY
BODMIN SELSEY

UTRECHT

Gand, St.-Pierre Roermond
Sint-Truiden
St.-Omer COLOGNE
Montreuil-sur-Mer Nivelles Andenne
St.-Riquier Aubigny St.-Amand
St.-Valéry Fosses Stavelot-
St.-Saëns Arras, St.-Vaast Malmédy
Fécamp Corbie Péronne TRIER
Montivilliers Logium St.-Quentin
Jumiège Noyon Barisis-aux-Bois
Meaux Laon, Ste.-Salaberge
Coutances Chelles Reuil Soissons
Paris Jouarre Beaulieu
St.-Maur-des-Fossés Rebais
Lagny Faremoutier Breuil
Orbais Bonmoutier
Troyes Montier-en-Der
Sens Moutiers-en-Puisaye Remiremont
St.-Pierre Fontaine
Indre Fleury-sur-Loire Auxerre Luxeuil
Bourges Lure Cusance St.-Ursanne St. Gall
Noirmoutier Navence Jouet-sur-l'Aubois Bèze Grandfelden
St.-Cyran Nevers Besançon
Nouaillé Flavigny Baulmes Disentis
St.-Benoît-de-Quinçai Charenton
Mazerolles St.-Amand-Montrond
Solignac Royat Chamalières
Brageac Manglieu

Cahors, St.-Amant Bobbio

Moissac Douzère
Grasellus

● monasteries founded between 590 and 640
● between 641 and 660
○ between 661 and 680
○ between 681 and 730
■ Anglo-Saxon and Celtic episcopal sees
□ dioceses founded and organized by Boniface

207. Monastic foundations which are the fruit of what is called the "Irish mission." Picture: the abbey of Echternach, today in Luxembourg. It was founded by the Northumbrian monk Willibrord in 708, whose grave is here. The abbey as it stands today dates from the Romanesque period.

4. THE CAROLINGIAN REFORM

ST. BENEDICT OF ANIANE

Under Pepin the Short (751–768) and especially under Charlemagne (768–814), Christianity and the church permeated all social phenomena in the empire. First, there was an extensive and rather widespread cultural and literary renaissance. Both the episcopal schools and the monastic scriptoria, in which the classical authors were copied and thus were not lost but came down to us, promoted the intellectual formation and culture of a part of society. The result was that a good deal of ancient culture was preserved; this in turn brought about the renaissance of the 13th century and the humanism of the 14th and 15th centuries. At the same time, these institutions tried to reform the morals of governors and people and the liturgical usages of the clergy, which were in full decline. Monastics became an educated class and educators of the people; the monasteries were active cultural centers, and some of their members became true teachers of the new peoples.

Almost imperceptibly, the rulers sought uniformity within their realms, being convinced that uniformity promoted unity and, in the end, their own power and the peace of the realm. Charlemagne, who was not a great founder of monasteries, asked the abbot of Montecassino for a normative copy of the Rule of St. Benedict; he then sent it to all the abbots of the empire and demanded that all monks follow it.

It was in this way that the Benedictine Rule was imposed on all monasteries. Yet, the spread was due not so much to an imposition from without as it was to the conviction of the monastics that this Rule was more measured than that of St. Columban and more suitable and balanced than the others in effect in different monasteries. In fact, St. Boniface and his Saxon monks were of the same opinion when they imposed on their monasteries the Benedictine Rule that had been brought to the British Isles centuries before. By the end of the 8th century, monastics regarded themselves as the sons and daughters of Benedict, whom they considered to be their sole patron and patriarch, without suspecting how novel this universal acceptance was.

St. Benedict of Aniane (c. 750–821), from a Visigothic family and knowledgeable about the Eastern monastic tradition, wanted

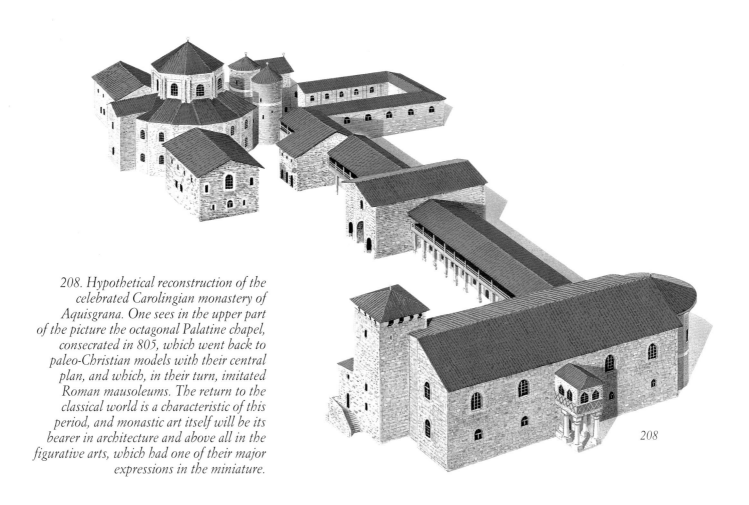

208. Hypothetical reconstruction of the celebrated Carolingian monastery of Aquisgrana. One sees in the upper part of the picture the octagonal Palatine chapel, consecrated in 805, which went back to paleo-Christian models with their central plan, and which, in their turn, imitated Roman mausoleums. The return to the classical world is a characteristic of this period, and monastic art itself will be its bearer in architecture and above all in the figurative arts, which had one of their major expressions in the miniature.

208

209

210

209. A masterpiece from the Carolingian scriptoria, this miniature of David playing an instrument, surrounded by musicians and his guards, acts as a frontispiece to the Book of Psalms in the Bible of Vivien (Tours, 845–846). The return to classical forms is obvious. Bibliothèque Nationale, Paris (Ms. Lat. 1).

210. This fountain of life where Christian symbols and classical and pagan elements are combined is part of the Evangelary of Godescalc. School of Charlemagne's court (782–783). Bibliothèque Nationale, Paris (Ms. Lat. 1203, new acquisition).

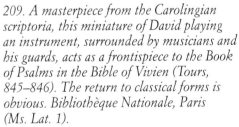

to live as a solitary and lead a very strict life. But, as we are told by Ardo, his biographer, "the grace of God inspired him with a different plan; in order that he might be a salutary exemplar to his brothers, God inflamed him with a love of the Rule of Benedict; leaving aside his solitary struggles, this athlete moved onto the field of battle in order to fight henceforth along with all the others." He founded an austere community near Montpellier and drew many disciples; he was also an effective promotor of monastic uniformity.

Benedict was certainly not opposed to the intellectual work of the monks, but he thought that this ought to be subordinated to their religious and spiritual roles. He was convinced that the variety of observances and the independence of the monasteries were one cause of monastic laxity. In his desire to revive the Rule of Benedict in all its purity he established important monasteries on which he imposed a demanding but balanced way of life.

Gradually, bishops and princes asked him to send monks capable of reforming other monasteries. Charlemagne and especially Louis the Pious supported him in this undertaking and made him supervisor of all the monasteries of the empire, thus making him their abbot general, as it were. Louis called him to the court in Aachen (Aix-la-Chapelle) and appointed him abbot of the new monastery of Inde (815), which had been founded in the capital, with the intention that he make it a model to be imitated. Louis wanted this monastery to become a nursery of abbots and to supply a body of inspectors who could reform existing monasteries.

The monastic synod of Aachen (817) instituted a "monastic capitulary": a set of often very detailed observances that were not always in accord with those of St. Benedict; there were seventy-five statutes that prescribed the principal duties of monks. In particular, the capitulary sought to ensure the economic subsistence of

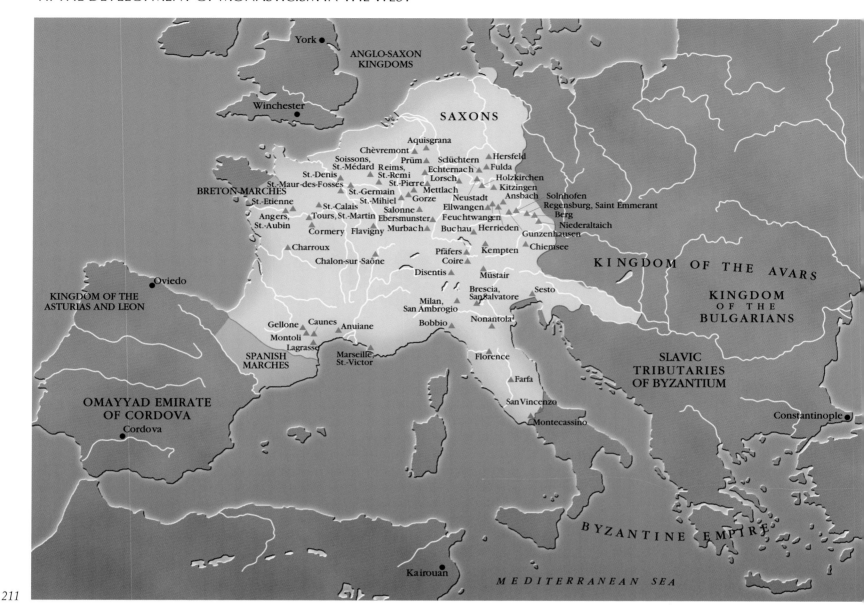

211

211. *Map of Charlemagne's empire showing the monasteries which received imperial donations.*

monasteries in face of the unscrupulous greed of abbots who held monasteries in commendam; this was a chronic cause of the decline of monastic observance and of the celebration of the Divine Office according to the principles of the Benedictine Rule.

Before all the abbots of the empire who were assembled for the synod, Benedict of Aniane "explained the Rule in detail; he made clear to everyone what had been obscure; he clarified difficult passages, rejected ancient errors, defended customs and useful additions. He caused everything to be approved unanimously and composed a capitulary which he presented to the emperor for his signature so that the emperor might then order its observance in all the monasteries of the empire."

A year later, another synod approved the rights and privileges Benedict wanted. At the same time, they approved some instruc-

tions for women monastics that would introduce a more demanding austerity into their lives. A rule inspired by the Benedictine model was prescribed also for the canons of cathedrals and parish churches and for the canonesses who were coming into existence at the beginning of the 8th century.

Benedict of Aniane was also responsible for a strong organizational centralization and a rigid disciplinary and liturgical uniformity that, to some extent, was an attack on the autonomy of the abbeys. In fact, Benedict revised the monastic Rule of Benedict on some points: giving greater prominence to the liturgy, strengthening the role of the abbot, adapting the food and clothing of the monks to climatic conditions in the Franco-Germanic kingdom, which were so different from those of southern Italy. All these innovations were accepted, and monastic renewal spread quickly.

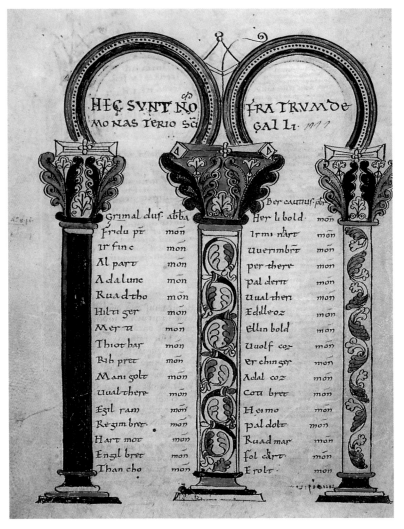

212

213

214

212. *Beginning of the list of the monks of St. Gall under Abbot Grimaldus (841–872), from the* Codex Fabariensis *("Liber Viventium") kept in the library of the same abbey.*

213. *Miniature from the Evangelary of Liuthar, kept in the cathedral treasury of Aquisgrana. Liuthar offers the book to Emperor Otto III.*

214. *From the abbey of Fulda comes this 10th-century miniature dedicated to the life of St. Killian, the patron of Würzburg, Germany. Niedersachsische Landesbibliothek of Hannover (Ms. 189).*

As often happened, the wealth and power of the monasteries attracted the greed of the feudal lords, who burdened them with taxes and tried to get hold of their revenues. They also were given the commendam, according to which monasteries found themselves subject to lay lords or abbots appointed by them, none of these being able to grasp the deeper meaning of the monastic vocation. The results were deadly to the religious life and discipline of many monasteries which passed through periods of decadence and helplessness, although some important monasteries continued to play a brilliant role, among them Fulda in Franconia, Corvey in Saxony, St. Gall in Swabia, and Reichenau near Lake Constance.

5. CLUNY

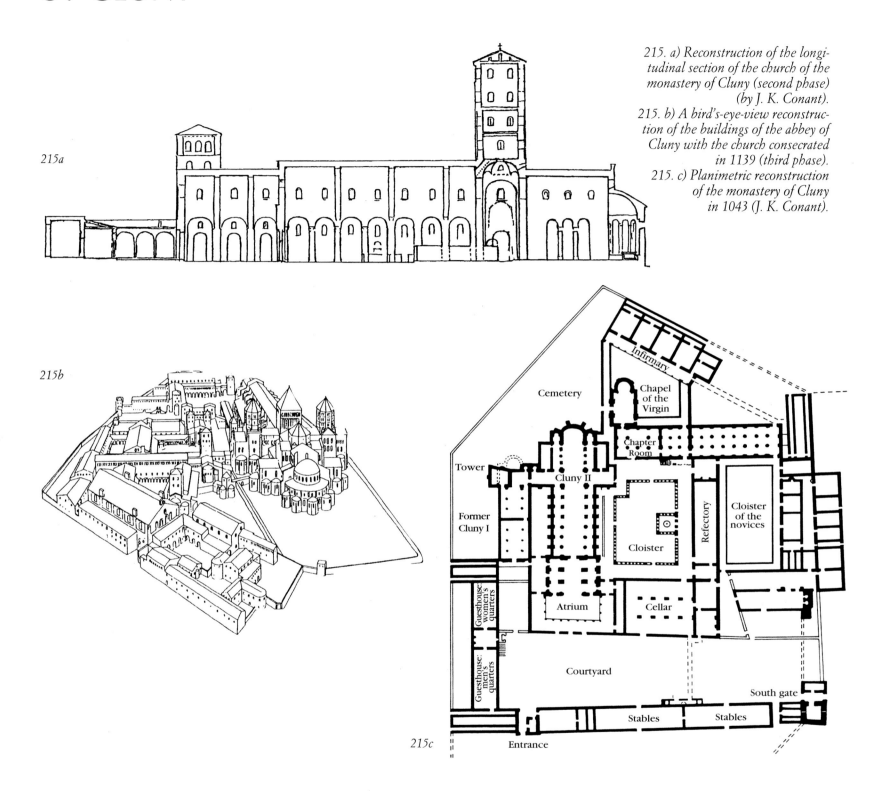

215a

215b

215c

215. a) *Reconstruction of the longitudinal section of the church of the monastery of Cluny (second phase) (by J. K. Conant).*
215. b) *A bird's-eye-view reconstruction of the buildings of the abbey of Cluny with the church consecrated in 1139 (third phase).*
215. c) *Planimetric reconstruction of the monastery of Cluny in 1043 (J. K. Conant).*

Labels in plan (215c): Cemetery · Chapel of the Virgin · Infirmary · Tower · Chapter Room · Cloister of the novices · Cluny II · Former Cluny I · Refectory · Cloister · Guesthouse: women's quarters · Atrium · Cellar · Guesthouse: men's quarters · Courtyard · South gate · Stables · Stables · Entrance

The reform of religious life, which became ever more necessary, came from the monasteries themselves. Some felt an irresistible need to return to the sources of the monastic vocation. The best known of these efforts and successes, and the one that would have a more lasting influence and take a more universal hold, was that of Cluny. In the so-called "dark century" the reformed monasteries succeeded in exerting a true moral influence on Christendom.

In 910, William of Aquitaine decided to build an abbey at Cluny "for the salvation of his soul," and he linked it to the "patrimony of St. Peter," that is, the papacy. The popes granted

Cluny a spiritual exemption and extended this to all the monasteries that became part of the new "order." In virtue of belonging to St. Peter, Cluny remained safe from the interference of bishops and feudal lords, and this autonomy, which broke the chains of the previous feudal system, was the basis of its greatness. Cluny became a real *civitas Dei* (city of God). The privileges granted by the popes caused conflicts with the bishops, but gradually all the monasteries and even entire religious congregations obtained from Rome the privilege of exemption.

The many monasteries that wanted to adopt the customs of Cluny (*Consuetudines,* 1068) were obliged to a strict submission

216

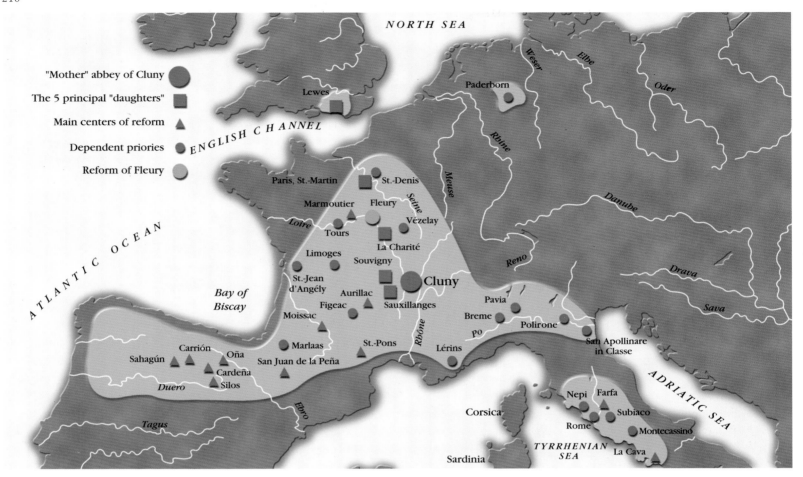

Legend:
- "Mother" abbey of Cluny
- The 5 principal "daughters"
- Main centers of reform
- Dependent priories
- Reform of Fleury

NORTH SEA

Weser · Elbe · Oder

Paderborn

ENGLISH CHANNEL

Lewes

Rhine

ATLANTIC OCEAN

Meuse

Paris, St.-Martin · St.-Denis

Seine

Marmoutier · Fleury · Vézelay

Loire · Tours · La Charité

Limoges · Souvigny

Danube

Reno

Drava

St.-Jean d'Angély · Aurillac · Cluny

Bay of Biscay

Figeac · Sauxillanges · Pavia

Moissac · Breme · Polirone · Sava

po

Carrión · Oña · Marlaas · St.-Pons · Lérins · San Apollinare in Classe

Rhône

Sahagún · Cardeña · San Juan de la Peña

Duero · Silos

Ebro

Tagus

Corsica

Nepi · Farfa

Rome · Subiaco

Sardinia

TYRRHENIAN SEA · La Cava

Montecassino

ADRIATIC SEA

216. *The congregations of Cluny, 10th–11th centuries.*

217. *Pope Urban II consecrates the main altar of the church of Cluny. Miniature from the* Chronicon cluniacense *of Saint-Martin-des-Champs, dating from the 12th century. Bibliothèque Nationale, Paris (Ms. Lat. 17716).*

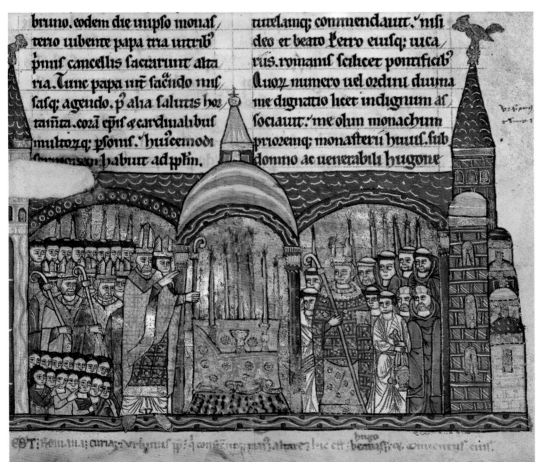

217

218

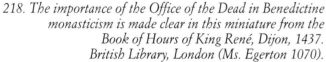

218. The importance of the Office of the Dead in Benedictine monasticism is made clear in this miniature from the Book of Hours of King René, Dijon, 1437. British Library, London (Ms. Egerton 1070).

219. The interior of the church of the monastery of Tournus in Burgundy, France, is an example of the purest Cluniac architectural style. Given the lack of sufficient remains from Cluny, Tournus here gives an illustration of how the Cluny of the year 1000 participated in the artistic and cultural revolution which would later on give birth to European Romanesque.

219

to the central abbey and to its abbot, who in fact became the only abbot of all the houses; all of them had to take a vow of obedience to him. The abbot and community of Cluny decided on regulations that pertained to all, and there was no general legislative assembly, although the monasteries remained independent in their daily life and in their specific organization. The community of Cluny grew from 50 to 700 monks, and the order ultimately had over 1200 houses in all the countries of Western Europe. All the novices made their profession at Cluny and lived there for the first three years of their religious life. This meant that the influence of the mother house was exerted more by the personal transmission of a spirit than by the imposition of rules, which, of course, were not lacking. In carrying out its role of guidance and teaching, Cluny relied on long-lived abbots, who were also exceptional personalities: Berno (910–927), Majolus (948–994), Odilo (994–1048), Hugh (1049–1109), and Peter the Venerable (1122–1157), a contemporary of St. Bernard.

The church at Cluny was for centuries the largest church in Christendom, while during the 11th century the abbey was the spiritual center of Western Christianity. Abbot Odilo instituted and established detailed regulations for the feast of All Souls. The feast began on the evening of November 1, the feast of All Saints, with the singing of psalms, the ringing of all the bells, and the

lighting of ten candles before the altar. Funerals, too, were regulated in every detail. The dead were regarded as among the blessed because they had entrusted themselves to the prayers of the monks, so sure were they of the efficacy of this intercession. Cardinal Peter Damian wrote, "I entrust my soul into your hands, so that it may be fed at the table of your prayers." The care of the dead is an element in all religions, but few institutions can match Cluny in offering the living so much security and hope in regard to the dead.

The trait most characteristic of Cluny was its liturgical life. The work of adoration and intercession for the Christian people, but especially for the deceased, which are proper to the Christian liturgy, was cultivated and developed in a splendid setting and magnificent style, although at times this was overly hieratic and formal. The monks gave over eight hours a day to the church and chapters, while manual labor was practically nonexistent and the work of copying manuscripts was dropped.

We read in a chronicle, "In that monastery . . . so great was the number of monks that Mass was celebrated continuously from dawn to mealtime; and it was a ceremony marked by such dignity, purity, and reverence that it provided a spectacle more angelic than human." But not much time was allowed for private prayer, since the monks acted as a compact group, with determined roles

220. All that is left today from the last phase of the great monastic establishment of Cluny is the so-called tower of the clock, which is the lantern of the right transept.

and defined objectives, in a Liturgy of the Word that was collective, accompanied by psalmody and processions, and truly fervent.

Also important was the part this monastery played in the Truce of God *(treuga Dei)* movement. The nobility, who were always in conflict among themselves and engaged constantly in bloody personal feuds, often accepted the peacemaking authority and appeals of these monks. Also, in the Spanish kingdoms the new monasteries dependent on Cluny played an important part in the history of the Reconquista, the reconquest of Islamic Spain by the Christians.

Cluny's part in the monastic renewal in the European countries was significant. The monks had close connections within feudal society, and their links with Rome (several popes had been Cluniac monks) led to their being frequently elected to the most important episcopal sees. This meant that the Cluniac reform also produced positive fruits for the reform of the Western church as a whole.

This monastic system was aristocratic, largely closed to ordinary people and, in general, to the movements of renewal that arose regularly among the rural population and the young people in the cities. In fact, not a few individuals began to condemn the scandalous wealth of Cluny, its frequent interferences in temporal matters, and, above all, its emphasis on two activities that were not originally part of monasticism: the prolonged periods devoted to the Liturgy, and the numbers, thought to be excessive, of monk-priests. St. Peter Damian, an exceptional thinker and renewer of monastic life, had harsh words for this style of monasticism. In his view, monastic life did not require monumental churches or trained choirs or lengthy chants or bell-ringing or valuable adornments.

Although the "Cluniac Order" continued to add foundations and extend its influence in the 12th century, it began to experience a severe and paralyzing crisis that threatened its entire organizational structure, which was too complex to be managed by the abbot of Cluny alone. Its religious effectiveness waned in the measure that its disciplinary demands multiplied.

On the following double page:
221. Map of present-day European Benedictine Congregations with the number of monasteries in each. For the spread of monasticism in Africa, Latin America, and Asia, see pp. 248, 259, and 261 respectively.

222. The west portal of the church of St. Mary Magdalen, Vézelay in Burgundy, which represents the acme of Romanesque architectural ornamentation, is a masterpiece of sculpture. Here we see the tympanum, which for some people illustrates the mission of the apostles (before the ascension), while for others is a portrayal of pentecost.

AUSTRIA		Croixrault	?	Vallumbrosan	8	CZECH REPUBLIC	
Austrian	15	Flavigny	?	Camaldolese	8	Slavic	3
St. Ottilian	1	GERMANY		Silvestrina	5	SCOTLAND	
Beuronese	1	Bavarian	13	Subiaco	19	English	1
Hungarian	1	St. Ottilian	10	Olivetan	11	Subiaco	1
BELGIUM		Beuronese	9	Swiss	2	SLOVAKIA	
Subiaco	4	Annunciation	2	Other Congregations	1	Hungarian	1
Other Congregations	1	Subiaco	2	LUXEMBURG		SPAIN	
Annunciation	5	ENGLAND		Solesmes	1	Subiaco	8
CROATIA		Subiaco	4	NETHERLANDS		Solesmes	4
Slavic	1	English	8	Dutch	3	SWITZERLAND	
FRANCE		Olivetan	2	Solesmes	1	Swiss	5
Subiaco	9	Solesmes	1	POLAND		Other Congregations	2
Solesmes	10	IRELAND		Annunciation	3	St. Ottilian	1
Annunciation	1	Annunciation	1	PORTUGAL		HUNGARY	
Olivetan	3	ITALY		Annunciation	4	Hungarian	4
Other Congregations	1	Cassinese	12				

On the following double page:
223–224. Between the end of the 10th century and beginning of the 12th, this impressive mural was painted in Sant' Angelo in Formis, a foundation of the abbey of Montecassino in central Italy. It is the first painted apse in the West after the paleochristian one in Santa Maria Antiqua in Rome.
Benedictine art thus gives its start to a model which will be repeated throughout the Romanesque period, the European art par excellence: Christ enthroned with the evangelists and the tetramorph from the Book of Revelation. In the enlarged detail on the left page, one sees Abbot Desiderius of Montecassino (1050–1087) offering God the new church of the monastery.

6. RETURN TO THE DESERT
A MONASTIC CHALLENGE TO MONASTICISM

Once again, the history of Western Christianity saw a pattern of great religious significance being repeated: the enrichment of monasteries, their sumptuous buildings, and relaxation in the monastics' manner of life led within the believing community to a sharp reaction in favor of a return to the real, innermost essence of monasticism: poverty, solitude, and identification with the cross. There arose spontaneously in the church a movement challenging the stagnation and the temporal involvements of the monasticism of the day, which was judged and condemned as too wealthy and comfortable. In fact, what happened once again, though in very different circumstances, was a return to the desert.

In St. Bernard's view, monastics were tormented by three fleshly concerns: food, drink, and clothing. These meant that the world was intruding, that the Evil One was tempting them, that they were entering "the valley of the shadow of death." Once monastics chose to flee the world, they ought to renounce every thought that linked them to it. Every challenging movement of reform struggled against the devil, the world, and the flesh in all their manifestations.

There was probably here a rejection as well of the juridical framework that seemed to smother all spontaneity and pluralism in religious life. Therefore, the reaction involved, in particular, a revival of eremitism, which always lurked beneath the surface of the life of Christianity, and of a greater personalization of religious life, an element that had become excessively weakened due to a thoroughgoing regulation. The need was felt for a radical return to the sources; a new concept of poverty, which was not only individual but collective; a revived respect for manual labor; a greater solidarity with the poor, who were so numerous at that time. Another influence, perhaps, was the arrival in great numbers of exiles from the empire of Constantinople, which had been invaded by the Turks; these newcomers brought with them the tradition of a rigorous and demanding life that was so characteristic of Eastern monasticism.

These reformist monastics were trying to recover the simplicity of monastic life and to achieve greater spiritual freedom, greater austerity and poverty, greater independence from feudal society, and greater solitude. These new monastics amazed their contemporaries and gave them hope, for they believed that they could renew Christendom.

St. Romuald

St. Romuald (950–1027) represents these aspirations perhaps better than anyone else. After a stay of three years at St. Apollinare in Classe (Ravenna), he lived for a while as a hermit near Venice and then for ten years at Cuixá in the Pyrenees, where he gave concrete form to the elements of his intuitive vision: a group of hermits living around a monastery, under a fixed rule and an acknowledged authority. Finally, back in Italy again, he began to establish hermitages with great success. In

1012 he founded the best known of these, at Camaldoli near Arezzo. The hermits kept the Benedictine Rule but with their own explanations and constitutions; they dressed in white. All of their houses were subject to the prior of Camaldoli until 1534, when the two branches—anchorites and cenobites—separated completely. Romuald set before his disciples a very demanding way of life: fasts, scourging, vigils, continuous prayer, and absolute poverty. He himself wore a hair shirt, never washed his garments, and ate only bread and herbs. Once again, a radical "contempt for the world" (contemptus mundi) had made its appearance.

In the Life of Romuald by St. Peter Damian we find the saint's idea of the eremitical life: an absolute poverty, a degree of communication with the members, obedience to a superior, a leaning mainly to the life of the hermit, a rejection of the way of life followed in the monasteries of his time, a selective acceptance of the Rule of St. Benedict, and the adoption of St. John the Baptist as the model of a true monastic. Romuald founded and reformed many hermitages and monasteries, but he did not legislate or offer a developed, regulated organization.

In the 11th century the laity interfered shamelessly in the life of the church, taking advantage of the collapse of the Carolingian organization and the decline of the papacy. In his Book of Gomorrah, Peter Damian, prior of Fonte Avellana and a disciple and biographer of Romuald, gives a striking picture of the vices of the clergy in his time. The situation led to a reaction among the people that resulted in the reform of the papacy and the church.

Damian, convinced that the eremitical life was the only valid one for zealous Christians, became the great propagandist for the new movements.

This was the period that saw the rise everywhere of groups of hermits and monasteries of women that all shared the same spirit; it was a period when not a few existing monasteries joined the reform movement by accepting its way of life. Among the Greek monks in southern Italy who had fled the Saracen invasions, the life of Nilus the Younger (910–1005), founder of the celebrated monastery of Grottaferrata, was venerated and followed.

Tuscany was one of the areas richest in new undertakings and experiments in spiritual fervor and wise reorganization.

One of the best-known reformers was St. John Gualbert (990–1073), founder of a colony of hermits who lived in huts in Vallombrosa (1038) near Florence; they kept perpetual silence and complete enclosure and did not do manual work. They soon developed in the direction of a cenobitic life under the Benedictine Rule, although, somewhat like the Camaldolese, the Vallombrosian monks could withdraw into the hills when they needed periods of greater solitude and recollection. In order that the monks might not be distracted and yet have their needs met, John Gualbert established a separate group of lay brothers (conversi).

Near each of the monasteries he founded over the course of his life, Gualbert erected a hospice for travelers and also a kind

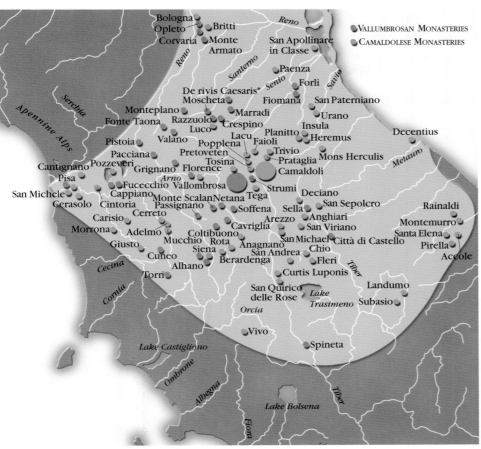

227

225

226

225. *In a rather limited territory of Italy between Emilia and the Latium, there is a high concentration of Vallumbrosan and Camaldolese monasteries.*

226. *Crucifix of Ariberto, today in the Museo del Duomo in Milan. In this masterpiece, completed about the year 1000, a new Western spirituality is expressed, no longer looking back to the classical world, but from now on facing the mystery of the cross as an opportunity to participate in the suffering of Christ and also to stand in opposition to the allurements of the world.*

227. *In this mural by Fra Angelico, dating from 1442, we find various saints who founded orders assembled together. At the foot of the cross, Sts. Benedict and Romuald, founder of the Camaldolese. Below, Sts. Francis, Bernard, and John Gualbert, founder of the Vallumbrosans.*

of boarding school in which aspirants to the priesthood lived, prayed, and were trained; often, these men were sent there by bishops who wanted to reform the life of their clergy.

In all these cases, then, we see an unconventional monasticism that challenged the status quo. Here were monastics seeking a greater share in the cross and a greater perfection; their solitude, however, allowed in some cases for community, and they never completely abandoned the pastoral life.

1. ATHOS AND THE CHANGES IN THE MACEDONIAN PERIOD

228. In the Protaton of Karyes, the "capital" of Mount Athos, we see this icon from the 16th century, representing Peter the Athonite.

Traditionally, Athos, which was first mentioned in the poetry of Homer, is a geographical name of the peninsula at the far eastern end of Chalkidikí. It was only in the Middle Ages that the name Holy Mountain came into use and became widely accepted. However, several centuries were to pass before that name became synonymous with the growing monastic practice on the peninsula, since monasticism was not actually easily and quickly accepted on Mount Athos. Its inland areas were comparatively unsuitable for economic activity, its shores were hostile, and it was far from the central regions of early Christianity. On the other hand, by the end of the 8th century, when the political situation on Chalkidikí and the mainland area closest to it improved, this spacious and rather secluded peninsula offered evident advantages for the life of a greater number of monks.

Thus, it is assumed that the first hermits may have retreated to the peninsula as late as the end of the 8th century, while their presence there was confirmed with certainty only in the first half

229. This mosaic in Santa Sofia in Constantinople shows Emperor Leo VI the Wise receiving divine wisdom from Christ. Leo VI is regarded as one of the first great supporters of Mount Athos.

230. The Metropolitan Church, called church of the Protaton, in the Great Laura on Mount Athos, thus called for being the see of the Protos, the primate among the representatives of Athos' twenty monasteries, the Protaton goes back to the 10th century.

231

231. This evocative view of the Athonite peninsula, which juts far into the sea, is what one sees from the summit of the Holy Mountain. Mountains are regarded by all civilizations as a symbol of the connection between human beings and the divine. The most ancient traditions and certain living traditions consider the mountain the place of the manifestation of the divinity. Because of this, monks chose (and still choose) to dwell on this long and mountainous peninsula for a twofold purpose: isolation and dialogue with God.

of the 9th: the liturgy in honor of St. Peter the Hermit, a renowned leading figure of early hermits, is first attested at this time. Soon, in 845, the final victory of the iconodules and the reestablishment of icon veneration led to the advancement of monastic life and practice, the reestablishment of monasticism, and the return of monks with fervent religious beliefs. In the beginning of the second half of the 9th century, several hermits came together in the first cenobitic communities. The prototype of monastic life, although very likely not the first of its kind, was a semi-eremitic community led by St. Euthymios the New, of Salonika, from 865 onwards. Such communities could have easily developed into cenobia, but they did not; and it was not in the central region of the peninsula that the first cenobitic community, Colobos, appeared, but on its outskirts. This fact was also confirmed at the beginning of the rule of the Macedonian dynasty by the first imperial charter ever given to Mount Athos; the dynasty's founder, Basil I (867–886), presented the community with the

sigillion (the royal seal) in June 883, by which "those who have chosen the life of hermits" were granted the protection of the emperor himself from any disturbance provoked by officials.

The *sigillion* of Basil I was of immense significance for monastic life on Mount Athos because the monastic community was thus granted independence and its integrity was proclaimed for the first time. Although monasteries had not yet been founded, the charter secured the possibility of their development. Thus the doors to the rise of monasticism were opened, and in all probability, the number of monks grew quickly until the end of the 9th century. These new conditions resulted in the independent governing of Athonite monasteries by the *protos* (the monk holding authority over all Athonite monasteries) even before the foundation of large monasteries, and Karyes became his seat. The first mention of the existence of a particular *protos,* the monk Andrew, is found in an act passed by the emperor Leo VI (886–912) in 908. In the following fifty years there is no

232. *Athanasius the Athonite (d. c. 1000) was the first great founder and reformer of monastic life on Athos. This mural from the 14th century belongs to the Macedonian School of the Protaton of Karyes.*

232

233. *Detail of a mural over the entrance to the refectory of the Great Laura. St. Athanasius is followed by Emperors Nicephorus, Phokas, and John Tzimisces, who were the benefactors of the monastic foundation.*

233

mention of any particular *protos,* and the organization of monastic communities in that period has remained unknown. The one certain thing is that by the end of the 10th century the Protaton, one of the oldest churches, had been erected in Karyes.

The greatest turn of events in the life of Byzantine Athos was caused by St. Athanasius the Athonite at about the same time. Athanasius reached Athos from Bithynia by the end of 957 and stayed. His almost three-year-long life of reclusion in the new place brought about immense changes both in monastic life there and its protection from Arabic raids, which threatened the existence of the whole community.

Athanasius was a well-educated monk, an exceptional calligrapher, but also a person with excellent political skills. Soon after his arrival he became a respected member of the community, partly because he was a spiritual father to the famous warrior Nicephorus Phokas. When in 960 Nicephorus first succeeded in an offensive on the island of Crete, which was then under Arabic rule, and thus removed a constant danger threatening Athos, he asked Athanasius to join him. The two friends decided to erect a small cenobitic monastery on Mount Athos. Nicephorus financed the work while Athanasius became the hegumen (head) of the new community.

The monastery was founded in 963, shortly after Nicephorus had already become emperor of the East (963–969). In 964 it was

given the name of Great Laura and granted complete independence; Athanasius became its first hegumen. The relics of St. Basil the Great and the fragment of the holy cross, which were given to the new monastery by the emperor, made it particularly respected. It is at this point that the history of monasteries on Mount Athos begins. The word "laura" came into use as a general term for the monastic communities there and thus had a meaning different from that of the early Christian period. Thanks both to the substantial funds at their disposal and the status of the Great Laura as an imperial foundation, the primary idea of building a small cenobitic monastery was abandoned and a grand edifice for 120 monks, surrounded by other buildings, such as its own hospital and scriptorium, as well as a port, was built.

The emperor John Tzimisces (971–976) gave support to the new monastery, which directly resulted in the codification of its organization and way of life. The Great Laura got its first typikon in 970/71, which followed the rule of the Studite cenobitic community, written in 799 by the reformer of Byzantine monasticism and hegumen of the Studion monastery, St. Theodore the Studite. According to his rule, which served as an example of monastic life, three basic principles had to be observed in the everyday life of a cenobitic community: communal life (without slaves), the law of absolute obedience, and compulsory work. The strict order

234

235

234. The Great Laura of Mount Athos seen from the sea.

235. Here one can see the complexity of the Great Laura.

of monastic life which was thus set by the typikon of the Great Laura became the prototype for organizing all the cenobitic communities on Mount Athos, including those which were founded later. Above all, it prescribed the strict internal organization of the monastery. The hegumen, elected by sixteen respected monks, had almost absolute authority granted for life and was considered a spiritual father to each member of the community. For the first time women were denied access to Mount Athos; it was even forbidden to keep female domestic animals.

As mentioned above, cenobitic communities which were founded later followed the principles of organization set by the Great Laura. Hegumens, elected for life, were heads of councils, the members of which were also elected for life. Everyday activities, including obligatory work, were communal and there were few personal possessions. Certain monks were entrusted with special life-long duties, such as the work of a priest, gatekeeper, librarian, cook, storekeeper, etc. Ascetic rules of life implied periods of fasting which lasted for two-thirds of the year. Each moment of spare time was to be devoted to prayers of self-purification.

Monks were mainly uneducated. Despite this limitation, both treasuring and copying religious manuscripts were encouraged,

141

236. Life on Athos maintains not only a scholarly tradition in regard to ascetical and liturgical practice, but also maintains the tradition of respect for the manual labor of the monks, who, apart from donations, must provide their own livelihood. In fact, agriculture continues to be practiced with traditional implements.

236

237

237. A monk with the simandron. *This ancient wooden instrument, which is struck with a mallet, is still used to call the monks to the liturgical offices.*

238. General view of the ancient refectory in the monastery of Vatopédi. In an atmosphere of intense azure, the walls completely covered with paintings, what the monks visualize, besides scenes from the Old Testament, is the entire story of monasticism through its main protagonists.

which consequently made Athos an important center of learning and spirituality in the Eastern Orthodox Church.

The prestige of the Great Laura soon caused some concern and unrest among other Athonites and in 972 Emperor John Tsimisces was forced to send a mission to Mount Athos, whose efforts resulted in the first general typikon on the organization of monastic life there. It is called the Tragos, since it is written on goatskin (*tragos* = goat), and is now kept in the archives of the Protaton. It provided for an assembly, the institution of supreme authority, which met three times a year. The protos and members of the assembly could not make important decisions without one another. This assembly was of extreme significance because five more monasteries were founded while Athanasius (d. c. 1004) was still alive and ten more by the middle of the 11th century. Eremitism was, however, still maintained as a fundamental form of monastic life and often significantly interacted with cenobitic communities in that most monasteries had a comparatively great number of kellia, recluses' cells, which more often than not became the kernels of new monasteries.

238

239

This place helps one to understand that the sacred character of monastic life does not belong just to the church buildings or the cells, but also—according to Pachomius' great teaching—to the moments when the community is assembled and the community in its turn feels itself in communion with Christ, the Mother of God, and all the holy monks who have preceded it.

239. The emperor Constantine Monomachus is seated at the right hand of Christ in a mosaic in Santa Sofia. In the middle of the 11th century, Constantine contributed to the harmonization of the various monasteries' life by giving them a common rule.

In the first half of the 11th century, almost at the end of the Macedonian dynasty, monasticism on the Holy Mountain was growing. However, it was also the time of maturation, and therefore a time of great instability as well. Problems with discipline became serious and caused great concern and difficulties since Athos was esteemed as the most renowned center of monastic life in Byzantium. Because their cenobia were "imperial lauras" and so under the patronage of the emperor himself, these problems were solved by an intervention of the highest order. Emperor Constantine IX Monomachus (1042–1055) sent his deputy, whose efforts produced, in September 1045, a new typikon, called Monomachus' Typikon. In it, the familiar name, Holy Mountain, was officially used for the first time. Monomachus' Typikon was of fundamental importance: it determined the order and organization of monastic life so thoroughly that for the next three and a half centuries there was no need for another general typikon. Moreover, the way of monastic life established by the reformer Theodore the Studite

240

240. The necessary buildings for any monastery are: the katholikon (= universal), the name given to the principal church of the monastery, the monks' cells, the refectory, the towers, and the fiáli, one of which is shown here, its interior completely covered with paintings and possessing a well, in the monastery of Dochiaríu.

The fiáli are, in fact, small octagonal or decagonal buildings open on the sides and roofed with a cupola supported by columns.

241

242

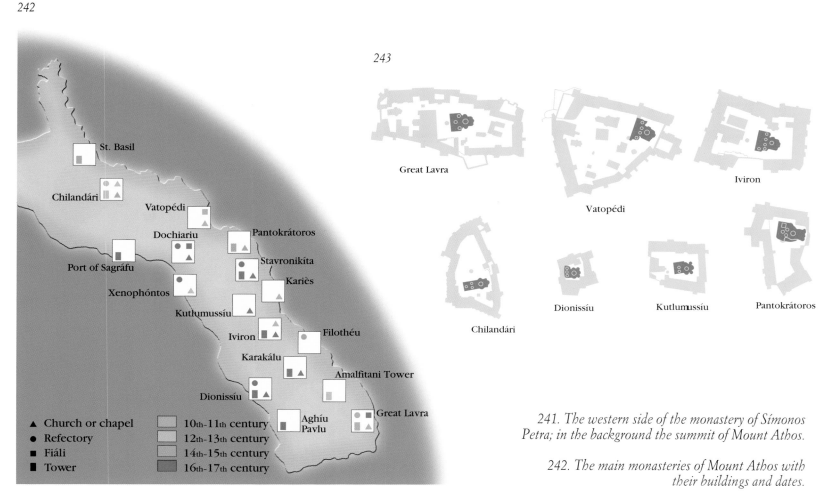

243

Great Lavra

Vatopédi

Iviron

Chilandári

Dionissíu

Kutlumussíu

Pantokrátoros

Map labels (fig. 242):
St. Basil
Chilandári
Vatopédi
Dochiariu
Pantokrátoros
Port of Sagráfu
Xenophóntos
Stavronikíta
Kariès
Kutlumussíu
Iviron
Filothéu
Karakálu
Amalfitani Tower
Dionissíu
Aghíu Pavlu
Great Lavra

▲ Church or chapel
● Refectory
■ Fiáli
■ Tower

10th-11th century
12th-13th century
14th-15th century
16th-17th century

241. The western side of the monastery of Símonos Petra; in the background the summit of Mount Athos.

242. The main monasteries of Mount Athos with their buildings and dates.

244

243. *The plans of the various monasteries with the highlighted* katholikon *in the interior court.*

244. *The monastery of Dionissíu. The tower, here in an excellent state of preservation, was particularly important for the monasteries which were situated directly above the sea.*

Xiropotámu

Sográfu

Dochiaríu

Karakálu

Símonos Petra

Aghíu Pavlu

Stavronikíta

...othéu

Xenophóntos

...igoríu

Esfigménu

Aghíu Panteleímonos

Konstamonítu

was not subject to any changes; on the contrary, its strict observance was required. All forms of luxury, economic expansion, trading with far-off places, and monks moving from one place to another were strictly prohibited. Organizationally, the unity of the monastic community was emphasized by their respect for the protos, who remained in office for life. The new protos was appointed in Constantinople, where he received the crosier and charter of appointment from the emperor himself. The protos made decisions regarding everyday activities by himself, while some more important matters were settled by five to ten hegumens. The most significant issues were discussed during the assembly, which was chaired by the protos and held three times a year at most.

Thus, by the end of the Macedonian period, the strengthened position of the protos finally began to symbolize the unity of the Holy Mountain's monastic community. However, the monasteries preserved their full autonomy; they were by no means reduced to the status of mere links in some hierarchically organized chain of institutions which were given orders by the protos. At that time the protos was elected from lower ranking monasteries so that he could not be imposed by the higher ranking ones from which he came. This order and organization finally transformed Mount Athos into the Holy Mountain. The great work of the Macedonian dynasty was finished and its achievements were passed on as a heritage to future Byzantine generations and, with all the changes made in the following centuries, to post-Byzantine ones.

2. BULGARIAN MONASTICISM

245

245. *Facade of the church dedicated to St. Clement at Ohrid in present-day Macedonia, at one time part of the Bulgarian empire. The great disciple of Cyril and Methodius he is considered one of the fathers of Bulgarian Christianity and monasticism.*

246. *Map of the centers of reference (Thessalonica, Athos, Constantinople) and of the foundation of Bulgarian Monasticism (Ohrid, Rila, Tŭrnovo).*

The beginnings of monastic life in Bulgaria were contemporary with the christianization of the Bulgarian people in 865. Before the official adoption of Christianity, it is only as a hypothesis that we can surmise the existence of some isolated monastic communities, about which we have no reliable information.

During the second half of the 9th century, in the area of the capital, Pliska, and later on in that of the Christian capital, Preslav, large monasteries already existed which were not only sources of Christian culture but also important centers of literary endeavors. From a marginal note in one of the copies of the *Theology* by John the Exarch, it is evident that the brother of Prince Boris Michael, Doxos, was a monk. He was also the organizer of the work of a whole generation of copyists and translators: Constantine of Preslav and John the Exarch—the disciples of Sts. Cyril and Methodius, who had come to Bulgaria—Clement of Ohrid and Naum. Following the examples of their teachers and mentors, the missionaries of the Christian faith, Cyril and Methodius, they established monasteries in the southwest of Bulgaria. These became centers of Christian culture and thus actively contributed to the use of the Slavonic language in the celebration of the Divine Office. Certain written sources show that the Bulgarian king, Peter, the son of Simeon the Great, also ended his days in a monastery and left us several books expounding the fundamental principles of Christian ethics. At the time of the First Bulgarian Kingdom, the task of monasticism was to spread the Christian tradition and teach the people the

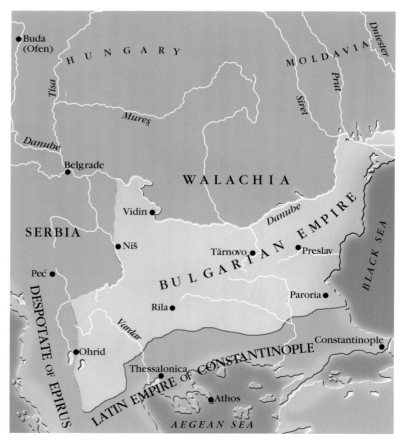

246

247

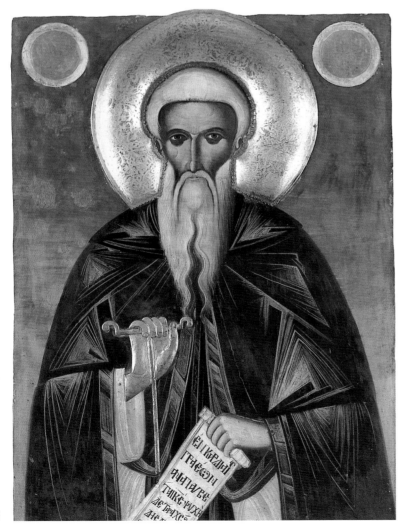

248

247–248. View of the interior courtyard of the great monastery of Rila showing the gallery and a part of the church dedicated to the nativity of the Mother of God, rebuilt between 1834 and 1837. This icon of St. John of Rila is kept there.

basic ethical norms of Christianity; such a task granted priority to a catechism concerned with morals.

The mystical and contemplative component of Christianity was introduced into Bulgaria by John of Rila (ca. 876–946), regarded as the first hermit-monk. He founded a cenobitic monastery on Mount Rila and became an example followed by several anchorites. According to legend, King Peter himself went to visit the hermit, whose blessing he received. Beginning in his own region, the veneration of John of Rila developed rapidly into a national devotion because the saint was considered the protector of all Bulgarians. The repeated transfers of his relics greatly contributed to his popularity. Under the reign of Asen I, the founder of the Second Bulgarian Kingdom, the saint's relics were transferred from Sofia to Tŭrnovo, the new capital, where they remained until the middle of the 15th century, protecting Orthodox Christians; they were then returned to the monastery of Rila, where they have been kept to our day. The hermit's influence and popularity spread also into Serbian territory, where hermits soon appeared: Gabriel of Lesnovo, Prohoros Psinski, Joachim of Osogovo (of Saranadapor), and Peter Koriski. The monasteries they founded are still in existence and celebrate commemorative offices in their honor.

At the end of the 12th century and in the beginning of the 13th, the monastic movement was strongly influenced by the new eremitical center of Mount Athos. These monasteries, in particular those of Sográfu and Chilandári and, to a certain extent, the

249

250

251

Great Laura, exercised an exceptional influence on the spirituality of the Bulgarian monks. Faithful to the idea of the moral purity of Orthodoxy and intransigent adversaries of any heresy, the monks of Mount Athos undertook to revise the Bible in order to preserve the faithful from any deviant interpretation of the holy Scripture. Such monks as the elderly John and his disciple Methodius were the pioneers of this project, which continued for decades and reached its climax in the 14th century thanks to the hesychast monks of Tŭrnovo: Theodosius, Cyprian, and Euthymius (ca. 1320–1330 to the beginning of the 15th century), the last patriarch of the Second Bulgarian Kingdom. The 13th and 14th centuries were marked by great achievements: in the 13th century, the foundations of a close and unbreakable association between the Bulgarian monasteries and those of Mount Athos were established, while in the 14th, the spiritual union of the Orthodox community in the Balkans was strengthened by a common adhesion to the teachings of hesychasm. Notwithstanding the contradictory opinions concerning this religious and philosophical doctrine, its final effect was inescapable in the

249. The transfer of the relics of John of Rila in a mural from 1863, executed by Nicholas Obrazopisov for the church of the Assumption in the metochion *of Orlitsa, dependent house of the monastery of Rila.*

250. Panoramic view of the monastery of Rila in a detail from a Bulgarian icon dedicated to St. John of Rila and executed between 1839 and 1840 by John of Samokov.

252

253

251. *A miniature from* King Ivan Alexander's Book of the Four Gospels, *which the Bulgarian monk Simeon executed for King Ivan Alexander (1331–1371). This miniature represents the king, his wife, and their two sons. British Museum, London (Add. Ms. 39627).*

252. *The Bulgarian monastery of Sográfu on the Athos peninsula seen from below. Like all Orthodox countries, Bulgaria has its own monastery on Athos, to which the Bulgarian people are especially devoted.*

253. *Evangelary from the monastery of Rila, dating from the first half of the 13th century (NMRM 1/13).*

context of the political dissolution of the feudal Balkan States and their invasion by the Ottoman conquerors: it succeeded in unifying the clergy and especially the monastics in the struggle to preserve the Orthodox traditions. In the 14th century, Bulgaria was under the sway of hesychast monks, most often trained in Constantinople or on Mount Athos, who considered themselves the disciples of the illustrious Gregory Sinaites, the founder of the monastery of Paroria, situated at the border of Bulgaria and Byzantium. This monastery became an important center of contact between Byzantium and the Slavic peoples during the late Middle Ages. This did not escape the attention of the Bulgarian sovereigns; thus, King Alexander (?–1371, crowned in 1331) promulgated charters of donations by which he gave real estate, gold coins, and precious stones to the monastery whose work he wanted to support. The monks of Paroria fostered more intense spiritual exchanges between Byzantine and Bulgarian hesychast monastics; one of the results was the production of lives of Bulgarian hesychasts written by Byzantine hagiographers,

in particular the *Life of Theodosius of Tŭrnovo* by the Byzantine patriarch Kallistos and the *Life of the Monk Romil of Vidin* by the Greek-born Gregory Dobropisec.

One of the first Bulgarian hesychasts was Theodosius of Tŭrnovo, born in 1300 in the region of Vidin. About 1335, he entered the monastery of Paroria and later on established the renowned monastery of Kilifarevo in Tŭrnovo where Euthymius, Cyprian, and Kyr Dionysios received their formation. After Theodosius' death, his successor, Euthymius, was ordained patriarch in Tŭrnovo in 1371. For his part, Euthymius founded the monastery of the Holy Trinity, which became a center of intense literary activity. Under his personal direction, the literate monks effected a thoroughgoing reform—linguistic, orthographic, and literary—of the holy books in order to bring them into conformity with the Byzantine norms in force at that time. Furthermore, the replacement of the canonical rules of Jerusalem by those of the Studion monastery, which had already been accomplished in Byzantium, was a result of Euthymius' efforts.

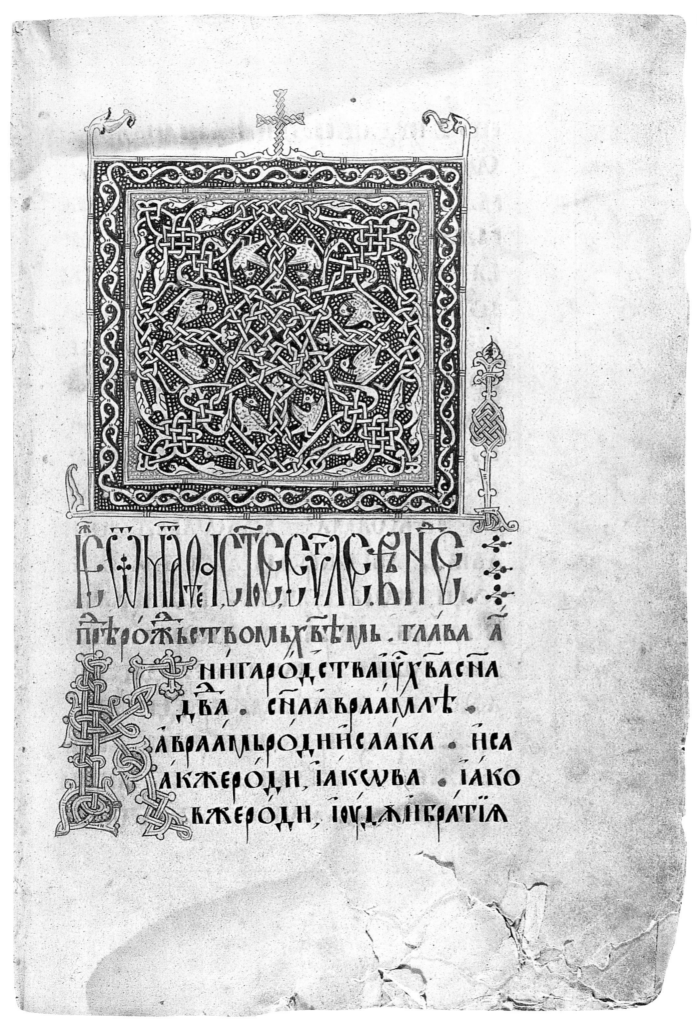

255

254. *Characteristic example of the calligraphy found in miniatures, from the book of the four gospels of Krupnik kept in the monastery of Rila. The heading is square with bird motifs and interlacings. The initial letter K is adorned with interlaced designs of a Balkanic type (NMRM 1/5).*

255. *Mural from 1603 in the refectory of the monastery of Bachkovo in which two pagan philosophers of antiquity are represented. The pagan philosophers were regarded as prophets of the coming of Christ into the Greek world.*

This was a document mandating the complete unity of Orthodox churches in the Balkans and elevating the role of monasticism to a level hitherto unknown.

Euthymius saw to the formation of a whole generation of scholars of Bulgarian literature who transmitted beyond the boundaries of their country not only hesychasm but also the literary traditions learned from their master. The work of the last Bulgarian patriarch was preserved and transferred to Russia by his confrere Cyprian, who became metropolitan of Russia. As to Gregory of Tsamblak (ca. 1364–1420), after having been the head of the monastery of Decani in Serbia and that of Neamţ, he assumed this position in Serbia, Walachia, and Moldavia; later on he was ordained metropolitan of Lithuania (1414) under the reign of Prince Vitovit. Devastated by conquerors and deprived of its sovereignty, Bulgaria nevertheless remained a center of knowledge and culture for the Orthodox Slavs, thanks to the efforts of some ten monks who, on leaving their homeland, took with them their spiritual heritage to preserve it and transmit it to future generations.

Despite the ruins which the conquerors had left behind in the territory of Bulgaria, in the 15th and 16th centuries the monasteries resumed their role as centers of both Christian consciousness and Slavic culture and civilization. Because they were financially supported by the Slav population, they functioned also as vestiges of a glorious past. In that respect, the monastery of Rila played the most important role: it was home to literate monks such as Vladislav Gramatik (15th century) and Dimitri Kantakouzenos. The indestructible bond with the monasteries of Mount Athos continued to be a source of spiritual encouragement to monas-teries in such difficult conditions. It was this same bond which in the 17th and 18th centuries was to contribute to the awakening of national consciousness at the time of the Bulgarian renaissance. In the period preceding this renaissance, the whole burden of literary and educational work throughout the country was carried by the monasteries. There were schools near several monasteries, especially those of Rila, Troyan, Etropole, Plakovo, and so forth. Some of these monasteries went as far as becoming centers of the armed struggle for national independence.

In the 18th and 19th centuries, owing to the efforts of monks who collected donations for the monasteries, the contacts between the members of the Orthodox community intensified. The major monasteries of Mount Athos—those of Sográfu and Chilandári—established houses in Bulgarian territory to shelter traveling monks. At the same time, they diffused literature in modern Bulgarian, thus contributing to the formation of the national consciousness. It is enough to mention that the author of the first history of Bulgaria, Paisii (1722–1773), a monk of the monastery of Chilandári since 1749, in the course of his journeys to Bulgaria made his book known in order to emphasize the role of monasticism as the driving force in the spiritual development of Bulgarian society. During the Bulgarian renaissance, monas-teries became authentic centers of national spirituality. It is in their midst that for the first time the ideas of an autocephalous church, of education in the Bulgarian language, and of national independence were born. Through all these endeavors they nurtured, the monasteries powerfully contributed to the rise of the movement for national liberation which culminated in the liberation of Bulgaria in 1878.

3. SERBIAN MONASTICISM

256. St. Sava in a medieval wall painting in the monastery of Mileševa in Serbia.

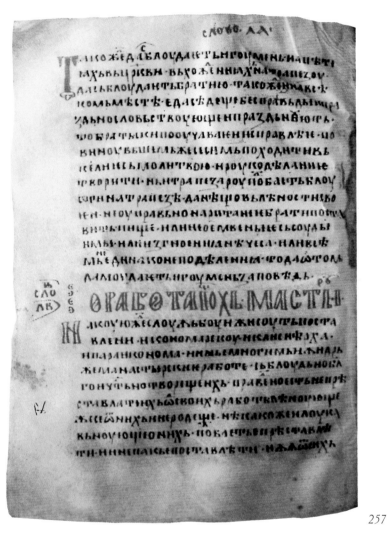

257. Copy of the typicon, that is, the rule, of the monastery of Chilandári on Mount Athos. The devotion of Serbian Christians toward Chilandari is most alive in our own times.

Monastic life and practice reached Serbia from the East and was established by 1219, before St. Sava was appointed archbishop in Serbia. It was greatly influenced by the Greek monastic tradition and developed somewhat more intensively owing to the influence of Sts. Clement and Naum of Ohrid. Hermits such as John of Rila, Joachim of Osogovo, Prohor of Pčinja, and Gabriel of Lesnovo were respected equally by all Orthodox southern Slavs. Monasteries of men and women alike were centers of monastic life. Thus, Kosara, King Samuilo's daughter, became a nun in 1015 in the monastery of the Mother of God of Krajina.

The founder of the Serbian state, Stefan Nemanja, who was given the name of Simeon when he entered one of the monasteries he built, St. Nicholas, set its monastic rule as its founder, which was accordingly called the Founder's Typikon (a manual of rubrics for religious services). After King Alexius III Angelos gave them permission, he and his son, the monk Sava, reconstructed

the monastery of Khilendar (Chilandári) in 1198 as the home of Serbian monks who wanted to practice monasticism on Mount Athos, which they have been doing now for the last eight centuries. After learning all he could about monastic life in the East, Sava reorganized Serbian monastic practice. Although he received his monastic formation in the cenobitic tradition, Sava was strongly inclined towards the eremitic tradition. Nevertheless, "The ideal monastic community," said one of the most learned monks of the 20th century, Filaret Granič, "should observe the principle of true collectivism in all fields of life, in both internal and external relations, which, in essence, implies the complete suppression of the individual and any special interest or ambition one may want to pursue."

Sava wrote three typika: in 1199 he inscribed the Karyes Typikon, a rule for hermits, into the stone walls of the hermitages in Karyes for himself and the monks who were to live in the same

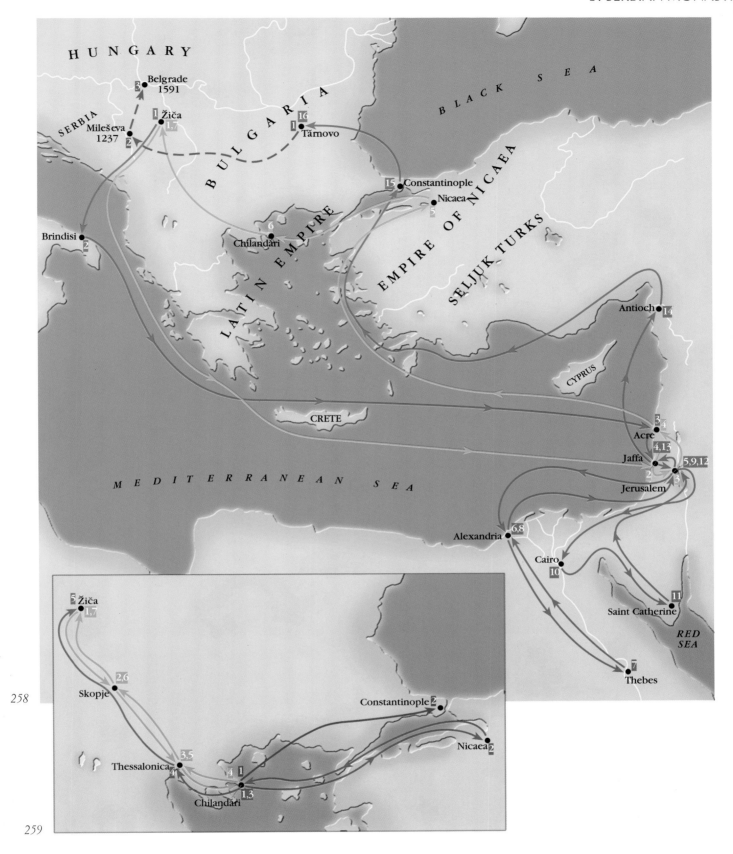

HUNGARY

Belgrade 1591

Žiča

SERBIA

Mileševa 1237

Brindisi

BULGARIA

Tǎrnovo

BLACK SEA

Constantinople

Nicaea

Chilandári

LATIN EMPIRE

EMPIRE OF NICAEA

SELJUK TURKS

Antioch

CYPRUS

CRETE

Acre

Jaffa

Jerusalem

MEDITERRANEAN SEA

Alexandria

Cairo

Saint Catherine

RED SEA

Thebes

258

259

Žiča

Skopje

Constantinople

Nicaea

Thessalonica

Chilandári

258–259. The monk and archbishop Sava traveled through the eastern part of the Christian world on different journeys for political or monastic reasons or on pilgrimage.
On the smaller map, are three voyages: from the monastery of Chilandári on Mount Athos to Constantinople (1198–1199, in blue); from the monastery of Chilandári to Nicaea and the monastery of Žiča (1219, in red); several trips from Serbia to the monastery of Chilandári (1191, 1207, 1216, in ocher).
On the larger map, the two pilgrimages are shown: to the Holy Places (1219, in ocher) and to the Holy Places, Sinai, and Thebes (1234–1235, in red).
The broken line in blue indicates the transfer of Sava's remains from Tǎrnovo to Mileševa and from there to Belgrade (by M. Blagojević).

260. *General view of the Serbian Monastery of Chilandári on Athos. The massive building in the center foreground is the refectory; in the center is the* katholikon *with a* fiáli, *half-hidden, on its left. Behind the* katholikon *stands the great tower of St. Sava while the bell tower is situated along the wall on the right. The monastic cells occupy the large building left of the tower of St. Sava. In the left foreground, the building on a high buttress which seems to protrude beyond the monastery is the guesthouse.*

cells after him. These monks need not necessarily have been priests since the monastic rule according to this typikon was comprised of psalms, prayers, and metanoia (prostrations). The practice in the Eastern Orthodox Church is to read the complete Psalter once a week during the Divine Office, and twice during the period of fasting before Easter. According to the Karyes Typikon the whole Psalter is to be read daily, a practice unique in the Eastern Orthodox Church.

Sava wrote the cenobitic Khilendar Typikon according to how the monastic life was practiced in that monastery during the period he spent there. This typikon served as one of the sources for worship in the Serbian Orthodox Church and was particularly helpful before 1319, when the complete Serbian Typikon was written.

261. *St. Athanasius the Athonite in a mural at Chilandári.*

262. *The splendid* katholikon *of Chilandári, built at the end of the 13th century by Milutin, king of Serbia; the* fiáli *is in the right foreground.*

262

264. *The centers of monastic life in Serbia. Shown in black, the monasteries founded between the 11th and 15th centuries; in red, those founded between the end of the 15th and 17th centuries, when Serbia was governed by the Ottomans.*

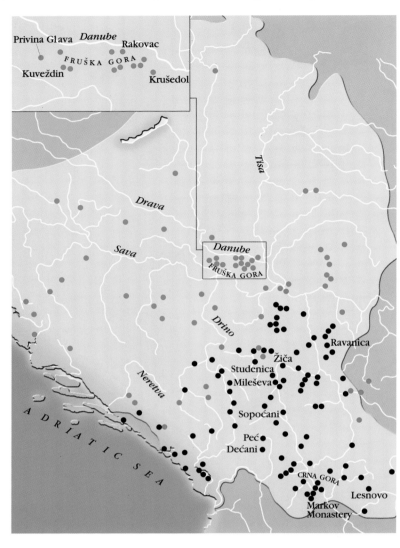

263

264

263. *The elegant church of the Presentation of Mary in the Temple, in the monastery of Kalenić in Serbia. Today there is a thriving community of women monastics there.*

265. *Aerial view of the monastic complex of the Studenica in Serbia, dating from the 12th to 14th centuries.*

266. *View of the apses of the churches of the Holy Apostles and of the Mother of God Odighitria and St. Nicholas, in the famous monastic complex of the patriarchate of Peć in Kosovo. This is the most important place of reference for both monasticism and Serbian Christianity from the historical and religious viewpoints.*

The third typikon associated with Sava's name is the Studenica (Studion) Typikon.

As for Sava's authorship of both the Khilendar and Studenica Typika, several different views are taken. Some researchers are convinced that both of them were written by one of Sava's associates, while others think that Sava wrote some parts of them. On the other hand, some experts claim that Sava is the sole author of the typika. Neither do researchers agree on the time the Studenica was written. It is usually believed it was written in 1206, but some say 1220.

The monastic life was as popular among women as among men in the Serbian Orthodox Church of the Middle Ages. Women from noble Serbian families became monastics. The same rules, those of the Jerusalem Typikon, were valid in monasteries of men and of women. This typikon was first translated from Greek into Serbian for the practice of the Serbian Orthodox Church and thus reached Bulgaria and Russia in its Serbian version. It comprises the complete typikon and consists of two parts: that concerned with worship and that referring to the organization of life in the monastery.

The number of monastics declined during Turkish rule, but monasticism, particularly in cenobitic monasteries, did not become extinct. The period after World War I saw the revival of monasticism, most notably in women's monasteries. Nowadays the Serbian Orthodox Church has monasteries for men and women in Serbia as well as in a diaspora (Romania, Hungary, Germany, America, Canada, Australia, Bosnia, Croatia, Dalmatia, and Slovenia), with Khilendar as the most renowned; however, the Ecumenical Patriarchate has jurisdiction over the clerics in this monastery.

4. ARMENIAN MONASTICISM

Some ancient traditions of this country go back to the preaching of Christianity there by the apostles Bartholomew and Jude Thaddeus, but the only reliable sources we have speak of the beginning of the 3rd century when a Greek embassy reached the Armenian court and made some conversions; these were badly received, however, and ended in persecution and martyrdom. Yet by the end of the century Armenia was already Christian.

The evangelizer of Armenia was St. Gregory the Illuminator, a member of the royal house, who was ordained a bishop in Cappadocia in 294. King Tiridates III, whom Gregory converted, issued a royal edict imposing Christianity on all his subjects. For this reason, Armenia is thought to have been the first nation in the history of Christianity that officially accepted it as the state religion.

Beginning with that official conversion, the historical lot of Armenia remained closely connected with that of the Christian religion. On June 2, 451, Supreme Commander Vardan Mamikonian addressed his troops thus on the eve of a crucial battle, "Anyone who believes that for us Christianity is like a garment will now understand that it cannot be taken from us, any more than we can lose the color of our skin." Seen in this light, Christianity can truly be said to be at the roots of Armenia's culture and nationality.

From the very beginnings of this history, monastics, their life, and their teaching were present at the implantation and development of Christianity. Hermits settled and monasteries were founded wherever there were memorials of the martyrs, thus closely linking the confession of the faith through martyrdom with the confession of the faith through a holy life. The deserts were filled with hermitages and the cities with monasteries.

This monastic tradition was fed basically by the monastic tradition of Cappadocia, which focused on the cenobitic life, and by the monastic tradition of Syria, as can be seen in the robust manifestations of a radical austerity and in the presence of the Syriac language in the liturgical books and rites.

In 354, the first national council of the Armenian Church was held, and it reflected on and legislated for monasticism. The fathers of the council decided to establish a number of monasteries as well as a number of lauras for hermits, for they realized the importance of these for the development of Christian life. Armenian monasticism was not strictly contemplative, but devoted itself also to the direct evangelization of the people and to charitable works. The council encouraged monks to establish hospitals, hospices, and homes for the elderly and poor.

At the beginning of the 5th century, two monks, Sts. Mesrob Vartapet and Sahak, invented the Armenian alphabet with its thirty-six letters and translated the sacred Scriptures and the works of the Fathers into this language. This activity put a stamp on the future of the church and of the Armenian nation as well.

These early monks provided a monastic model that would play a decisive role in the life of this church. It is a model that reminds us of the one set down by St. Augustine: monks well-educated, celibate as distinct from the married clergy, and devoted to the study of the Scriptures and the instruction of the people. In the monasteries, which were at the same time universities, the monks became the spiritual guides of the people.

Armenian monastic life experienced a remarkable flowering. We know today the location of over 460 monasteries, to which

267. St. Gregory the Illuminator, the evangelist of Armenia. Miniature from 1658 in a synaxarion. Armenian Catholicate of Cilicia, Antelias, Lebanon.

268. Remnants of the monastery of Marmashen in Armenia.

269–270. Ruins of the church of the Armenian monastery of Tänahti Vank' (13th century), an outstanding example of Armenian monastic architecture. On the left one sees the splendid ornamental details of the external sculpturing.

must be added the many Armenian monasteries built in Palestine and other countries.

In the time of Justinian, because of his oppressive policies bent on domination, the Armenians separated from the imperial church in order to preserve their religious and cultural identity: the differences between the two churches were not so much a matter of diverse doctrinal stances or assertions (there was a time when the Armenian Church adopted Monophysitism) as of the conviction of the Armenians that the Byzantine demand for liturgical and doctrinal uniformity would lead to their assimilation.

268

269

270

271. Armenian miniature: Jesus'
washing the feet of the disciples,
in the Evangelistary of
Vaspurakan, dating from 1450.
Sam Fogg Gallery, London.

272–273. Two miniatures taken
from an Armenian hymnal
dating from 1591. Armenian
Museum of France, Paris.
On the left, Christ as the Good
Shepherd; on the right, a composite
representation of the Martyrs of
Sebaste in which the icy lake is
depicted as a cup while, according
to the Byzantine iconographic
tradition, the souls ascend to
God in the form of crowns.

Arab rule (7th to 11th centuries) did not lead to a cultural decline in the Armenian Church, for it was able to keep up a remarkable artistic and architectural activity.

The Armenian rite is one of the five main rites of the Eastern Church. The liturgy in use today comes substantially from the second half of the 5th century, with later additions due to Byzantine and Latin influences exerted especially in the 11th to 16th centuries.

The basic focus of medieval Armenian culture was theological and philosophical, due in great measure to the fact that the entire system of higher education centered on these two disci-

plines; the system was shaped almost exclusively by the church, the only force of unification amid the existing fragmentation and the absence of any autonomous political authority. Thus, monastic institutions were the real agents of the development and transmission of the culture.

In a territory constantly exposed to invasion by the Arabs, Seleucids, Mongols, and Ottomans, the monasteries with their capacity for resistance, due in part to the favorable geography of the region, represented the continuity of a tradition that was not only religious but also cultural and historical and that, while rooted in the East, also had profound links to Western culture.

275. Interior of the church of the monastery of Makaravank. One clearly sees the play between apse and cupola achieved with deeply cut stone.

276. Interior view of the gavit with its crossed arches in the monastery of Mshkavank.

274. Plan of the monastery of Sanahin.
1. Church of St. Astvatzatzin (934); 2. Gavit with three aisles (1211); 3. Church of St. Amenaprkitch (966); 4. Gavit of the church of St. Amenaprkitch (1181); 5. Academy (11th century); 6. Church of St. Gregory (1061); 7. Matenadaran (library) (1063); 8. Portico in front of the library (13th century); 9. Bell tower (12th–13th centuries); 10. Tomb of the Kiurikian; 11. Tomb of the Zakarian family; 12. Khatchk'ar; 13. Entrances.
The colored part indicates the two gavits, architectural proof of the educative and social function assumed by the Armenian monasteries.

275

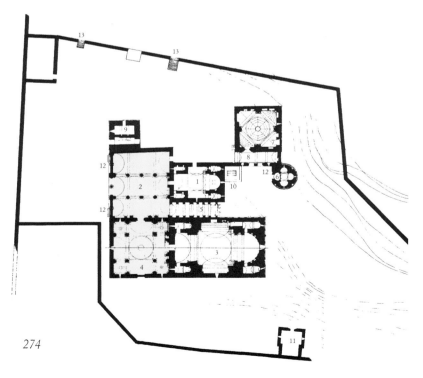

274

276

277

278

277. *Ruins of the monastic complex of Kirants, built from the 13th century on. They are an anomalous example because they show that baked brick and glazed ceramic were used here.*

278. *Main monastic sites of Armenia.*

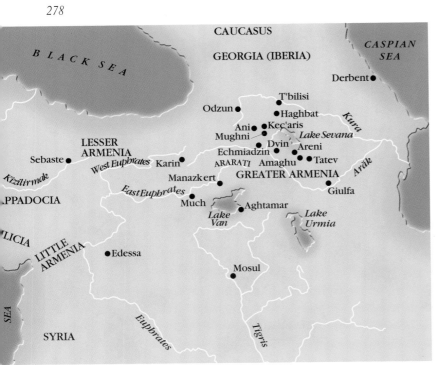

From the beginning of the 18th century at the monastery on the island of San Lazzaro in Venice, Armenian monks of the Mequitarist Congregation have kept the Armenian language, literature, and history alive through their products, translations, and publications, thereby carrying on the rich tradition of Armenian monasticism.

This critical role of the monasteries explains the presence of an architectural feature peculiar to them, the *gavit*: a large covered space in front of the church, a space which, though it can also be used for religious purposes, is used primarily as a lecture hall and a room for meetings, assemblies, and the administration of justice.

During the long centuries in which the Armenians had no independent state and lived scattered around the world, the church was the strongest preserver of national feeling.

5. Georgian Monasticism

279a
279b

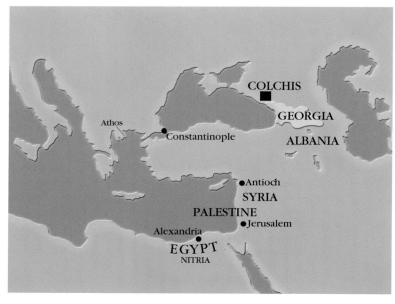

279. a) Principal monasteries of Georgia.

279. b) Georgia in the geographic context of the Middle East.

One of the great teachers of asceticism in Asia Minor was Eustathius of Sebaste, a controversial figure as a churchman, a bishop, and a theologian, for he adopted an extremely puritanical kind of asceticism. He inaugurated monastic life and propagandized for it among the Armenians, the Paphlagonians, and the inhabitants of Pontus.

Georgia was converted to Christianity around 337, surely due to the activity of a young slave girl named Nina, who succeeded in converting King Merian and Queen Nana, who were attracted by her virtue and her piety. It was a sudden conversion but a profound one and had lasting consequences. Moved by the miracles performed by Nina, King Merian sent to the emperor Constantine to ask for priests, with the result that the entire population embraced Christianity. The king even proclaimed Christianity the religion of his people. There was a bishop in the kingdom as early as 331, and from Georgia Christianity spread eastward to Albania (in Antiquity and the High Middle Ages, the region of the Caucasus west of Georgia, part of present-day Azerbaijan) and westward to the region of the Colchians.

When we speak of Georgian monasticism, we must distinguish between Georgian monastics outside their homeland and those within it since one of the traits of this monasticism is its tendency to go abroad and found monasteries in various places, while preserving its own characteristics. The first Georgian monk known to us is Evagrius Ponticus (345–399), who became famous among the monastics of Nitria in Egypt. In Jerusalem there was a well-known "monastery of the Iberians (Georgians)," that of St. Theodore, where we find the oldest inscriptions in the Georgian language (430). In Syria, Clibanion was a center for translations of the Fathers

from Greek into Georgian, while other centers of Georgian monks arose in Palestine and Egypt, near the pillar of Simon Stylites, in the first case, and at Mar Saba, in the second. Later on, there would be a famous colony of Georgian monks on Mount Athos.

This surprising flowering of monasteries of Georgian monastics outside their native land can be explained only if there existed a healthy monastic life within the country. The odd thing is that

280

281

we find no mention of its existence before the 5th century, when King Vachtang had two monks come from Greece who became successively the Catholicos of the Georgian Church (the catholicos was the supreme national religious figure, with functions identical with those of the patriarchs of the empire); in other words, the Church of Georgia became autocephalous.

The acceptance of orthodox christology led the Church of Georgia to follow a different course than did the other churches of the Near East, in which Monophysitism or Nestorianism acted as a spiritual force for the preservation of their rites against the expansionism of Constantinople. Georgia accepted the Byzantine rite, but this did not at all mean any loss of identity and ethnic pride.

King Vachtang also founded a monastery at Opiza that later became famous both for its religious life and for its activity in meeting the needs of the Georgian people. In defense of the national identity, this and other monasteries promoted the local language (Georgian) by using it for all ecclesiastical needs, both in the liturgy and in an interesting literature that made use of the most disparate genres: apocrypha, exegesis, dogmatics, hagiography, ascetics, and canon law. In other words, these monasteries were the centers of a varied cultural activity that would leave its mark on every aspect of the Georgian people's lives.

Monastic expansion, properly so-called, began in Georgia with the "Thirteen Syrian Fathers," as they are called, who came to Georgia from Mesopotamia in 550. They reorganized existing monasticism, developed it, and spread it. It was they who also played a decisive role in the final collapse of Monophysitism in the country.

280. As has been seen for Bulgaria and Serbia, Georgia has its own monastery on the Athos peninsula. Iviron is one of the monasteries that stand by the sea; consequently, its port is in direct contact with the monastery.

281. Elevation of the church of the monastery of Opiza (9th century), founded by King Vachtang in the 5th century.

282

283

284

*282–284. Rock-hewn monastery of Udabno in David-Garedža
in the district of Sagaredžo and view of the remains of the
Great Laura of Garedža established in the 6th century by
the hermit St. David. The monastery was completely
covered with paintings wherever the community gathered,
as can be seen from the exterior and interior of the refectory
with the monks' seats also carved from the rock.*

285

288

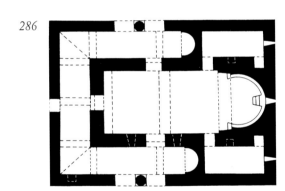

286

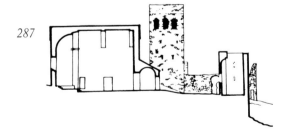

287

285. *Ruins of the upper room of the "palace" (8th–9th centuries) of the monastery of Nekresi, district of Kvareli, in the ancient region of Kahetia.*

286–287. *Plan and longitudinal section of the church of Nekresi with the adjacent buildings. It is easy to see that this edifice is a most interesting example of a basilica with three aisles.*

288. *Church of the monastery of Martvili, district of Gegečkori in the historical region of Mingrelia. The building, whose western facade we see here, goes back to the 7th century.*

The Thirteen Fathers came with the blessing and support of St. Simeon Stylites the Younger; this explains the devotion to this monk and the influence of his life on the traditions of the Georgian Church. Eremitism, especially in its itinerant form, always found a good number of followers among the monks of Georgia, even after cenobitic monastic life had become general.

Under Arab rule, which lasted from 650 at least until the 9th century, there was a notable expansion of monastic life, which became the center of the cultural and religious life of the country. The cultural heights reached in the 12th century coincided with a brilliant period of political expansion, when the realm extended from the Black Sea to the Caspian, from Trabzon to the Caucasus. However, a decline began with the Mongol occupation.

A special characteristic of Georgian monasticism was the priority it gave to the apostolic life, to the point of ordaining all qualified monks to the priesthood so that they might give themselves more easily to the direct apostolate.

Despite the Arab invasions and the intermittent exercise of Arab control, and despite all the resultant political difficulties, the process of territorial reunification was completed in 1008. At this point, the second important period in the nation's life began (11th–13th centuries). The most illustrious personage of this period was undoubtedly David the Builder, who established the capital at Tbilisi, organized a feudal system with a strongly centralized government and a redoubtable army, and gave the church a role in the management of the national state (he watched carefully over the election of bishops). He built churches and erected monasteries, one of which, Gelati, became a famous university center.

The fall of the Russian monarchy in 1917 restored the independence of the Georgian Church, which at the beginning of the 19th century, when Georgia was annexed by Russia, had been absorbed

289. *Painting from the 16th century in the church of the Mother of God in the monastery of Gelati, district of Tkibuli in the ancient region of Imeretia. It shows the monk David, who after the reunification of Georgia, which happened about the year 1000, became the major founder and builder of monasteries, among which is that of Gelati.*

290. *The lesser church of St. George, located at the rear of the katholikon of the monastery of Gelati.*

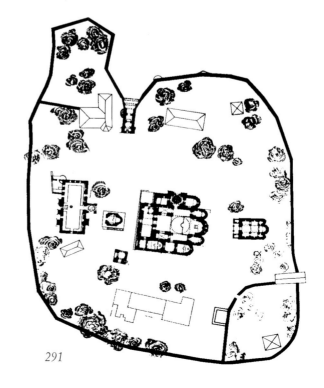

289   290

291. *Plan of the monastery of Gelati between the 12th and 13th centuries. In the center is the vast complex of the* katholikon, *the monastery's principal church.*

by the Russian Church. The difficulties caused by the Communist regime were the same as in other lands where this ideology was in control, but here the resurgence of Christianity has been rapid and has been linked from the outset with important cultural and social phenomena in the country.

The birth of the Republic of Georgia in 1991 marked the beginning of a new era for the local church, whose prestige is growing from day to day. Today there are some three million faithful.

291

292

292. Like the katholikon, *the lesser church of St. George was entirely covered with paintings, and despite the murals' state of disrepair it is still possible to admire the splendid chromatism of Georgian monastic art.*

On the following double page:
293. Ananuri, district of Dušeti in the ancient region of Kartlia, is an excellent example of a fortified Georgian monastery. The present-day aspect is due to a restoration accomplished during the 17th and 18th centuries.

6. Italo-Greek Monasticism

294

294. *The* katholikon *of a monastery in the vicinity of Stilo, Calabria, is in an extremely good state of preservation. Its plan, a Greek cross inscribed within a square, is easily seen.*

295. *Italo-Greek monasticism in southern Italy and Sicily flourished equally under the government of the Byzantine and that of their enemies, the Normans. On the map the Italo-Greek monasteries are indicated by a red triangle; the beige line shows the extent of the reconquest of the southern territory by the emperor Basil II in the beginning of the second millennium.*

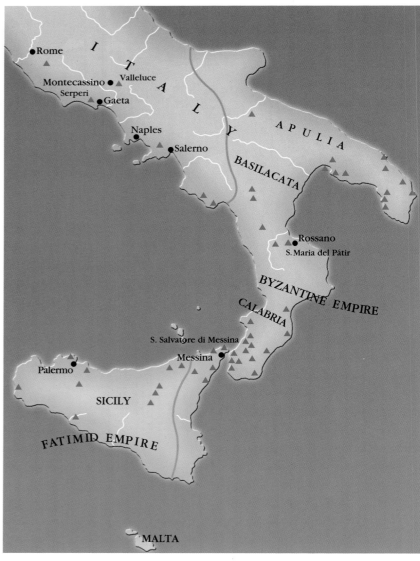

295

During the Middle Ages we find a rich and varied manifestation of Greek monasticism in southern Italy and Sicily. This was the area known as Magna Graecia, where the Greek tradition remained alive down the centuries, but these lands were also favorable to Byzantine expansion when this reached its apogee. Through the centuries the eremitical life, lauras, and small monastic centers all multiplied there. In wretched huts and in isolated caves a multitude of ascetics lived who devoted themselves to prayer, fasting, and bodily penances; they were admired by the surrounding populations for their austere life and their reputation as prophets and miracle workers.

After the troops of Justinian had conquered these regions (6th century) and after the exodus from the East of monastics who were fleeing the Persian invasion (7th century) or of monastics fleeing persecution by iconoclastic Eastern emperors (8th cen-

tury), the number of Italo-Greek monastics grew considerably. When the Arabs invaded Sicily in 831, many monastics fled to Calabria and there founded new monasteries, turning the region in a new Thebaid. When the Normans conquered Sicily, the monastics returned there in the middle of the 11th century and restored the island's monastic life in its ancient splendor.

Basilian monastics eventually possessed over three hundred monasteries in Calabria and a sizable number in Sicily, and they turned these into centers of Byzantine culture. Other monasteries followed the Rules of Theodore the Studite or St. Anthony of Mount Athos. The situation roused the distrust of the Normans, who suspected the Basilians of siding with the Byzantine government. This was the main reason for the Norman policy of protecting the Benedictine monastics and promoting the extension of their Rule.

296

298

296. *Roger II, king of the Normans in Sicily, is crowned by Christ. Mosaic in the church of the Martorana in Palermo.*

297. *Mosaic in the nave of Santa Maria del Pátir near Rossano in Calabria. Here the representation of a centaur is a proof of the continuing influence of Greek classical culture on the Greek monasticism of southern Italy.*

298. *Façade of the church of Sts. Peter and Paul in Forza d'Agro in eastern Sicily, south of the Strait of Messina. One of the traditions presents it as a restoration which Roger II conducted in 1116 for the Greek community at the request of the monk Gerasimus. In fact the church is an example of Byzantine art's love of color.*

297

Despite this, the devotion of the people to the Italo-Greek monastics was so constant that the Normans finally accepted and protected them; in fact, in 1105 the famous monastery of Patrion obtained the privilege of exemption from episcopal jurisdiction, the first Greek monastery to enjoy this favor. It was under Norman dominion that the Greek monks of Calabria showed their greatest vitality, with a multitude of saints and a considerable influence on the studies and art of their age. Indeed, they were effective transmitters of Greek culture to the ensuing centuries of Italian humanism.

In 1131, the monastery of the Savior in Messina won from Roger II the right to have all the other Basilian monasteries of the diocese (over thirty of them) be subject to its archimandrite and not to any other religious or secular authority. This concentration of authority recalls what had happened at Cluny, but surely the

299

299. This mosaic of the three great Fathers of the Eastern church, St. Gregory the Theologian, St. Basil, and St. John Chrysostom, stands out in the palace chapel, the most celebrated edifice of the palace of the Normans in Palermo. The Normans, whose culture is one of those which have most effectively determined the formation of Europe, were to live in close contact with Eastern Christianity and allow the people to hand down the memory of their own roots.

300

300. Italo-Greek monasticism reached as far as Rome; the most important foundation to endure until our own times is the abbey of St. Nilus in Grottaferrata, which will complete its first millennium in 2004. Here we see the reproduction of a page from a text of monastic literature written in St. Nilus' (the founder of the monastery) own hand (Ms.B. ἀ 189).

most direct model for it was the system that existed on Mount Athos, where the administration of the monasteries was directed by a council under the leadership of an archimandrite. This new monastic legislation, which promoted regular life and avoided the dangers of isolationism, also promoted the flowering of the ancient Basilian traditions in Sicily; this had important effects in the areas of spirituality and culture.

Beginning in the second half of the 13th century, under the domination of the Angevins, the Basilian monasteries began to decline, partly because the Greek element in them had radically decreased, partly because the struggles between the Angevins and the Aragonese led to the disappearance of the Greek rite. Thus ended the impressive epic of Byzantine monasticism in southern Italy.

Yet Greek monasticism did not completely disappear from Italy because a glorious abbey near Rome would remain down to our time: the abbey of Grottaferrata, founded by St. Nilus.

Nilus was born in Rossano (Calabria) around 910 to a noble family of Italo-Greek origin. After leaving his wife, he became a Basilian monk, spending his time in prayer, penance, and the study of sacred Scripture and the Fathers, without neglecting Greek

literature; he himself excelled as a cultured poet. During this period of life as a hermit, he experienced once again the trials and victories of the ancient Fathers of the desert. The insistence of his disciples led him to build a monastery near Rossano. Traveling ever northward from there, he kept building monasteries, among them that of Valleluce near Montecassino and that of Serperi near Gaeta, where he was visited by the young dreamer Otto III, who as a sign of respect and veneration placed the imperial crown in Nilus' hands. The monk's final foundation was in Grottaferrata, where he died at the age of ninety-five, leaving behind a long line of admirers and enthusiasts among both the hellenized inhabitants of Calabria and the people of Latium, and venerated both by the Italian princes and the emir of Salerno.

Even though Nilus founded a number of monasteries, he lived most of his life in strict solitude, and the Rule of St. Basil, which he adopted for his monasteries, including Santa Maria de Grottaferrata, was altered by a tendency towards an extremely rigorist asceticism and a strong feeling for eremitism.

In 1024 Pope John XIX consecrated Grottaferrata to Mary the Mother of God; the oldest document to use this title is a bull of Benedict IX from 1037. Ever since that time, the monks of this

301

301. *Mosaics on the triumphal arch inside the church of St. Mary Odighitria in the abbey of St. Nilus. St. Nilus is represented on the lower left, opposite St. Bartholomew, who carried out the building of the abbey.*

302. *The Romanesque construction of Grottaferrata is a clear proof of the full acceptance of Italo-Greek spirituality within a Western architectural tradition.*

302

monastery have faithfully imitated their founder in devoting themselves to the study of Scripture and the Fathers and in restoring and preserving ancient manuscripts; their work has had a marked influence on hagiography, hymnography, and philology. They have kept the Italo-Greek iconographic tradition alive down the centuries.

Abbot Vitali of Grottaferrata took part in the Council of Florence (1438–1450), which was attended by the patriarch of Constantinople and many Greek bishops; the famous Cardinal Bessarion, who was commendatory abbot of the monastery, promoted studies and the Greek liturgy during the years when Constantinople fell into the hands of the Turks.

In our own day, the monks still devote themselves to the direct apostolate and to Oriental studies. Their library contains an exceptional collection of Greek manuscripts, chiefly in the areas of the liturgy and Byzantine music.

The importance of Nilus, above and beyond his foundations, consisted in the new vigor he instilled into Italo-Greek monasticism, enabling it to enter energetically into the Latin and Italian religious tradition and to contribute its own culture and specific religious sensibility.

7. MONASTICISM IN KIEVAN RUS'

303

303. *Tomb of Jaroslav the Wise located in the famous cathedral of Saint Sofia in Kiev, the ancient capital of Rus' (ancient Russia), today capital of the republic of Ukraine. Prince Jaroslav promoted monastic life in Rus', just recently converted to Christianity.*

304

304. *The icon of the Mother of God in the celebrated monastery of the Caves in Kiev, founded by Antonii Pečerskii. Christianity, which had entered Rus' through the conversion of the reigning class, became popular mainly through the monks' work, and this image became one of the most venerated in Christian Kiev. Here we see a copy from the 13th century of the Mother of God of the Caves (Svenskaya) represented between the founders of the monastery, Antonii and Feodosii. Tretyakov Gallery, Moscow.*

The beginnings of Christianity among the eastern Slavs of Kievan Rus' go back to before the 10th century. In fact, there are clear early testimonies to a monastic presence even at that time. But it was only with the baptism of Grand Prince Vladimir and his subjects in 988 that the foundations for some stable forms of monastic life organized according to Byzantine models were laid. From that time on, monasticism made a very important contribution to the interiorization of the Christian message among the eastern Slavs, giving it the monastic imprint characteristic of Eastern Christianity. Byzantium, from which Vladimir had received baptism, had emerged barely two centuries earlier from the iconoclast struggle; this struggle had ended with the victory of the monastic party (Second Council of Nicaea, 787), which was so strengthened by it that it became the decisive force in the Byzantine Church. It is to be assumed that the missionaries who came to Kiev were monks and that these instilled their own spirit into the newborn Russian Church. Beyond a doubt, monasticism immediately sank deep roots among the christianized people and quickly exerted a great religious, social, and cultural influence.

The monasteries of the Kievan period were of two basic kinds. There were monasteries founded by a prince and closely connected with the family of the founder. Alongside these, there gradually arose monastic centers focused on the personal and charismatic experience of a monk; these were better able to translate the

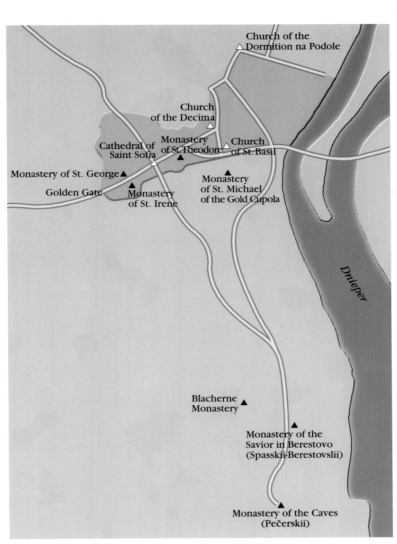

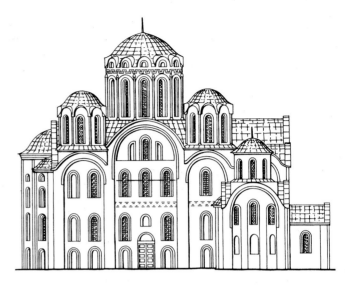

305. Map of the area of Kiev where the cathedral of Saint Sofia and the various monasteries are located; the most remote is the Caves.

306. Map of the principality of Kiev at the beginning of the 11th century.

307

307. Section of the elevation of the north facade, cathedral of the Dormition of Mary, monastery of the Caves (by N. Logvin).

characteristics of the people into ascetical experience. In the earliest chronicle of the eastern Slavs, the Chronicle of Nestor (Povest' vremmenych let), we find the first chronological testimony to the two types of monastic foundation. In 1037 Jaroslav the Wise founded in Kiev two monasteries of the Byzantine type, in which it was usually the founder who decided on the rule (typikon) and conferred privileges; in 1051, drawn by the experience of Anthony, a solitary, disciples gathered and originated a properly Slavic monastic life. In a few but significant phrases, the Chronicle contrasts this monastic experience with Jaroslav's two foundations: "Many monasteries were founded by rulers and boyars and built on wealth, but they differed from those founded on tears, fasts, prayer, and vigils. Anthony had neither gold nor silver but founded his monastery on tears and fasting."

It was therefore only with the coming of Anthony of the Caves (= *pečery*) (Antonii Pečerskii, d. 1073) that monasticism began to sink its roots into the consciousness of the people of the Rus'. After having been introduced to monastic life on Mount Athos, Anthony chose the caves on the tufa hill overlooking the river Dniester in which to live a hermit's life; this was near Berestovo, where another hermit, Hilarion, a priest, had already lived for a short time. Under Theodosius of the Caves (Feodosii Pečerskii, d. 1074), this newborn monastic movement changed from eremitical to cenobitic. Thus there arose the monastery known as "of the Caves," which in 1169 was awarded the title laura (Kievo-Pečerskaja Laura) and was destined to become the starting point and center of a movement of asceticism and a transmission of spirituality among all the eastern Slavs.

Theodosius adopted as his rule the *Hypotyposis* as given in the edition of Alexius the Studite of Constantinople and thereby

308. General view of the monastery of St. George of Novgorod in the north of the ancient principality of Kiev. With the arrival of the Mongols, it was mostly in the north that monks took refuge and with them the center of reference of Russian Christianity.

linked his monastery to the Byzantine tradition that went back to St. Basil, but without surrendering the monastery's own characteristic traits. The most authentic traits of this early Russian-Ukrainian monasticism are to be found in the testimony of the sources that tell of the lives of the first monks of this great monastery of Kiev: the *Life of St. Theodosius,* written by the monk Nestor a few years after the death of the saint, and the *Paterikon,* which was composed during the first half of the 13th century. The ascetical tradition received its classical formulation in the *Kievo-pečerskii Paterik,* which was composed on the model of the ancient "Books of the Fathers" but, unlike these, does not simply report sayings but tells the lives of many monks from the Monastery of the Caves.

Despite its legendary elements, the *Paterik* is a valuable source because it enables us to trace the development of Russian monasticism, which did not simply reproduce Byzantine models but gave rise to traits of its own that were peculiar to the Slavic spirituality which was aborning. These are, for example, the forceful recalling to common life or to humility as taking the form of a preference for menial tasks. Another characteristic is the tendency to a "passive" asceticism, that is, to see asceticism as taking the form of the endurance of adverse geographical and climatic conditions and the necessity of hard manual labor, without seeking out other means familiar in the East and in Byzantium.

The Studite Rule emphasized the idea of service to the community and to society rather than obedience in the strict sense; but Theodosius went further when he looked upon his own role of hegumen (head of a monastery) as a "service" and went looking for the lowliest tasks and wore the poorest garments. Theodosius' way of interpreting traditional monastic poverty was one of his most characteristic traits. He not only prohibited private ownership by individual monks but insisted on a complete poverty for the entire community (take no thought for the morrow! cf. Matt 6:34);

309. Inside the thoroughly Western psalter of the archbishop Egbert of Trier, we do not find any miniature of the Kievan Rus'. The codex became part of the dowry of Gertrude, who came as the spouse of Prince Izjaslav Jaroslavić. Here we see Christ crowning Prince Jaropolk and Princess Irina, who was remembered as a great foundress of monasteries.

310. View of the river Volchov near the monastery dedicated to St. Anthony in Novgorod, one of the major centers of Christianity at the time of the principality of Kiev.

311. Extraordinary fragment of a wall painting representing a saint in the monastery of St. Anthony in Novgorod.
Russian monastic art, fully faithful to the Byzantine tradition, had now assumed its own particular identity within the local schools of iconographers and mural artists, capable of an extraordinary power of expression which prompted a strong popular support and became an efficacious instrument of devotion.

in doing so, he was trying to combine the Basilian model of common life with the poverty typical of hermits, which was understood as a complete self-abandonment to divine providence. A similar phenomenon would be seen later on in the Mendicant Orders of the West. Also worth noting is the collegial spirit at work in the election of new hegumens, even if this gave rise to critical situations.

In fact, it can be said that in the *Paterik* we can find, in seminal form, the antinomies which the Russian Church kept trying to resolve down the centuries: the ideal of common life and its organization versus the continual openness or receptivity to solitude and idiorrhythmia (life according to the individual's pace); a spirituality of flight from the world versus an openness to hierarchy and society; the desire for mastery of book-wisdom versus the inclination to become "a fool for Christ" (*jurodistvo*).

In some of the 12th- and 13th-century monks described in the *Paterik* of Kiev we can see a gradual weakening of this harmony between asceticism and monastic life, solitude and community, that Theodosius had embodied. This led to exaggerated forms and methods of asceticism and, above all, to the weakening of the cenobitic life.

We see in the 12th and 13th centuries how the increasing material wealth produced by benefices and donations and the ever closer links between prince and monastery caused the Laura of the Caves in Kiev and the other monasteries that arose in Novgorod, Suzdal', Vologda, and Vladimir to have an ever increasing social and cultural influence, but they also led to a spiritual decadence.

The Mongol invasion of 1240 put an end to life in the Laura; that life would be renewed later on, but without regaining the same importance as before. The Laura was closed after the October Revolution and turned into a museum by the Bolsheviks. It was partially rebuilt after having been bombed during the Second World War and is now the most important Orthodox monastery of the Ukraine.

8. SINAI, BYZANTIUM, ATHOS AND THEIR INFLUENCE

312–313. Two contrasting views of the celebrated monastery of St. Catherine on Mount Sinai. Like Mount Athos, this monastery has remained through the centuries one of the centers of Eastern Christian spirituality, recognized as a point of reference by all countries which are Orthodox and of all Eastern Christianity. In addition, the monastery has remained a place of pilgrimage for all of Christianity, including the West, a goal—and not a secondary one—of pilgrimages to the Holy Land.

Gregory Palamas (1296–1359) was the last great Byzantine theologian and gave hesychasm (a quietistic system of meditation) a metaphysical foundation, thereby permanently influencing the entire Orthodox spirituality and theology that regards Palamism as its highest expression. But in order to understand this man we must go back to the very beginnings of monasticism.

The tradition of the ancient Fathers was given its systematic development by Evagrius Ponticus (345–399), the "Doctor of the Desert." Without speaking in so many words of the prayer of the heart, Evagrius did emphasize a number of themes that recur in all subsequent Eastern spirituality: custody of the heart, stripping of the spirit, simplification of prayer, and struggle against

"thoughts." The "Sinaitic School," Byzantine mysticism, and the Athonite hesychasts all go back to him.

The most original interpreter of "Sinaitic spirituality" was John Climacus (d. 649?), who continued the tradition of the hermits of Sinai that is attested as early as the 4th century. Around 557 the monastery of Batos was founded (renamed St. Catherine in the 11th century) on the traditional spot of the burning bush seen by Moses (Exod 3:2).

Before becoming its hegumen (head), John lived a hermit's life there for forty years. In his book (from which he derives his name "Climacus"), *Ladder of Paradise (Klimax tou Paradeisou)* with its thirty chapters, he instructs both solitaries and contemplatives on

314. Icon from the 13th century dedicated to the great interpreter of Sinaite spirituality, John Climacus; here we see him between St. George and St. Blaise. Russian Museum, Saint Petersburg.

the spiritual struggle and the acquisition of the virtues, relying for his teaching on Evagrius Ponticus, other Fathers, and his own experience. The *Ladder* is a true summa of the spiritual life and easily wins over the reader by its practical tone and methodical psychology; it has been widely read in both East and West.

For both Climacus and Evagrius, prayer grows through a gradual elimination of images and thoughts. Whence the necessity of a monology (prayer "using a single word") or a short and continuously repeated invocation of Jesus, which disposes the spirit and nourishes a constant remembrance of the Lord. According to Climacus, this remembrance and its oral expression must become "one with the breath." This remark would give rise to a school of thought, although it is difficult to say whether the author understood it as describing a method. His spiritual descendants would lay a much greater emphasis on this point, among them Hesychius Sinaites (8th–9th centuries) and Philotheus (end of the

12th century). In any case, Climacus would remain a classical author and would become the least challenged inspirer of the hesychastic renewal on Mount Athos in the 13th and 14th centuries. As late as the 19th century, when Russian bishop Ignatii Bryančaninov was warning beginners against the dangers of psycho-physical methods, he spoke of "the method of Climacus" as the simplest and safest for attaining to prayer of the heart.

Continuing the tradition, Hesychius Sinaites set forth a very simple idea of spiritual perfection. In his view, everything depends on attention, simplicity, and interior quietude *(hēsychia)*. To distinguish between thoughts and put a stop to those that are wicked, that is, imaginative representations, is to remain free of the sin that originates in these thoughts. According to Hesychius, the most effective weapon in this struggle is a monological invocation, that is, the prayer of Jesus. Both Nicephorus Hagiorites and Gregory Palamas would take over this doctrine as

315. *Icon representing the famed ladder of paradise as described by John Climacus (see fig. 179, pp. 106–107). This icon was probably painted in the second half of the 12th century in the monastery of St. Catherine itself, where it is preserved.*

it stood, while also enriching it, the former with a breathing technique and the latter with the vision of the light of Tabor.

Simeon the New Theologian (917–1022), author of a great many catecheses and poems that show him to be one of the greatest, if not the greatest Byzantine mystic, is an important link between the tradition and Athonite hesychasm. His theological thought is based on the supposition that baptized persons do not truly experience the effects of their baptism unless they attain to a consciousness of the Holy Spirit present in them and unless they see the light of the glory of God. In adopting this view, Simeon is also located within another great spiritual current, one that coexists with Evagrian intellectualism but, unlike it, seeks the sensible experience of divine grace. It is this element, along with the vision of the divine light, that makes Simeon the New Theologian an author on whom Athonite hesychasm gladly relied (this hesychasm began in the 13th century and had Nicephorus as one of its key figures).

Nicephorus the Solitary (second half of the 13th century), also known as the "Hesychast" or "Hagiorite," was the first and most authoritative witness (who can be dated with certainty) to the prayer of Jesus in combination with a breathing technique. According to Irénée Hausherr, he was the true author of the famous text *A Method for Holy Prayer and Attention,* which tradition, however, attributed to Simeon the New Theologian and which entered the *Philocalia* under his name. The text describes the bodily posture, the manner of breathing, and the psycho-physical effort required for attaining as quickly as possible to the vision of the light.

The true and proper hesychastic restoration of the 13th and 14th centuries is dominated by the figure of Gregory Sinaites (1255–1346), so called because he lived on Sinai before going to Mount Athos. Nourished as he was by the teaching of Climacus and Simeon the New Theologian, Gregory too understood the spiritual life as an experiential recovery or, better, rediscovery of

316. Monastery of Grigoríu, whose katholikon *is seen in the center of the buildings, a characteristic view of a monastery on the coast of Athos.*

the "energy" given in baptism and as an experiential perception of the light. Like Nicephorus, he saw the prayer of Jesus, accompanied by control of the breath, as the shortest way to the goal. Gregory, however, does not dwell at length on the rhythm of breathing but describes what the invocation of the name of Jesus is, refers to a degree of physical pain in using the method, and explains in greater detail its psychological effects.

When Gregory reached Athos, where the monastic life had been cultivated since the 9th century, he was struck at finding not the contemplative life but only the observance of external practices of asceticism and prayer. He therefore settled in the skete of Magulà and there instructed a group of disciples in hesychasm. It was probably at this time that he met Gregory Palamas. Because of the Turkish invasions Gregory was forced to leave the Holy Mountain in 1325. A long journey brought him to, among other places, Bulgaria, where he promoted hesychasm among the monastics and helped put down the Bogomil sect.

Despite his relatively short presence on Athos, he gave, by means of hesychasm, a powerful impulse to the monasteries there, which henceforth became trustees of the Orthodox monastic tradition. This would make its way out into the entire Orthodox world and would fructify both Romanian and Slavic (especially Russian) monasticism: both Nil Sorskii and later Paisii Veličkovskii would draw from Athos as if from the source of the hesychastic tradition before beginning their work of monastic reform in the 15th and 18th centuries respectively.

Between the two World Wars, the "neohesychastic" movement, started by the publication of the *Philocalia* (Venice, 1782)—which had been compiled on Athos by Macarius of Corinth and Nicodemus Hagiorites—and even more by its translation into Russian (Moscow, 1793), moved beyond the borders of the Orthodox world and entered ever more fully into the Catholic world as well.

9. St. Gregory Palamas and Hesychasm

317

317. Eastern view of the katholikon *of the Great Laura on Mount Athos. As a monk in this laura, St. Gregory Palamas defended the* hesychast *spirituality which imbued all the monasticism of the Byzantine tradition.*

Mystical Orthodox theology, called hesychast, reached its apex in the 14th century, thanks to St. Gregory Palamas, its most fervent defender. Palamas was born in 1296 into an aristocratic family of Constantinople and received an excellent education in philosophy. About 1316, he took the monastic habit and became a hermit near the Laura on Mount Athos. Afterwards, he sojourned in several places and various monasteries on the monastic peninsula, including the famed ones of Vatopédi and Esphigménu, and for a period he was the hegumen (head) of the latter. Palamas' theological thinking is the pure fruit of the hesychastic tradition, whose origin goes back to a much earlier period. Hesychastic theology is closely related to the mystical experience which aims at enabling human beings to participate in the uncreated energies of God. From the 4th century on, a mystical theology developed, centered on the unceasing invocation of the name of Jesus, a practice promoted by St. Paul in his letters. Such a prayer takes place in the heart of the praying person. The continual repetition of Jesus' name was the inspiration for the mystical doctrine of the great spiritual masters, a doctrine which evolved later and blossomed in an extraordinary way.

In the 14th century, the hesychastic prayer was practiced by the most austere hermits and cenobites of Mount Athos. During this

318

319

HMCTA   IC   XC   MOP ФЄОΣIΣ

318. A 15th-century portable icon of Gregory Palamas. Museum of Fine Arts, Saint Petersburg, Russia.

319. An 18th-century icon of the transfiguration belonging to the Venerable Archconfraternity of the Purification in Livorno, Italy. Hesychasm, with its continuous invocation of the name of Jesus promoted

by Gregory Palamas, tends to lead the faithful to the contemplation of the "light of Tabor," that is, the light of Christ, the experience of the apostles during the mystery of the transfiguration—the presage —of this light. Therefore, this mystery and this feast will be particularly venerated in the Eastern tradition, including its far reaches, such as southern Italy and Sicily.

320

320. Evocative scene of a monk on Mount Athos in contemplation before the sea. In the background stands the monastery of Stavronikíta.

century, the practice of the prayer of the heart was given a new vitality thanks to the activity and spiritual teaching of Gregory Sinaites (d. 1346). Originally from Asia Minor, he had successively sojourned in monasteries of Cyprus, Sinai, and Crete and had transmitted the traditions he had encountered there to the Athonite peninsula. Gregory Sinaites' teaching was a systematization of this prayer, whose psycho-physical method aimed at contemplation. Contemplation was attained by the "return" of the intellect into the heart and the conditioning of breathing and heartbeat so that they coincide. Thus, with every heartbeat, the divine name is repeated under the form of a short prayer, "Lord Jesus Christ, Son of God, have mercy on me, a sinner." Little by little, the practitioner of this prayer arrives at the contemplation of the very light which the apostles Peter, James, and John saw at the transfiguration of Christ. Moreover, through the prayer of the heart, the hesychast is introduced into divine realities which are unattainable by the intellect alone. Thus theology becomes inner experience rather than knowledge linked to reason.

The hesychasts' teaching about prayer met with a fierce adversary in the person of Barlaam, a Greek monk from Calabria, whom the emperor had entrusted with the teaching of philosophy in Constantinople. Being well-grounded in philosophy, Barlaam confronted the hesychastic doctrine, which he believed was a deviation from orthodoxy because, according to him, it was contrary to the principle of the unknowability of God. Barlaam found untenable the hesychasts' claim that they participated in the uncreated energies of God, such as the light of the transfiguration. What made matters worse was that he knew of the hesychastic beliefs through monks who were pious but simple and unable to pursue a theological discussion. Soon others joined the adversaries of the hesychasts: Gregory Akindynos, a monk; John XIV Kalekas, the patriarch of Constantinople; Nicephorus Gregoras, an eminent historian; and other prelates and scholars. In the battle over the hesychastic doctrines, Palamas took upon himself the role of principal defender by refuting the arguments of Barlaam and his followers. To this end, he

321. *In this miniature from the 15th century we see the synod presided over by the emperor John Cantacuzenus in the Blacherne palace in Constantinople. The synod was held in 1341 to resolve the dispute concerning hesychasm, fomented by the Calabrian monk Barlaam.*

322. *The church of St. Catherine in Thessalonica, Greece, was already in existence at the time Gregory Palamas became bishop of the city after having left Mount Athos.*

wrote a series of theological treatises entitled *Triads in Defense of the Holy Hesychasts* in which he insisted that one must make a clear distinction between the knowledge of God, which is unattainable, and the knowledge of God's energies, which, however, is accessible to human beings.

The "hesychastic disputes," already begun earlier, had shaken the ecclesial life of Byzantium and had divided theologians into two factions. However, Palamas' theological arguments attracted more and more theologians to the hesychastic doctrines. In 1341, the hegumens of the Athonite monasteries had convened a synod at which an important document (*Tomos agioreitikós*) supporting the hesychastic theses and written by Palamas was unanimously endorsed. In spite of this, the opponents persisted, and the situation having become acute, Emperor John VI Cantacuzenus and the regent, Anne of Savoy, convened a synod in 1347. It sided with Palamas and the hesychasts and excommunicated their adversaries; that same year, Palamas was promoted archbishop of Thessalonica. In 1351 and 1368, two more synods dealing with the same question also ruled in favor of the hesychasts. Thus, the

hesychastic monastics of Byzantium and the neighboring regions of the Balkans, where the hesychastic movement had found a very favorable reception, were vindicated. Palamas had nothing to do with this; his mystical doctrine had already grown deep roots in the life of the church and ushered in a new theological age. Hesychastic prelates were called to replace many of those who opposed their doctrines.

Palamas was a prolific writer. Besides the *Triads* mentioned above, he wrote a great many letters addressed either to his adversaries or to his followers. Some of these are, indeed, treatises of profound theology, but all of them deal with the important question of the distinction between the essence of God and the uncreated divine energies. His devotional writings are proof of the depth of his spirituality while his homilies manifest his pastoral zeal for the church of Thessalonica. However, although a bishop, Palamas remained at heart an Athonite monk, as fervent as in the beginning of his career when he was a hermit on the Holy Mountain. He died in 1359 and was canonized by the Church of Constantinople in 1368.

10. St. Sergius of Radonezh

HIS TRADITION AND HIS HEIRS

323

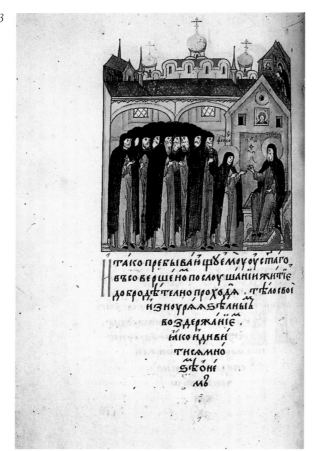

324

323–324. Miniatures from the famed Russian codex of the late Middle Ages containing the life of St. Sergius of Radonezh and also concerning his confreres.

St. Sergius of Radonezh, founder of what is today the most important Orthodox Russian monastery (Troice-Sergieva Laura), is one of the principal monk-saints of the Russian Orthodox Church. He is also looked upon as a national saint because of the important role he had in the birth of the Muscovite state in the 14th century. The laura which he founded also houses the Theological Academy of Moscow and is the burial place of the Russian patriarchs.

Bartholomew Kirilovich, the secular name of the future monk Sergius, was born in 1313 or 1319 near Rostov the Great but very soon moved with his family to Radonezh in the area of Moscow. Even as a little boy he wanted to be a monk, but it was only around 1340, after the deaths of his parents (who became monastics just before dying, in accordance with ancient custom), that he was able to withdraw into solitude. He received the monastic habit in 1342 and changed his name to Sergius. In 1353 he became hegumen of the monastery he himself founded and to which he gave the name Holy Trinity. He died on October 8, 1392, at the age of seventy-eight, after more than half a century of ascetical life, and was buried in his own laura, which still bears his name: Troice-Sergieva Laura. He was canonized in 1448, and his memorial is celebrated twice a year, on July 18 and October 8. He is also included in the Eastern Catholic calendar.

A vocation to the monastic life meant for Sergius a vocation to the eremitical life. He inaugurated a great movement of hermits *(pustynniky),* a new type of monasticism that would spread throughout the territory of the dawning Muscovite state and would foster its religious, cultural, and political rise because Kiev, which the Tatars had destroyed in 1240, would not again acquire the importance it had before the invasion.

Sergius spent about two years in solitude on the site of the future laura. During this period, as we read in his *Life,* he had to endure many tribulations: cold, bears, wolves, and other savage beasts, whose good will he managed to acquire in the course of time. These experiences led to the "passive" type of asceticism that is characteristic of Russian monastics, who, unlike the Byzantines, did not seek out special ascetical practices since work and the endurance of climatic and natural conditions constitute a very harsh mortification.

As in so many similar cases (see, for example, the life of St. Theodosius Pečerskii), Sergius, too, after living a life of solitude, was joined by others desirous of imitating his asceticism and living the monastic life. Thus in the course of a few years a community of twelve monks was formed and became the nucleus of the future monastery. Sergius accordingly moved with them from the solitary to the cenobitic life and became the founder of the monastery of the Holy Trinity, which was already the title of the church he had built for himself in his solitude. While Sergius was the founder, Metrophanes was elected the first hegumen. Only after the latter's death (1353/54) did Sergius himself become

325. Present-day view of the laura of the Most Holy Trinity, founded by St. Sergius on a site close to Moscow; later, it took the name of laura of the Trinity of St. Sergius. It became the main center of Russian monasticism and still occupies an exclusive place in the spirituality of the Russian people.

325

326

326. Apsidal view of the cathedral of the Trinity, built over the saint's tomb, in the laura of St. Sergius.

head of the community. On that occasion he was ordained a priest. But because of internal disagreements Sergius soon left the monastery and withdrew again into solitude; he returned, however, at the insistence of the community.

Complying (it is said) with a request of Alexius, metropolitan of Moscow, and of Philotheus, patriarch of Constantinople, Sergius introduced a cenobitic rule of the Studite type, which later on became widespread in Russian monasteries. But for the liturgy the rule of Jerusalem was adopted.

The building of the monastery of the Holy Trinity in this deserted place led to a colonization of the area. Around it arose the small town of Sergiyev Posad (changed to Zagorsk by the Bolsheviks, but now changed back to the original), seventy kilometers from Moscow. The monastery soon became a religious, cultural (with its scriptorium for copying manuscripts), and even political center. Through his advice and interventions Sergius had a considerable influence on the activities of the various Russian rulers of the time. The grand dukes of Moscow came to the monastery. Alexius (1300–1378) entrusted Sergius with the mission of making peace between the dukes of Novgorod and Ryazan' and those of Moscow. Finally, Alexius wanted Sergius to succeed him in the metropolitan see, but Sergius was "harder than a diamond" in refusing the offer. The most important political event connected with the name of Sergius is the battle of Kulikovo, September 8, 1380. Dimitrii Donskoi, grand duke of

327. The hospitality of Abraham, better known as the icon of the Trinity (c. 1411), the most celebrated of all Russian icons, the work of the great master Andrei Rublev. For a time, it was at the center of the iconostasis in the cathedral of the Trinity of St. Sergius. Tretyakov Gallery, Moscow.

Moscow, fortified by Sergius' blessing, won a decisive victory over Khan Mamay, thus inaugurating the gradual liberation of Russia from the yoke of the Tatars.

Shortly after 1400 Epiphanius the Wise, one of the greatest Russian hagiographers, wrote a *Life* of Sergius (expanded in 1415). Despite the legendary elements in this work, the traits both of Russian monasticism as such and of the personality of Sergius come through, making the *Life* more than mere hagiography.

One example is the radical way in which Sergius lived monastic poverty. Following Theodosius Pečerskii, he wanted to pledge the entire community to a rigorist interpretation of poverty as understood in the eremitical tradition, that is, keeping nothing for the morrow. The resultant penury, however, dissatisfied the monks to such an extent that Sergius had to yield and help in the gradual acquisition of wealth by his monastery. But he himself, even as hegumen, kept his preference for the most shabby clothing.

The rise of trinitarian spirituality in Russia is linked with the name of Sergius. The first church which he built in the forest was dedicated to the Holy Trinity, and he gave the same name to his monastery. It was in this mystical setting that Andrei Rublev (1360–1430), who belonged to the laura, created the famous icon of the three angels visiting Abraham near the oaks of Mamre (Genesis 18); this is one of the most sublime pictorial representations of trinitarian theology.

The foundation of several dozen monasteries is attributed to Sergius, who placed his disciples at the head of them (eleven of these are venerated as saints). For this reason he has been de-

328. General view from Lake Beloye, near Lake Kubenskoye, of the monastery of St. Cyril of Belozërsk, northeast of Moscow; it has become a center of great importance for the Russian people.

329. View of the cathedral of St. John in the laura of the Trinity of St. Sergius; on the left, one sees the cell of Cyril.

330. Icon of Cyril of Belozersk, a work of 1414 attributed to Dionisii of Glušhchitskii. The icon comes from the monastery of St. Cyril. Tretyakov Gallery, Moscow.

330

scribed as "the father of monasticism in northern Russia." Lauras spread not only southward (toward Moscow) but also to the north, where a new monastic center came into being, the so-called "Russian Thebaid." Four of these northern monasteries became exceptionally famous:

The monastery of St. Cyril of Belozërsk. Cyril (ca. 1337–1427), the son of a boyar, entered the Simonovo monastery of Moscow, where he became its hegumen in 1390, but as early as two years later he became first a recluse and then a hermit in the region of the White Lake (Beloye Ozero), along with Ferapont, a monk. Each of them founded a monastery. Following in the steps of Sergius, Cyril also influenced the civil society of his time. Three letters have been preserved which he wrote to the rulers of that age, reminding them of the duties they owed, as Christian rulers, toward their subjects. Cyril's monastery remained one of the most important in Russia; it was there that, among others, Nil Sorskii (1433–1508), the father of Russian hesychasm (a quietistic system of meditation), received his training.

The tradition of Sergius of Radonezh was also continued by the monks of the forests of Komel', who established a monastic center across the Volga. St. Paul of Obnora (1317–1429), one of Sergius' disciples, lived for some years in the trunk of a linden tree (an ancient ascetical practice of the so-called "Dendrites"). He had a great love of silence and is therefore thought to have been a hesychast. He was joined by another solitary, Sergius of Nurom (d. 1413), who came from Mount Athos but had likewise had his training at the laura of Sergius.

331. The spectacular painted interior of the church of the Nativity of the Mother of God in the monastery founded by the monk Ferapont, a disciple of Cyril, also in the famed region of Lake Kubenskoye.

332. A northern landscape, to which monks had a great attraction, on Solovetskiy, an island in the White Sea; here one sees the small church dedicated to St. Andrew.

333. Icon representing the monastery of Sts. Zosima and Savvatii on Solovetskiy.

There were also the monks of Lake Kubenskoye. Among the various monasteries they founded, the most famous is Spasso-Kamennii. Among others who lived there was the "Russian Gonzaga," Prince Andrei Zaozersk (d. 1453), whose religious name was Josaphat. After renouncing all his possessions, he died after only five years of monastic life.

Another great monastery of the North was the one on the island of Solovetskiy. Sadly, in recent times it became known as the most dreaded of Stalin's gulags; there, in 1937, Father Pavel Florensky, one of the most promising of Russian religious thinkers, died.

334. Present-day view of the monastery of Sts. Zosima and Savvatii, on Solovetskiy, today called the monastery of Solovetskiy.

335. Map of the major Russian monasteries which can be visited today.

336. Evocative winter view of the monastery of the Tolga in Yaroslavl'. Tradition has it that in the 14th century Bishop Prochor, on his way back from the White Sea, had a vision at the confluence of the river Tolga with the Volga. There appeared to him a radiant icon of the Mother of God. It is told that the icon was found by him and his companions and that the monastery was built on that spot.

334

335

11. ROMANIAN MONASTICISM

337

338

337. General view of the monastery of Neamṭ, an ancient foundation made by Petru Musat at the end of the 14th century. It is traditionally attributed to the disciples of the blessed Nicodemus of Tismana, the founder of hesychastic cenobite life in Romania. Petru Musat was the first metropolitan of Moldavia, a region, formerly province, of Romania, and the monasteries of Neamṭ and Putna are renowned for their artistic activity: scriptoria, music schools, liturgical embroidery.

Despite the important place of monasticism in the religious life of the Romanian people, there are few sources, and even bibliographical material is scarce. One of the rare original documents is the *Teachings of Prince Neagoṣ of Bessarabia to His Son Theodosius,* a work written in Old Church Slavonic at the beginning of the 16th century. It was not until the years 1980–1988 that Father Ioanichie Bǎlan, a monk of the monastery of Sihǎstria, would publish his trilogy on the history, past and present, of Romanian monasticism.

The origins of monasticism in Romania may go back to the period of the Roman empire inasmuch as the presence of real monastic centers is attested for the provinces of Scythia Minor and Dacia; from these came such monks as John Cassian (d. 435), Germanus, and Dionysius Exiguus (the Little, d. 545), as well as the so-called "Scythian monks" at the beginning of the 6th century.

The lot of monasticism during the subsequent period is not attested until the 14th century. It is clear, however, that there were cenobites and hermits in Moldavia (an autonomous principality beginning in 1359) before the 14th century. Many monasteries, such as Neamṭ, that were founded in the 14th century, were established by Serbian monks who were followers

339

338. *Detail of a mural of the Last Judgment in the exterior narthex of the monastery of Moldoviţa. Here we see Moses and the Hebrews, the Turks, and the people of the West.*

339. *The church of St. George in the monastery of Voroneţ in Moldavia, founded by Stephen the Great in 1488. The monastic churches of Moldavia are frequently characterized by exterior murals as well as completely painted interiors. The goal is to teach sacred history—Old and New Testaments—liturgy, and theology.*

340

341

340. Like other Orthodox countries, Romania has its monastery, founded by Moldavians, on Mount Athos. View of the Romanian skete of the Prodromu, that is, John the Precursor.

341. The monastery of the Prodromu on the Athos in an etching from 1779, attributed to Zaharija Orfelin.

of Nicodemus of Tismana and by monks from the lands south of the Danube who were fleeing before the advancing Turks. It is certain that Nicodemus (d. 1406) played an important role as organizer of cenobitic monastic life in Walachia (a principality in southern Romania, autonomous since 1330). Nicodemus was a native of Serbian Macedonia and had been trained in asceticism on Mount Athos, where he made his profession in the Serbian monastery of Chilandári. After a probable stay south of the Danube in Krajna (under Serbian control), where he seems to have founded two monasteries, he went on to Walachia, where he founded Vodiţa (1369) and Tismana (1375–1378).

The monastic tradition in Romania reached its greatest growth toward the end of the 18th century, when the Athonite Philocalian renewal reached Romanian monasticism thanks to the work of starets Paisii Veličhkovskii (1722–1794). Paisii came from the spiritual school of Basil of Poiana Mărului (1695–1767); both were Slavs who had taken refuge in Romanian territory. The spiritual personality of Paisii was the dominant influence in Romanian monasticism during the first half of the 19th century and thus linked the Oriental tradition with modern times. Paisii based life in his large monasteries on four pillars: cenobitic life, the study of the writings of the Fathers, the practice of the Jesus Prayer, and the daily manifestation of thoughts to a spiritual father; he thus adapted the hesychastic ideal, originally lived by hermits, to large cenobitic monasteries. Paisii had a noteworthy ability to keep monks from various nations in harmony, especially the Romanians and Russians. The latter, after being formed in the school of Paisii,

342

343

later returned to Russia where they gave birth to the spiritual renaissance of the 19th century.

The Romanian spiritual descendants of Paisii were the startsy Gheorghe (1730–1806) and Calinic (1787–1869).

The special trait that Romanian monasticism displays is its hesychastic inspiration. In Romania, in fact, the very word *hesychast* has played a part not matched in the rest of the Orthodox world. Evidence of this is the countless mountains, hills, rivers, and places whose names derive from terms of monastic origin that recall the name of this or that hesychastic monk who lived in the area. Moreover, hesychasm was received in an original way in Romania; thus, it is possible to speak of a "Romanian hesychastic tradition" as a typical phenomenon which has lasted to our time.

The main centers of Romanian hesychastic life, the "hesychasteries" (in Romanian, *sihăstrie,* from the Greek *hesykasterion*), are in the Romanian regions of Dobrogea, Moldavia, Walachia, Banat, and Transilvania. Their numerical development is a phenomenon almost unique in the Orthodox world. The hesychastic and Philocalian ideal has remained alive throughout the entire history of Romanian monasticism, above all in the large cenobitic monasteries.

Some of these, founded by Romanian princes in Walachia and Moldavia in the 14th and 18th centuries, are true monuments because of both their architecture and murals. The architecture is a unique synthesis of the Byzantine and Gothic styles with that of the Renaissance. The murals, both on the outside (another characteristic phenomenon) and inside, embody an entire implicit theology, the meanings of which are still to be deciphered.

342. General view of the monastery of Sucevița in Moldavia. The monastery, begun in 1583, was built by Gheorghe Movila and his brother Ieremia, the future prince of Moldavia. The buildings and the paintings were completed within the year 1596.

343. Mural from 1535 representing four holy monks, Sts. Germanus, Nikon, Timothy, and Theophan, church of the Dormition in the monastery of Humor in Moldavia.

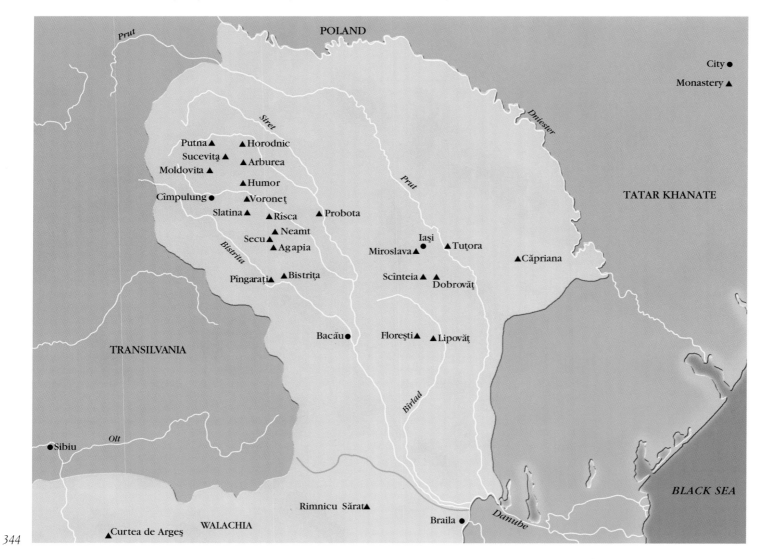

344

345

344. *The monasteries of Moldavia between 1365 and 1606 (by C. C. and D. C. Giurescu,* Istoria românilor, *Bucharest, 1976).*

345. *Map of Eastern Europe between the Baltic and Black Seas showing the location of Moldavia and the region of Walachia.*

346. *Detail of a mural which represents the famous hymn, the Acathistus, in honor of the Mother of God. The use of this hymn is especially prevalent in the monastic liturgy. The detail represents verse 24, on the veneration of the icon of the Theotokos (the Mother of God). The painting is on the exterior wall of the church of the Annunciation in the monastery of Moldoviţa.*

On the two following pages:
347. *This impressive mural of the Last Judgment from 1547 is on the eastern facade of the church of St. George in the monastery of Voroneţ.*

12. THE *PHILOCALIA*

348

348. Gregory of Nazianzus in the act of writing. Miniature from a codex containing his homilies (Sinait. 339). He used the term "philocalia" for his collection of Origen's works.

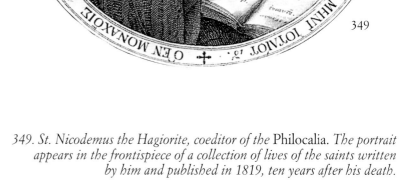

349

349. St. Nicodemus the Hagiorite, coeditor of the Philocalia. *The portrait appears in the frontispiece of a collection of lives of the saints written by him and published in 1819, ten years after his death.*

The *Philocalia* is an extensive anthology of ascetical and mystical texts having to do especially with hesychastic prayer. It was compiled by Macarius (Notaras) of Corinth (1731–1805) and Nicodemus Hagiorites (1749–1809), both of whom were monks of the Great Laura on Mount Athos, and first appeared in Venice in 1782. It was the most important work published in the Greek Orthodox world during the Turkish domination, a period in which Greek Orthodoxy went into a gradual decline. The *Philocalia* bears witness to the effort to promote a spiritual renewal through a "return to the sources" of Orthodox spirituality; this effort was part of the movement of the so-called "Kollyvàdes," who supported a deepening of liturgical and sacramental theology, as well as a return to the patristic and Byzantine heritage. The Greek word *philokalia* means, literally, "love of the beautiful and the good." St. Augustine identifies the word with "philosophy," but Eusebius had already used it to signify anthologies of texts. Basil and Gregory of Nazianzus gave the same title to their collection of texts from the works of Origen.

The *Philocalia* of Macarius and Nicodemus is a vast work of 1200 folio pages in its first edition and contains both extracts and

entire works of about 36 authors from the 4th to the 15th centuries. It is the largest collection of texts having to do with hesychasm and reflects the spirituality of the men and women who withdrew into solitude and silence in order to unite themselves with God through continuous prayer and thereby to achieve *theosis* (the deification or divinization of the human being). This ideal of Eastern spirituality is a thread that unifies the entire *Philocalia.*

Very quickly, Paisii Veličkovskii published an edition in Old Church Slavonic in St. Petersburg in 1793; it was titled *Dobrotoljubie* and was reprinted at least eight times by 1920. It is not a simple translation, because Paisii had already worked on the same patristic texts. While the influence of the (Greek) *Philocalia* remained limited to monastic circles, the *Dobrotoljubie,* which was recommended by Russian startsy, had a wide readership and influenced even popular piety (see the heartfelt accounts made by a pilgrim to his spiritual father: Kazan', 1881).

Another who met the felt need of a translation into Russian was Bishop Theophan the Recluse, whose five volumes were sponsored by the Russian monastery of St. Panteleimon on Mount Athos (1877–1889). While taking into account Paisii's Slavonic

350

350. The refectory of the monastery of Dionissíu on Mount Athos, where St. Nicodemus made his religious profession.

version, Theophan based his own translation as far as possible on the Greek original. His translation is, however, much more voluminous than the original because he made his own selection of texts, adding some and excising or changing others, for example, those having to do with the psycho-physical method of hesychastic prayer. His pastoral intention is clear: to make it possible for not only hermits but also cenobites and laypersons to practice hesychasm, perhaps the reason that Theophan's *Dobrotoljubie* was widely read in Russia before the revolution and is being reprinted today, lately in an abridged, pocket-sized edition.

It was this Russian *Dobrotoljubie* that served as the basis for the first translations into Western languages, initially as collections of selected texts, such as the English-language *Early Fathers from the Philokalia* (London, 1951), which was used in turn for translations into French (1953), German (1956), and Italian (1960). Recently, complete translations of the Greek *Philocalia* have been published, in four volumes, in English (1979–1995) and Italian (1982–1987). The soil in which such an interest in the *Philocalia* grew in the West was prepared by the "heartfelt accounts of a Russian pilgrim to his spiritual father";

this was translated into a number of Western languages beginning in 1925 (German; 1946, Italian); it became famous in English as *The Way of a Pilgrim.* The book consists, in fact, of an account of how the teachings in the *Philocalia* may be translated into life.

Thus the *Philocalia* had, and continues to have, a very important role in the revival of prayer and the renewal of the spiritual life in both East and West; it shows that the "Philocalian movement" that came out of Russia in the 19th century is still alive.

The *Philocalia* deals with prayer and with the dispositions and conditions which prayer requires. Among the dispositions the main one is custody of the heart and a watchfulness of spirit that excludes every wandering of the mind and is therefore called *nēpsis* ("vigilance"); in fact, in the subtitle the words "of the Vigilant" occur. Is it possible to speak of a typical spirituality? The first writers did not have such an intention, even though they applied a standard in choosing texts: Christian dogmas should be experienced in a prayer that divinizes and gives peace (deification). As a way of reaching this goal, the *Philocalia* sets down, first and foremost, the Jesus Prayer, which, if recited

351

352

351. *General view of the monastery on the island of Solovetskiy, which became an influential center of diffusion of the* Philocalia *in Russia.*

352. *A papadikiya is a collection of monastic hymns. Papadikiya, ca. 1670, monastery of Iviron (cod. 1250) on Mount Athos.*

On the two following pages:
353. *View of Esfigménu, a monastery on Mount Athos, from the sea. Athos, with its history of spirituality, remains an indispensable source for understanding the great movement of the startsy.*

354. *Itinerary of Paisii Veličkovskii and the expansion of the startsy movement. From today's Ukraine Paisii went to Athos where, having*

become a monk, he entered deeply into the mystical dimension. Then he went to Moldavia, Romania, and was the originator of a school for startsy. His disciple Theophan (Feofan) and the starets Leo made the monastery of Optina in Russia the center of the movement.

355. *Panoramic view of the monastery of Dragomirna in Moldavia, which must already have looked this way in 1763 when Paisii arrived and stimulated its renewal.*

diligently, will lead the person to prayer of the heart. It suggests that in order to reach this goal more quickly, the person use the psycho-physical method developed by the hesychasts of Mount Athos in the 14th century; this consists of certain bodily postures during prayer and the regulation of one's breathing. This Athonite hesychasm received its theological and philosophical justification in the thought of Gregory Palamas, which maintains that under certain conditions a person can have a mystical experience in which he or she participates in the uncreated energies of God, the "light of Tabor."

It must be noted, however, that what has been said does not exhaust the *Philocalia*. The work also presents the broader conception of hesychasm, which involves the seeking of continual prayer amid interior peace: an aspiration of monasticism since its very beginnings.

The *Philocalia*, therefore, reflects various spiritual tendencies that came into existence in the course of the ten centuries represented in the work. Thus, while the predominant element in the work is the Evagrian current of "pure prayer," the vision of God by the intellect alone, which has been emptied of every concept, form, or image, there is also present the Pseudo-Macarian current of "feeling." This presence of different spiritualities, however, makes the *Philocalia* a work not easy to read.

The difficulty seems to have always been recognized, which explains why the editor of the Russian *Dobrotoljubie,* Theophan Zatvornik, was not content with a simple translation, but gave the work a style that met the pastoral needs of his time. The same was true of Dumitru Stăniloae (1903–1993), author of the monumental Romanian *Philocalia;* and while speaking of the *Philocalia,* we must not forget the Romanian hesychastic tradition (Stăniloae's edition, begun in 1946, reached its tenth volume in 1981). At an earlier date, Ignatii Bryančaninov (1807–1867) had gone even further in this direction; his ascetical writings are an anthology of Philocalian writers with commentary. Nor may we forget that Paisii Veličkovskii himself not only produced the first Slavonic edition, but also trained in his monastery the startsy, the spiritual fathers who transmitted Philocalian spirituality via their own personal, living words. This necessary link between Philocalian spirituality and spiritual guidance by a starets can be seen in *The Way of a Pilgrim.* Even though *The Way* is probably based on the experiences of a real pilgrim, the text is the fruit of a careful and gradual development that is directed by a precise intention: to make hesychastic spirituality accessible to all, while eliminating the danger of possible confusion. Thus understood, *The Way of a Pilgrim* is an introduction to the *Philocalia* by one who was himself a starets.

13. THE STARTSY AND RUSSIAN PIETY

IN THE 18TH AND 19TH CENTURIES

353

The reforms of Peter the Great (1672–1725), which were intended to modernize his vast empire by opening it to the West, produced a period of traumatization. Even from the viewpoint of monasticism, the 18th century, taken as a whole, was a period of decline that culminated in the disappearance of monasticism from Russian political and social history through a progressive secularization of monastic centers (1701–1764). Throughout the 18th century, especially under Catherine the Great (d. 1796), the number of monasteries dropped from 1200 to 387, the rest being taken over by the state's organization and bureaucracy.

Yet within this critical situation, the first glimmers of a spiritual renewal began to appear. The rediscovery of the contemplative dimension and of the idea of the spiritual father as essential elements of the monastic experience had a profound effect on two men of that century: St. Tikhon of Zadonsk and Paisii Veličkovskii.

In Tikhon of Zadonsk (1724–1783) we see the union of two classical types of Russian holiness, that of the bishop, the pastor of souls and witness to the gospel (Tikhon was bishop of Voronezh from 1763 to 1767), and that of the monk, the starets, who thirsts for silence and solitude but at the same time remains near and open to every human being (in 1768 Tikhon withdrew into solitude in the hermitage of Zadonsk). His spirituality displays the predominant characteristics of Russian monasticism: the desire for an intense union with God, love of the suffering Christ, a thirst for the complete transfiguration of human beings in the kingdom of heaven, and a compassionate love for the poor. Above all, however, Tikhon was able to harmonize, in the person of the starets, the two essential components of monastic experience: life in God and love of neighbor.

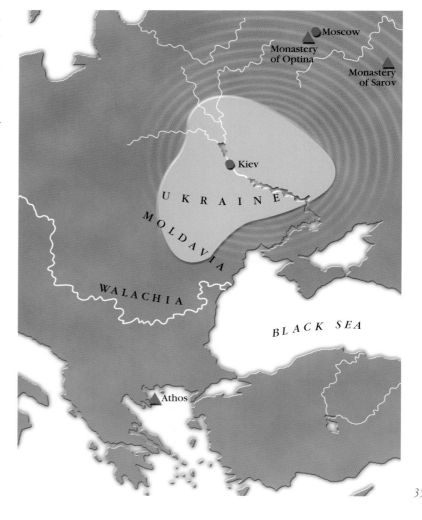

354

355

A Ukrainian monk, Paisii Veličkovskii (1722–1794), gave a new, vital impulse to Russian monasticism, along with a rediscovery of spiritual fatherhood (starčestvo) within the community. His eager search for the authentic sources of the monastic tradition took him to Mount Athos (1746), where he became a monk and rediscovered the mystical dimension of monasticism in the writings of Nil Sorskii and the hesychastic authors. In 1763, Paisii, together with the disciples who soon gathered around him, moved to Moldavia (in modern-day Romania), where he became a stimulus to the renewal of a series of monasteries (Dragomirna, Sekul', Neamţ). There he began a true school of startsy, thereby recapturing the earliest basis of Eastern monasticism: the spiritual father (or mother). An innovation, however, was the "communal" aspect of Paisii's spiritual intuition, for the Jesus Prayer, the study of sacred Scripture, and an emphasis on the personal dimension of the journey to God were integrated into the balanced framework of a cenobitic life that was supported by liturgical prayer and work, both intellectual and manual.

Through starčestvo, then, Paisii succeeded in adapting the hesychastic ideal to life in his large monasteries, thus opening the way to an interior renewal of Russian monasticism. In order to supply solid patristic and ascetical foundations for his model of monastic life, Paisii translated into Old Church Slavonic a classic of Eastern spirituality, the Philocalia (Slavonic: Dobrotoljubie). The influence of this work on the Russian spiritual world was not limited to monasticism but reached all social classes, not only ecclesiastical but lay (see The Way of a Pilgrim).

The link between the spirituality of Paisii Veličkovskii and the "Philocalian renewal" of the 19th century appears in the startsy,

who set a decisive mark on the role of monasticism in Russian society and on its impact on the spiritual formation of the people.

Two monasteries stand out in the history of that period: the hermitage of Optina, made noteworthy by a real dynasty of startsy, and the monastery of Sarov, which is linked with the name of one of the greatest monks and mystics of the Russian Church, St. Seraphim.

In 1800, Theophan (Feofan), a disciple of Paisii Veličkovskii and one permeated by the spiritual experience of his teacher, gave a new impulse to the hermitage of Optina. But it was through starets Leo (Leonid Nagolkin, 1768–1841) that Optina became the center of Russian starčestvo. The term staretz (literally: "old man, elder") means, in the context of monasticism, the spiritual maturity of one who is henceforth able to direct others. Leonid was a living example of this role: he was the father of the humble who sought out his words, which were drawn from the texts of the Scriptures and Fathers, as a comfort in their physical and spiritual sufferings.

Other traits were to be seen in the person of Macarius (Makarii Ivanov, 1768–1860). He was a contemplative and learned man who opened the hermitage of Optina to literary men and scholars (Dostoyevskii, Solov'ëv, Leont'ev, and others). Makarii spread the writings of Paisii Veličkovskii and began an edition of patristic texts, the reading of which would lead the Hegelian philosopher, Ivan Kireevskii, to convert to the Orthodox faith.

The best known of all the startsy of Optina was certainly Ambrose (Amvrosii Grenkov, 1812–1891). In his person the compassion of the heavenly Father for humanity was renewed. Attentive as he was to the individual and her or his every activity, Amvrosii possessed the extraordinary gift of immediately

356

358

357. The prophet Elijah in the desert. From a 15th-century icon, Museum of Decorative Arts of Karelia, Petrozavodsk, Russia. When Eastern monasticism wanted to recover its original eremitical spirituality, the figure of Elijah returned as an Old Testament model.

357. St. Seraphim of Sarov during a vigil in the forest. Russian icon from the 19th century.

357

358. A well-known painting from 1889 which we owe to the Russian artist Mikhail Nesterov. It shows the figure of a hermit, which will often be identified in the Russian tradition with a starets. The starets, a true "spiritual father," is the one who is capable of guiding others and therefore of helping the monastic community to recover its original spirit.

359

359. Icon of Pentecost (Moscow School, 1405) by Prochor of Gorodets. Pentecost is a feast which represents the premise of the startsy's spirituality; they intended to lead monastics and laypeople to the rediscovery of the meaning of the descent of the Holy Spirit on the community of believers. Iconostasis in the cathedral of the Annunciation, the Kremlin, Moscow.

understanding the spiritual state of the person speaking with him and of finding the "word of salvation" for that person's soul. "My desire," he wrote, "is to give every human being the blessed joy of God, to help everyone, whatever the circumstances of their lives." Tolstoi gave a brief but telling description of Amvrosii: "It is when one speaks with human beings like him that one feels the closeness of God."

In the monastery of Sarov lived one of the most shining figures of Russian monasticism: the starets Seraphim (1759–1833). His life, which was simple and all of a piece, reveals a synthesis of aspects from both Russian spirituality and the most authentic monastic tradition: a yearning for the transfiguration of every creature in God through the Holy Spirit dwelling within it and permeating its entire being (see the well-known *Conversation with N. Motovilov*). In addition, the life of Starets Seraphim embraced all the dimensions of monastic experience: as a monk in the monastery of Sarov (1779–1793), he felt the call to asceticism and a solitary life, which he spent immersed in prayer, yet was linked to the people and their vicissitudes. During Napoleon's invasion of

Russia, Seraphim spent three years (1804–1807) as a stylite on a rock, the only instance we know of stylitism in the 19th century. A period of complete silence followed (1807–1810), after which Seraphim lived as a recluse in a tiny cell (1810–1825). This period of silent prayer, which "is more powerful than anything else that exists because it brings down the Holy Spirit," prepared the way for the final stage of this monk's life: his openness to all comers and his service as a spiritual father. He received the crowds of people who streamed to Sarov and gave to each of them the message summed up in the words of salvation with which he greeted whoever came to him: "Christ is risen, and he is my joy!"

It can be said, then, that to the startsy goes the credit not only of having formed the popular Russian piety of the 19th century (following the lead of the *Philocalia*) but also of reconciling with the church the Russian intelligentsia that had traditionally remained alienated from it. Through their "personalist" approach, the startsy showed the church and Russian monasticism a way out of their crisis of secularization. This way was unfortunately blocked by the Bolshevik revolution.

14. Contemporary Orthodox Monasticism

360. Mount Athos remains a reality more alive than ever for the Eastern monasticism of our time. Here we see a picture of the monastery of Aghíu Panteleímonos, also called the "Russikon," a constant point of reference for the monasticism of Russia.

361. The Russian skete (monastery) of the prophet Elijah on Mount Athos is another point of reference for the monasticism of Russia.

360

361

In attempting to give a more or less objective picture of contemporary Orthodox monasticism, one cannot avoid making a distinction between the countries with an Orthodox majority that used to be members of the Warsaw Pact, and those that remained connected politically with the West. Only Greece can be placed in this second category. Therefore the phenomenon of monasticism is to be seen in conjunction with the events that left their mark on these countries after 1917.

Russia was, and is, the largest territorial entity with an Orthodox majority. The fate of vocations to the monastic life in that country can be taken, by and large, as a model.

During the reign of Nicholas II (1894–1917), the last czar before the rise of Communism, Russian monasticism grew notably. We know that in 1917 there were 1257 monasteries of men or women, with about 33,572 men and 73,462 women. In other words, while there were more monasteries of men (about 550) than of women (about 475), there were far more female than male monastics. Except for the large lauras and some important foundations, there were about thirty to fifty monks in each monastery, whereas all the communities of women had more than a hundred members. Only in five dioceses (Vyborg, Kiev, Kursk, Moscow, and Charkov) did the monasteries of men contain over a thousand members in all; on the other hand, women monastics reached that number in a good twenty-five dioceses (Kiev, Moscow, Nizhniy Novgorod, Orël, Penza, Samara, Tambov, etc.). A

monastery had more members depending on the reputation for holiness of its spiritual mothers and fathers and on the strictness with which its rule was observed.

At the beginning of the 20th century, attempts were made to establish, alongside the traditional ascetical way of life, a type of active religious life among both men and women that was very like the Western religious congregations. While retaining some elements of monastic structure, these communities had missions that included the apostolate, help for the poor, and social work. These were attempts to integrate the consecrated life into the fabric of society and its problems. Examples of this new type were the foundations established by the grand duchess Elizabeth Romanov (d. 1918) and John of Kronstadt, a priest (1829–1908); in 1902, the latter's "House of Labor" had workshops, schools, libraries, orphanages, and hospices, and employed seven thousand people.

After the October Revolution, the policy adopted by the state was one of repression and confiscation that would have eliminated monastic life completely if some communities had not adopted the device of registering themselves as labor cooperatives. But the prohibition against allowing those who had previously been religious to enter these communities ended up thinning their ranks. Between 1918 and 1921 alone 722 houses were closed so that by 1930 not a single monastery existed in the entire Soviet Union.

362. It is 12 June 1988. Outdoors, in the monastery of St. Daniil, which has become the new see of the patriarch of Moscow, the solemn Liturgy of the "Millennium" honoring the birth of Christian Kievan Rus' is being celebrated, with the Russian patriarch Pimen presiding and the other Orthodox patriarchs concelebrating.

363. The faithful arrive for a liturgical service in the laura of the Trinity of St. Sergius not far from Moscow. The Monastery, as it is called, remains the center of the Russians' Christian devotion.

362

363

Survival was assured in neighboring countries (Finland, Estonia, Lithuania, Poland, Romania, etc.) and in countries more distant (Serbia, Czechoslovakia, France, the United States, Canada, Australia, and South America), while monasteries founded in China disappeared after Mao's revolution.

The presence of Orthodox monasteries of men and women in the Western world was always dependent on members who were Russian or of Russian descent along with some sympathizers.

Monasteries that had come into existence outside of Russia (Holy Land: Ain Karim, Mount of Olives, Gethsemani, etc.; Mount Athos: St. Panteleimon, sketes of St. Andrew and St. Elias, etc.; St. Catherine of Sinai) gradually lost their inflow of members. An example: in 1900 there were 3496 Russian monks on Mount Athos, in 1925 the number dropped to 560, in 1945 to 280, in the 70s to 61, and in 1988 there were only 25.

After the Second World War, when the Soviet Union annexed neighboring territories (Ukraine, Transcarpathia, Belarus, Bessarabia, Moldova, the Baltic republics), there were a good 104 monastic institutions in those countries, but by 1965 their number had shrunk to about 20.

In the seventies and eighties the number of monasteries dropped to 16; in 1970 the total number of monastics, men and women, was 1275.

On the occasion of the millennium anniversary of the christianization of Russia, about twenty monasteries were returned to the church. In the report which Metropolitan Vladimir of Rostov presented to the Holy Synod in Moscow in 1990, he spoke of 35 monasteries, 17 of men and the rest of women.

The Russian model applies pretty well to all the countries of the Warsaw Pact. After the fall of the Berlin Wall, there was a revival of traditional monastic life, but at the same time with new aspects deriving from the experiences which women and men had had in the Western world. The revival is undoubtedly considerable, but not exceptional, due obviously to the emigration of young people to the West.

Mount Athos, on the other hand, can serve as a kind of yardstick measuring the progress of monasticism within Orthodoxy. In 1903 there were 7432 monks, of whom 3496 were Russians, 3276 Greeks, 307 Bulgarians, 286 Rumanians, 51 Georgians, and 16 Serbians. In 1985 the monastic population had shrunk to 1309, of whom 95% were Greeks.

The pole of Greek monasticism is Mount Athos and the revival of some Meteorite houses, transformed from male to female monasteries.

Some Athonite monasteries have had a good increase in numbers, but with the members coming from conservative movements that are not always open to dialogue.

The drop in vocations applies to all of the Orthodox Church, but its course differs according to the diverse realities. Regarding this subject, the course Bulgarian monasticism has taken is

364. For the Greeks a spiritual point of reference today is still the complex of monasteries of the Meteora, partially excavated from the rock, in the north of the country.
The very landscape in which the monasteries are situated is a symbol of the search for heavenly things. Here is a view from below of the monastery of St. Nikolaos Anapavsas.

365. Interior court of the monastery of Bachkovo in Bulgaria. One sees part of the church of the Assumption of the Virgin, which dates back to the 17th century. The monastery is completely renovated and is a center of intense spirituality.

364

365

366. There is a rebirth of women's monasticism in Bulgaria. Here in Samokov we see the inside of the monastery dedicated to the shroud of the Virgin.

significant. After the Liberation of Bulgaria from Ottoman rule (1878), a certain number of Bulgarian monasteries found themselves outside the borders of free Bulgaria. While there were only some ten monasteries for women in the first half of the 19th century, after the Liberation several monasteries for men, which had become depopulated, were transformed into monasteries for women. In 1890, Bulgaria had 90 monasteries with 530 monastics (346 women and 184 men); by 1936, the number of monasteries had reached 105 with only 234 monastics (208 women and 26 men). According to the latest surveys in 1994, the number of monasteries is 164 with 228 monastics (122 women and 106 men). Many of the monasteries are practically empty and are maintained by the priests of the closest town or village; others are inhabited by one or two monks. Not all the 106 monks reside in monasteries. More than half are part of the hierarchy: the patriarch, the metropolitans, the bishops, the rectors of the two seminaries, and so forth. In any case, at present the monks who reside in monasteries are a rather heterogenous group: the younger ones have received a theological formation, but older monks—who are in the majority—have simply chosen to spend the rest of their days in the quiet and recollection of their hal-

366

367. *A recently painted iconostasis in a small monastery of women not far from the monastery of Kalenić in Serbia.*

368. *This photo taken in the winter of 1988 shows the impressive building site of the new cathedral of Belgrade dedicated to the founder of Serbian monasticism, St. Sava.*

367

368

lowed monasteries. The same thing is true for monasteries of women in which most of the nuns are older than sixty.

At the present time, the monasteries of Rila, Bachkovo, Troyan, and Rozhen are completely renovated and have a more intense monastic life.

The situation seems to be somewhat different in Serbia. After the First World War, the patriarchate of Serbia (which was restored in 1920) had 209 monasteries with 442 male and 69 female members. Women's monasticism received an unexpected increase with the arrival of refugee nuns from Russia, who brought with them a spiritual renewal known as the "devotional movement." As a result of the increase, the monasteries of Hopovo in Fruška Gora and of Kuveždin were able to found monasteries in the dioceses of Niš, Ohrid-Bitolj, Šabac, Žiča, Bačka, Banat, Braničevo, Timok, Skopje, Zletovo-Strumica, Belgrade, and Karlovača. Consequently, in 1940 the patriarchate had 348 male and 397 female monastics in 27 monasteries. The monasteries established schools and ateliers of iconography that produced a large number of iconographers.

The Second World War struck hard at the entire monastic movement because it affected not only buildings but persons as well. Yet after the war was over, many religious, men and women, returned to their destroyed monasteries and began to rebuild them. In 1969 the Serbian Orthodox Church had 87 monasteries with a good 845 nuns. Their life, however, was not simple or easy, nor would their social activities on behalf of orphans and the handicapped bring them favor over the subsequent fifty years. Yet today the Serbian Church has 119 monasteries of men with 446 members, and 122 of women with 818 members.

The 19th century was one of the most difficult for Romanian monasticism.

The founding of modern Romania, after the union of the principalities of Walachia and Moldavia in 1859, brought with it a laicist and anticlerical conception of public life, the confiscation of monastic possessions, and the suppression of monasticism (1863). After that date, only women and men over 60 could become monastics. Of the 250 monasteries and sketes only 75 remained open; the rest were turned into parish churches, prisons, and psychiatric asylums. Of the 3500 male and 3045 female monastics at the end of the 18th century only 820 men and 2250 women remained. The majority were exiled to Mount Athos, Palestine, and Russia. The state's interference in the life of the Romanian

369. Believers and non-believers alike come in numbers to Moldavian monasteries, to recover the original spirit of Orthodoxy and to admire the extraordinary artistic monuments decorated with murals, veritable catecheses painted on the walls.

370. A monk of Mount Athos lights a lamp before an icon, a sign of daily devotion. All faithful are invited to come face-to-face with the spirituality of Orthodox monasticism because this spirituality is seen by all of Eastern Christianity as a paradigm for everyone since each person is destined to make room in his or her life for the concrete presence of Christ.

Orthodox Church (which had been declared autonomous in 1865 and had obtained Constantinople's recognition of its autocephaly in 1885) caused monasticism to stagnate.

A balance was achieved after the nation had gained a degree of political stability, namely, after the First World War. At that point, monasticism began to recover and also to enter more deeply into the ancient Philocalian tradition. This was the period of the life and work of the greatest Romanian Orthodox theologian, Dumitru Stăniloae (1903–1993), who began the monumental edition of the Romanian *Philocalia* (the first volumes appeared in Sibiu in 1946–1948, but it was not possible to publish the next six volumes until 1975–1981). The harsh repression of monasticism by the Communist regime made it necessary for it to reorganize on the basis of its usefulness to society; this meant having the monasteries become cooperatives for production, with the emphasis placed chiefly on their preservation as museums.

When the Communist regime ended, Romanian monasticism had been reduced to about 1500 female and 1000 male monastics in 122 monasteries and skete. Yet paradoxically something of a new flowering had been going on due to the influence of about ten spiritual fathers, authentic startsy such as Father Paisie Olaru

(1897–1990) and Father Cleopa Ilie (1912–1998). Another person who was especially influential during the time of persecution was poet and journalist Sandu Tudor (1896–1961), who became a monk and then a schemomonk (a wearer of the "great schema" or habit, which was a sign of an elevated ascetic state) and took the name Daniil. In the monastery of Antim in Bucharest he drew around him a group of intellectuals known as the "Burning Bush," which signaled a reconciliation of the Romanian intelligentsia with the Orthodox Church. Conscious that a whole world and an entire hierarchy of values were collapsing, these individuals rediscovered the spiritual foundations of the human person in the Jesus Prayer and in hesychasm, which had been passed on to them by Ivan Kulighin, a monk from Russia who had taken refuge in the monastery of Cernica, but was later deported once again to Siberia, where he would die in 1950. Father Tudor died in 1960 in a Communist prison, as did so many others of the group.

Orthodox monasteries, both of men and of women, that were founded in the diaspora, chiefly in the United States, Canada, and Australia, have a good many young monastics who are living in depth the spirituality and liturgy of the ancient Byzantine tradition.

370

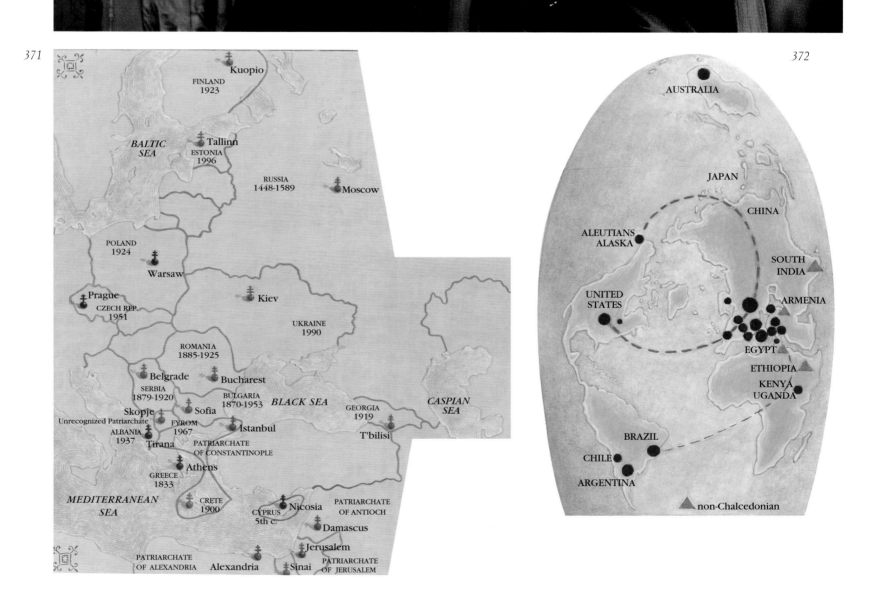

371

372

371. The Orthodox Church with its patriarchates in Europe, the Caucasus, and the Mediterranean basin.

372. Spread of Orthodoxy and the Orthodox monastic presence in the world. The green triangles indicate the non-Chalcedonian churches.

15. MONASTICISM IN PRE-CHALCEDONIAN CHURCHES

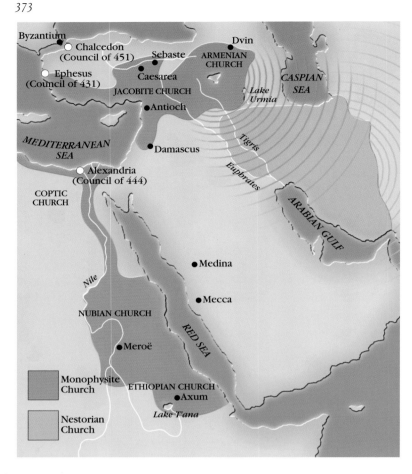

373. *Spread of Eastern pre-Chalcedonian monasticism.*

374. *St. Cyril of Alexandria. Mural in the monastery of St. Moses the Ethiopian in Nebk, Syria.*

The Fourth Ecumenical Council, held at Chalcedon in 451, is to be seen as a kind of watershed for Christianity. After that event, new religious and political arrangements came into being that enable us to understand the present state of affairs in the Christian East.

In Constantinople, Eutyches, an archimandrite, took as his starting point what had been decreed by the Council of Ephesus (431) and what had been said by Cyril of Alexandria (d. 444). On this basis, he maintained that after the incarnation there was no distinction between divinity and humanity in Christ but only a single nature. The council of Ephesus in 449, which approved this theological perspective, was held amid disorder and riots.

For this reason, the empress Pulcheria and emperor Marcian convoked a council to meet in Chalcedon in 451. Here the fathers defined that Christ has two natures (human and divine), united in a single person and single individual.

The result was a radical split, still not healed, between the supporters (the dyophysites) and the opponents (the Monophysites) of this dogma.

Anti-Chalcedonianism or Monophysitism immediately became the political banner of separatist and nationalist drives, especially in Egypt and Syria, which saw in it an excuse for a struggle against Byzantine imperialism.

In many Eastern churches the result was the coexistence of two hierarchies, one accepting the Chalcedonian faith, the other Monophysitism. The former, representative of a state-approved orthodoxy, was supported by the dignitaries and bureaucrats of the imperial administration and followed by an increasingly smaller number of faithful, chiefly Greek-speaking, who had settled in the large commercial cities on the coasts. They were called, contemptuously, Melkites (from Syriac *malka* = emperor, king, sovereign), that is, servants of Byzantine imperialism, collaborators.

The Melkites, despite the opposition from those around them, were able to ensure the survival of their own church. They followed their traditional rites down to the 12th–13th centuries, when, as a result of the centuries-long bond of communion with the Byzantine Church, they finally borrowed its rite; they now used Greek and Arabic as their liturgical languages, with the hierarchy remaining mainly Greek-speaking. Even today, in fact, the patriarchs of Alexandria and Jerusalem are Greek-speaking.

The term "Melkite" later came to signify the churches of the Middle East that follow the Byzantine tradition but are in communion with Rome.

The hierarchy that adopted the Monophysite faith, with strong support from the people, was clearly nationalistic and engaged in a struggle for political independence from Constantinople.

375

376

375. Church of St. Hrip'sime in Vagarsapat in Armenia. The church, dating from the 7th century, is venerated as one of the sources of Armenian spirituality.

376. Outside of the church of Mar Yakub in the region of Tur'Abdin today in Turkey. It is a place of pilgrimage, and tourism for those who want to encounter the impact of Syrian monasticism.

As a matter of fact, Monophysitism, which served as a mask for various independence movements, cannot, generally speaking, be traced back to the christology of Eutyches ("authentic Monophysitism") but rather to the Cyrillian tradition ("apparent Monophysitism"). This latter is essentially an opposition to Chalcedon that is more formal than substantial; that is, it can be traced back to a simple matter of terminology having to do primarily with different understandings of the word *physis* (nature).

"Authentic Monophysitism," in fact, was not very successful. The followers of Eutyches did not last long but were eliminated by the criticisms not only of the Chalcedonians but also of the "apparent Monophysites." The latter included respectable thinkers, such as Severus of Antioch (d. 538), who would leave a tradition behind them.

The post-Chalcedonian disintegration of the church led the Byzantine emperors to seek a middle ground, which, although intended to simplify the problem and bring the sides together, often had quite the opposite effect.

Some centuries later, because of the original tragic misunderstanding the nationalist, anti-Byzantine Monophysite movements of Syria and Egypt would end up promoting the lightning expansion of the Arabic Muslims and their occupation of those lands.

The pre-Chalcedonian churches also included the Eastern Assyrian or Nestorian Church, the Syrian Orthodox or Jacobite Church, and the Armenian and Coptic Churches. All these, in proportion to their numbers in their respective homelands or in the diaspora, possess a flourishing monasticism, but one that is largely closed in its own religious reality.

The Eastern Assyrian or Nestorian Church, begun by Nestorius, who was condemned at the Council of Ephesus in 431, spread initially in Mesopotamia and Persia, but its great missionary expansion in the Middle Ages reached India and China. After their repression in Iraq in 1933, a great many Nestorians emigrated to the United States, Canada, and Australia. At the present time, the faithful number about 130,000 in the diaspora, 110,000 in the Arab world, and 120,000 in Turkey and Iran.

After 1968 there occurred a schism that produced two patriarchates: one with its center in Morton Grove, Illinois, and the other with its center in Baghdad. The schism is presently being healed in favor of the catholicos living in the United States, who

377

378

377. View of the monastery of the Syrians in Wadi al-Natrun. Today, Egyptian monasticism is experiencing a season of impressive rebirth, partly attested by the work of restoration on buildings as well as the artistic heritage.

378. Interior of the church of the monastery of St. Anthony in Egypt with the liturgical furnishings prepared for the Divine Office.

represents the legitimate succession. In 1994 this patriarch and the Roman pontiff signed a declaration of their common christological faith. The church has many monastic communities that are living the traditional monastic life; many appointments to the hierarchy are made from these communities.

The Syrian Orthodox Church is also known as the Jacobite Church because of the one who organized it, namely, Jacob Baradaeus, bishop of Edessa (d. 578). After a moderate expansion in the East, this church suffered much from the Mongol invasion under Timur in the 14th century. In 1984, the patriarch, who resides in Damascus and has the title of patriarch of Antioch and the Entire East, joined the pope of Rome in signing a document in which they professed a common christological faith. The faithful number about 300,000 in the Middle East and about 150,000 in the diaspora, which includes northern Europe, the United States, Canada, and Australia. Monasticism flourishes with the monastics often well educated; it follows the ancient Syrian customs.

The Coptic Church comprises the faithful of the ancient patriarchate of Alexandria. Estimates of their numbers vary from a minimum of 3 million to a maximum of 8 million, located primarily in Egypt, with about 400,000 in the diaspora (Europe, the United States, Canada, and Australia). In 1996 two dioceses were erected in Italy (Milan and Turin). In 1973 and in 1988, the patriarch, who resides in Cairo, subscribed with the Roman pope to a document professing their common christological faith. Coptic

379

379. View of the monastery of St. Pshoi, also in the region of Wadi al-Natrun. We see here the slender and soaring architecture of the new campanile.

380. This drawing of a triumphal cross in a Syriac manuscript from the 17th century recalls Eastern spirituality, which expresses in the cross the passion and the resurrection.

monasticism is flourishing today, and the ancient monasteries of St. Anthony, St. Pachomius, and others, boast of vocations of individuals very well prepared intellectually and desirous of reviving the ascetic way of life of their tradition. The Coptic monastic centers display a great openness.

The Armenian Apostolic Church recognizes as its supreme authority the catholicos, who resides at Echmiadzin in the Republic of Armenia. The faithful of Lebanon, Syria, Iran, and Greece, and of the diasporas of these countries are under the jurisdiction of the catholicos of Cilicia, who resides at Antelias (Lebanon). The patriarch of Jerusalem has Palestine, Israel, and Jordan under him, while the patriarch of Istanbul has Turkey. The faithful number about one million in the Middle East and several million in the diaspora, chiefly in Europe, the United States, Canada, and South America. In the diaspora there is a comprehensive organization with dioceses and parishes. Monasticism flourishes, but, like the Armenian Church, is "turned inward" (as a symbolic expression has it: "All things Armenian in Armenian for the Armenians.").

Ever since 1700 the monastic community founded by Abbot Mechitar (Peter Manuk) on the island of San Lazzaro in Venice has done great cultural service.

On the whole, it can be said that in all the pre-Chalcedonian churches there is a revival of monasticism, especially for men, whereas in the corresponding Catholic churches there has been a sizable decline.

380

1. St. Anselm

381. Romanesque campanile of the church of St. Orso in Aosta, the symbol of the Aostians' Christianity. It is from Aosta that Anselm departed to go and renew monasticism in France and England.

382. The ancient Roman road which from Aosta led to the Rhône valley and from there to Gaul and Brittany.

381

382

St. Anselm was born in Val d'Aosta, Italy, studied in France, became a monk, prior, and abbot of Bec, and was appointed archbishop of Canterbury; yet he always remained in every respect a monk. He left behind as an abiding legacy his aspiration to conquer divine truth insofar as this is possible for a human being. He made his profession at the age of twenty-seven, after a period of troubled and irregular life, and spent the first three years in silence and prayer, deepening his monastic vocation.

He studied unceasingly under Lanfranc, prior of the monastery and a man regarded in his time as the wisest person in Christendom. Lanfranc often urged the younger men to devote themselves to intellectual work, although he also reminded them of the danger that study might be prejudicial to observance of the Rule. In order to respond to the requests and concrete needs of his

brothers, he also began to write spiritual and theological works; he was in fact the principal agent of monastic renewal in his time.

At the death of the monastery's founder, Anselm was appointed abbot. Eadmer, his biographer, writes: "He was a father to those in good health and a mother to the sick, or, rather, a father and a mother to all. So it was that when someone, especially among the youngest, was keeping something secret, he hastened to reveal it to Anselm as to a mother."

Anselm was appointed to the primatial see of Canterbury and was ordained a bishop on December 6, 1093, after months of struggling with himself, for as a monk he felt a complete repugnance to honors, power, and glory. He was faithful to the Holy See and its ideas, and this led to his banishment for six years. In his new office he was faithful to his state as a monk and never departed from the

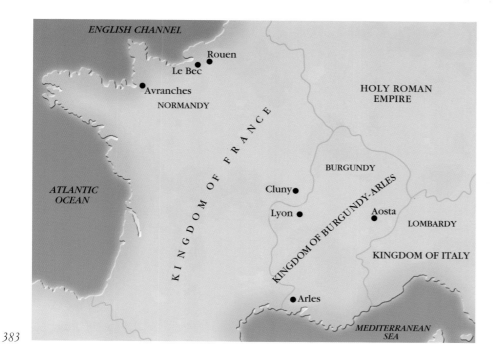

383

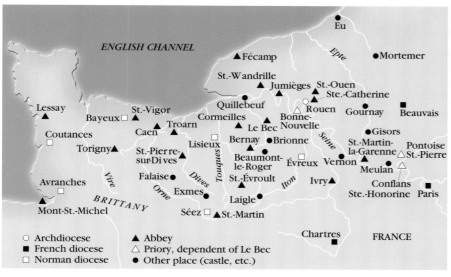

384

383. Map of France and a part of adjacent countries at the time Anselm came to the monastery of Bec in Normandy in the north of France.

384. After he arrived at Bec in Normandy in 1059, Anselm stayed there as a monk and became prior, then abbot, and remained there until 1092. In this period, the possessions and dependent houses of the monastery multiplied in Normandy and England. Having become archbishop of Canterbury in England, he still sojourned at Bec in the summer of 1103 and from July 1105 to August 1106.

requirements of his monastic vocation. "I can very truly assure you," his biographer says, "that I often heard him say he would rather live in a monastery among children and tremble before the teacher's rod than be the head of the Church of England."

He wrote a great deal and was the author of speculative treatises and of meditations and spiritual reflections, but all of these works were responses to the petitions and interests of his monks. "Faith that seeks understanding" (his own well-known phrase that sums up his writings) meant to meet the concrete needs of his brothers by helping them to prepare their souls through love and fear of God and a better knowledge of themselves.

Anselm was basically a contemplative, and his entire work is a search for truth and the experience of God. His intellectual method takes as its point of departure his personal experience of

God, which he desires should be ever deeper and more luminous. He seeks sure truth about God and wants to feel and perceive the divine presence in a sensible way. It is love that moves his intellect to undertake rational investigation, that is, the speculative path to the knowledge of God. At the beginning of the *Proslogion* we find this prayer which sets forth an entire program: "Let me seek you, Lord, by desiring you and desire you by seeking you; let me find you by loving you." Anselm's search originates in prayer; it advances accompanied by prayer; and it ends in prayer. His thought is completely permeated by a biblical culture.

J.-P. Pouchet, a scholar writing of Anselm, points out the means used by the saint in his study of the mystery of God: "the inviolable priority of prayer, the observance of the divine commandments, meditative reading of the *sacra pagina,* fervor in prayer, observation of nature, rational research, contemplative intuition." The faith that seeks understanding fills an intellect that in its turn starts with faith. The Bible, the liturgy, the Fathers, and the traditional teaching of the church are the soil that nourishes his abilities and his method, which is that of a modern, original thinker.

The following passage from the *Proslogion* may serve as the expression of Anselm's method and spirit: "Come, little man, set your cares aside for a moment; enter for a moment into yourself, far from the tumult of your thoughts. Cast out of yourself the worries that oppress you; set aside your painful anxieties. Give some time to God and rest for a moment in him. Enter into the chamber of your soul; shut out everything except God and what can help you to seek him. Then, with all the doors shut, seek God. Then say with your whole heart, say to God: 'I seek your face, O Lord, I seek your face.'

"And now Lord my God, teach my heart where and how to seek for you, where and how to find you.

"Lord, if you are not here, where shall I look for you in your absence? I know that you dwell in inaccessible light. But where is this inaccessible light? How shall I draw near to it? Who will lead me to it and guide me into it, so that I may see you in it? And then, what signs do you give of yourself and behind what face shall I seek you? I have never seen you, O Lord, my God; I do not know your face.

'What am I to do, O Most High Lord, what am I to do, this exile who is far from you? What is your servant to do, who yearns for your love and is cast far from your face? I desire to draw near to you, but your dwelling is inaccessible. I burn with longing to find you, but do not know where you dwell. I want to seek you, but I have never seen your face.'"

This fine passage not only sets forth the permanent and agonizing dilemma faced by human beings who sincerely seek God, often without finding an answer to their anxious plea. It also gives the secret of religious life, the explanation for the attraction of the desert and of monastic life.

Perseverance in a monastery means that one persistently seeks God and that one advances daily in knowledge and love of God. This is because the essence of monastic life is to do everything possible in order to know God who reveals the divine self in Christ, to plumb the meaning of revelation through understanding and love, and to place one's entire life under obedience to Christ.

Throughout his monastic life, in his writings, and in all his spiritual direction, Anselm urged the need of prayer and obedience, which are the real "peregrination" of monastics as he saw it, and of the flight from the world. He also preached these abiding methods for a Christian life, methods that constitute the essence of the monastic vocation: hospitality, care of the sick, detachment, patience, stability, purity of heart, friendship, and fraternal charity.

385. Map of England at the time Anselm was archbishop of Canterbury.

385

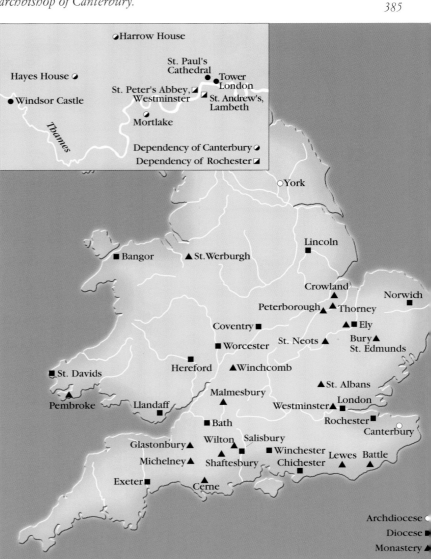

386

387

388

386. Incipit in a copy of the celebrated Monologion *of Anselm. The miniature is an initial letter decorated with the figure of Anselm enthroned between two monks. Bibliothèque Municipale, Rouen, France (Ms. 359).*

387. Portrait of Anselm in a miniature. Bodleian Library, Oxford (Ms. Auct. D. 2.6).

388. Anselm presents his Orationes sive meditationes *to Matilda of Canossa, countess of Tuscany. Detail of a miniature. Stiftsbibliothek, Admont, Austria (Ms. 289).*

389. Plan of the abbey of Canterbury from a period slightly after Anselm's time.

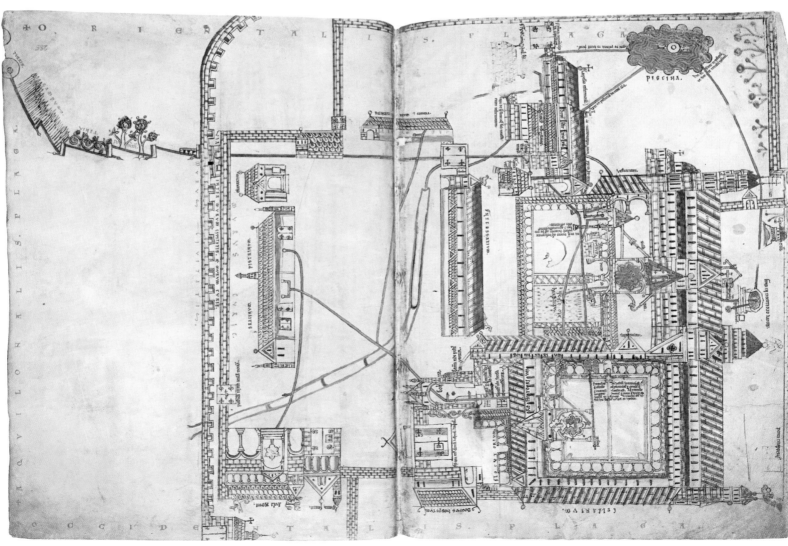

389

2. THE CARTHUSIANS

390

St. Bruno was born in Cologne around 1027; he was an enthusiastic student of art and theology in Rheims and was appointed teacher in the cathedral school, where he taught theology for twenty years and belonged to the chapter of canons. One of his disciples was the future pope Urban II, another was Hugo, bishop of Grenoble. But the excessively worldly life of the clerical world and of medieval Christendom in general did not satisfy his yearnings for a demanding spiritual perfection. He decided, together with some friends, "to abandon the fleeting world in order to win what is eternal, and to take the monastic habit." In 1084, after spending some time at Molesme with St. Robert, founder of the Cistercians, he withdrew with six disciples to the solitude of Chartreuse, an uninhabited Alpine valley some thousand meters high. His only desire was to live alone with God.

Bruno did not belong to the Benedictine tradition and sought something fundamentally different: the hermit's solitude. He built some crude huts of logs around a small chapel. In the arid bleakness of the mountains these men could freely lift their souls to the regions of the divine contemplation they were seeking. They lived literally the ideal life described by St. Paul in his second letter to the Corinthians: "Let us show ourselves in every way as ministers of God: in much patience, in labors, in vigils, in fasts, chastity, and knowledge; as distressed, yet always rejoicing; as having nothing, yet possessing everything."

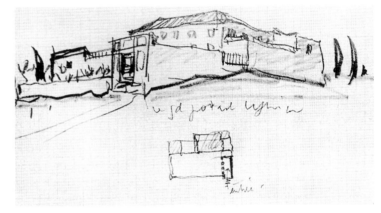

391

The different character of the new order could be seen in its white habit, a woolen robe that was not dyed; in the formula of profession of the lay brothers, who devoted themselves to manual labor but were professed monastics and who, unlike the other monks, lived in community; in a liturgy characterized by austerity, being simple in its ceremonies and not having any musical accompaniment (in fact, the churches of the Carthusians do not have an organ). Fasting was almost permanent; the monks never ate meat, and ate fish only if it was given to them. On Tuesdays, Thursdays, and Sundays they could have eggs and cheese; on the other days they were content with bread and water. Except on certain feasts, they recited the offices of the Blessed Virgin and of the dead daily. When they died, they were buried uncoffined and wrapped only in their habits, and nothing but a wooden cross, without any name on it, marked their graves.

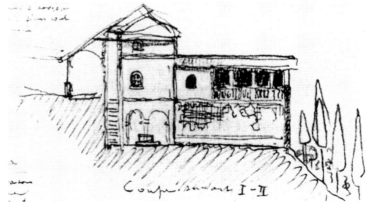

392

Urban II summoned Bruno, his former teacher, to Rome as an adviser in 1090, but given his deep-rooted vocation as a solitary, the saint found it very difficult to endure the busy life of Rome. The pope allowed him to establish another hermitage in Calabria, named San Giovanni Battista della Torre. There the holy founder died. It was from this hermitage that he wrote to his brothers in Chartreuse: "To you, beloved brothers, I say that 'my soul proclaims the greatness of the Lord,' for I see how richly God's mercy is shown to you. I rejoice that, lacking as you do the knowledge of letters, almighty God with his finger engraves in your hearts not only love but the knowledge of the holy law. For by your works

393

394. *Idealized reconstruction of a Carthusian monk's dwelling.*

391–393. *In his youth the great French architect Le Corbusier was struck by the expressive force of the monastery of Ema, and he drew various sketches in his notebook. For the father of the "modern movement" in architecture this "silhouette" made of "cubes," which, being divided, were particularly fit for the monks' life, was a stimulus to think of buildings afresh as, on the one hand, strongly geometrical and, on the other, as adapted to the human dimension. It is not by any arid rationalism that Le Corbusier characterized a building by its "lyricism."*

395. *Part of a diptych by an anonymous Dutch painter of the Renaissance. We see here a Carthusian donor with St. Bruno. Royal Museum of Fine Arts, Brussels.*

you show what you love and what you know. It is clear that you are wisely reaping the sweet and revitalizing fruit of the sacred Scriptures, because you carefully and zealously practice that true obedience which consists in fulfilling the commandments of God, that obedience which is the key to the entire spiritual life and the guarantee of its genuineness. This obedience is never found apart from deep humility and exceptional patience and is always accompanied by pure love of God and by true charity. Remain, then, my brothers, in the state you have reached."

Bruno's disciple, Guido, wrote of him: "Master Bruno was well-known for his religious spirit and his knowledge; he was a model of int.egrity, dignity, and complete maturity. . . . He was a man with a deep heart."

After the death of the founder, who probably never thought of himself as having established a new order, his followers called themselves "Poor Men of Christ." The first Consuetudines (customs established by rule) date from 1128 and were imposed on the entire order by the chapter of 1142; the "Statuta Antiqua" date from 1259; and the "Statuta Nova" from 1368. In 1581, all previous rules and customs were collected and organized in the "New Collection of Statutes," a document that is still in effect. The prior of La Grande Chartreuse was always to be general of the entire order, with vicarial jurisdiction over the various autonomous houses, an account of which he must render to the eight-member

396

body of Definitors to whom he offers his resignation every three years, which they can accept or reject.

The common library was an extensive one, and the basic work of new monks was the copying of manuscripts, although they also did carpentry, etching, and gardening. They built their cells around a cloister that abutted on the oratory; the whole was surrounded by a protective wall. The monks worked, slept, ate, and prayed in their separate houses, leaving their cells only on three occasions: for the night office, for Mass, which in the beginning was not celebrated every day, and for Vespers. On Sundays and feast days they ate together in the refectory. All this means that the Carthusians are a mixture of cenobites and hermits. As hermits, they live separately and independently; as cenobites, they gather in the choir for the lengthy Matins and Lauds at midnight, for the conventual Mass, and for Vespers. Silence, one of their characteristics, was broken when they thought it necessary to speak, and on the obligatory walk which they took once a week. The house/cell of a Carthusian consists of a lobby, a room for study, a workshop, an oratory, a bedroom, and a garden.

Prior Guido (1173–1180), in his *Letters on the Contemplative Life,* insisted on the need of combining asceticism and contemplation: "One day, during manual labor, I began to think of how people are to exercise themselves spiritually, and suddenly there came to my mind four spiritual steps: reading, meditation, prayer, and contemplation."

The Carthusians had the good fortune of not spreading rapidly, as reformed orders did. On one occasion Bruno wrote to a friend, "The children of contemplation are less numerous than the children of action." As a result, they did not suffer through the crises of the large orders. Neither were they caught in the net of politics, even church politics. For these reasons and because of their resolute policy of accepting only candidates who show the right spiritual, social, and physical aptitude, it has been written of them that they have never been reformed because they have never become deformed (*quia numquam deformati*).

The women's branch of the Carthusians was not founded by Bruno. Fifty years after his death, the ancient monastery of Prèbayon asked to be affiliated with the order and its request was

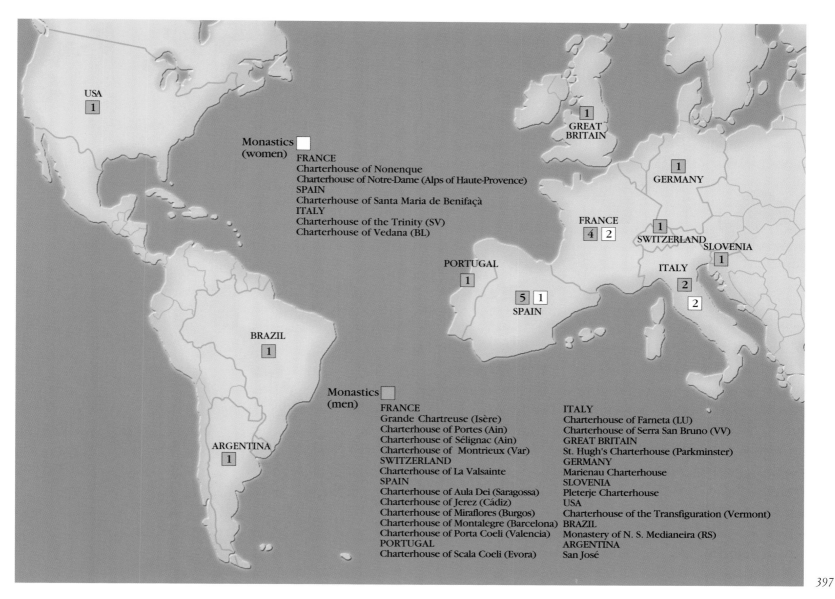

USA
1

Monastics
(women)
FRANCE
Charterhouse of Nonenque
Charterhouse of Notre-Dame (Alps of Haute-Provence)
SPAIN
Charterhouse of Santa Maria de Benifaçà
ITALY
Charterhouse of the Trinity (SV)
Charterhouse of Vedana (BL)

GREAT
BRITAIN
1

GERMANY
1

FRANCE
4 2
SWITZERLAND
1
SLOVENIA
1

PORTUGAL
1

ITALY
2
2

5 1
SPAIN

BRAZIL
1

Monastics
(men)
FRANCE
Grande Chartreuse (Isère)
Charterhouse of Portes (Ain)
Charterhouse of Sélignac (Ain)
Charterhouse of Montrieux (Var)
SWITZERLAND
Charterhouse of La Valsainte
SPAIN
Charterhouse of Aula Dei (Saragossa)
Charterhouse of Jerez (Cádiz)
Charterhouse of Miraflores (Burgos)
Charterhouse of Montalegre (Barcelona)
Charterhouse of Porta Coeli (Valencia)
PORTUGAL
Charterhouse of Scala Coeli (Evora)

ITALY
Charterhouse of Farneta (LU)
Charterhouse of Serra San Bruno (VV)
GREAT BRITAIN
St. Hugh's Charterhouse (Parkminster)
GERMANY
Marienau Charterhouse
SLOVENIA
Pleterje Charterhouse
USA
Charterhouse of the Transfiguration (Vermont)
BRAZIL
Monastery of N. S. Medianeira (RS)
ARGENTINA
San José

ARGENTINA
1

397

396. Built between the 15th and 16th centuries, the monastery of Pavia, south of Milan, is without any doubt one of the most extraordinary works of Carthusian art. Today it is no longer a charterhouse, but remains an example of the art of the Renaissance, in which a particular taste for color and ornamentation was grafted onto the rigor of the classical forms. In the charterhouses, the monks devoted themselves to art and crafts.

397. Map of the diffusion of charterhouses throughout the world.

granted. The prior of La Grande Chartreuse composed for the women a rule inspired by the original customs of the order. Later on, other monasteries of women were founded. The nuns do not live in separate houses but in cenobia and take all their meals together. Their daily schedule resembles that of the male Carthusians, as do the fasts they practice.

3. THE CISTERCIANS

Because of its desire for authenticity and generosity, the church's life is a constant return to its origins. At the end of the 11th century ecclesial reform took different directions: one was a violent breakaway, in the case of the Cathars and the Waldensians; one was heretical, seeking salvation outside the church; still another was institutional, that is, it went on within the church as can be seen in the reform of Pope Gregory VII, which consisted in the search for a religious and ecclesial life more in accord with and faithful to the gospel. The religious reformers of that century turned their eyes to the Fathers of the desert and St. Benedict as models to be followed.

This was the path followed by the founders of the Cistercian Order: Sts. Robert of Molesme, Alberic, Stephen Harding, and Bernard. In 1098, Robert, abbot of Molesme, a monastery which he himself had founded, and seven other monks expressed a desire to form a community that would observe the Rule of Benedict more strictly and faithfully, more austerely and perfectly than previously. Thus the Cistercian Order came into existence at Cîteaux in the heart of Burgundy. Robert dreamed of the desert as the ideal of monastic life, and we can glimpse in the founding of Cîteaux a reflection of the work of Pachomius.

In 1100 Pope Paschal II placed the new foundation under the protection of the Holy See so that it might be "free of pressure from an ecclesiastical or secular person," and he granted it canonical approval and juridical status.

At Easter of 1112 Bernard of Fontaine, then 22 years old, asked to enter the monastery. With him came 30 members of the best families of Burgundy, among them four of his own brothers and two maternal uncles. This unexpected influx shows how quickly and surprisingly the new Order expanded. At the age of 25, Bernard became the first abbot of Clairvaux (1115). He stood out because of his spirituality and character, his literary gifts and personal teaching, and he exerted an exceptional influence on the church of his time. Some writers consider him the last Father of the Church. In the course of his lifetime he founded 66 abbeys.

Bernard, when he called monasteries schools of charity, developed and applied what Benedict meant. The primary objective of monastic discipline was to restore human nature, made in the image and likeness of God, that is, as created for love and personal self-surrender.

According to Bernard, the renunciations of monastic life can be accepted only through knowledge and experience of God. To reach this goal, monastics must enter into themselves, and this is possible only in solitude and silence. In his view, this solitude was incompatible with the exercise of pastoral duties outside the monastery. He fiercely criticized the size and wealth of Cluniac churches, the profusion of fantastic figures on the capitals of columns, the sumptuous liturgical vestments, the lifestyle, and the material of the habits: "The habit is to be a sign of humility, and yet they make them out of luxurious materials; monasticism means a rejection of the world, and yet monks affect to be the lords of the province." The result was the creation of a simpler and more austere architectural style and personal esthetic, known as "Cistercian."

In its spirit the new order sought renewal and strength by connecting directly with the spirit of the Benedictine Rule: it obeyed the prescriptions of that Rule in everything having to do with food

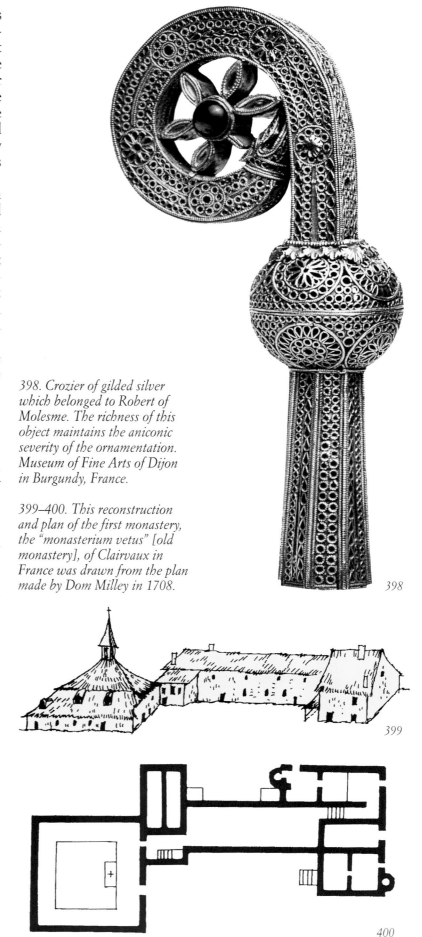

398. Crozier of gilded silver which belonged to Robert of Molesme. The richness of this object maintains the aniconic severity of the ornamentation. Museum of Fine Arts of Dijon in Burgundy, France.

399–400. This reconstruction and plan of the first monastery, the "monasterium vetus" [old monastery], of Clairvaux in France was drawn from the plan made by Dom Milley in 1708.

398

399

400

401

401. Stephen Harding, third abbot of the Cistercian order, at left, and the abbot of Saint-Vaast in Arras, France, offer each his own abbey to the Virgin. This miniature is in the fourth book of the commentary on the book of Jeremiah by St. Jerome. Bibliothèque Municipale de Dijon in Burgundy, France.

and clothing, rejected all ecclesiastical levies as a source of enrichment and corruption, and rejected both the institution of priories, which would introduce the principle of a hierarchy that is contrary to the spirit of charity, and recourse to serfs. In Bernard's eyes, luxury was culpable, sinful, a child of the devil, and contrary to what Christianity taught: it was damnable in monastics, who thereby denied the humility proper to their profession; it was an intolerable scandal in pastors, including the pope, who thereby thoughtlessly showed themselves children of the world and despoilers of the poor. According to the Rule, "the monks are to sleep clothed . . . so as always to be prepared." According to Benedict, the monastic is a soldier on a campaign; that is how he puts it in the prologue of his Rule.

Cistercian abbeys, which had only a dozen monks in accord with the prescription of Benedict, were not built in wastelands but in forests or where the land could be made suitable for agriculture. These abbeys became real monastic cities.

According to the Charter of Love *(Carta caritatis)* of Stephen Harding, the third abbot and real organizer of the order, Cistercian abbeys are completely autonomous but remain united by a covenant of friendship, by a way of life, and by a shared charity. The abbot of Cîteaux annually visits the Cistercian abbeys in order to watch over Cistercian unity; he does not intervene in temporal administration except in extreme cases. A general chapter of the abbots is held at Cîteaux every spring for the purposes of discussing the affairs of the order.

The order expanded with surprising rapidity from Portugal to Sweden, from Ireland to Estonia, from Scotland to Sicily. At the end of the 12th century there were 530 monasteries of Cistercian men (the "white Benedictines") and many monasteries of women.

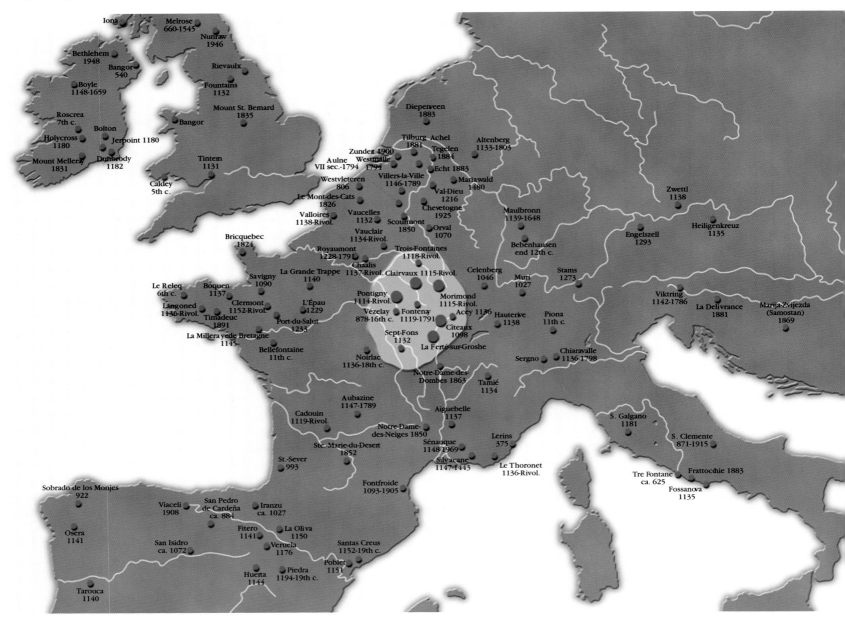

402

402. The map illustrates the extraordinary and rapid spread of the Cistercians.

403. St. Bernard preaching in chapter. Miniature from the Book of Hours of Etienne Chevalier painted by Jean Fouquet in the 15th century. Condé Museum, of Chantilly, France.

404–407. View of the sites which were the heart of the great Cistercian reform. They are also called the four-leaf clover: upper left, Pontigny, upper right, La Ferté, lower left, Morimond, lower right, Clairvaux.

403

404

405

406

407

On the two following pages:
408. The cloister of the abbey of Chiaravalle, today almost at the gates of
Milan. Even now, Chiaravalle is an important Cistercian monastic
center and a center of study.

The success of the order and its uncontrolled growth caused, in a sense, the ruin of the spirit that marked its founding. The abbot-father could not visit all the abbeys, and all the abbots did not attend the general chapters. The abbeys were in fact left to their own resources, and the outcomes were very unequal. Once again, the basic spirit was sapped by wealth acquired through gifts or the success of agricultural enterprises, which were often of enormous extent (the monastery of Clairvaux owned 20,000 hectares, the abbey of Alcobaca owned 40,000).

The Cistercian model broke with the reigning feudal system. A Cistercian house was a self-sufficient unit that met the needs of a community which divided its time between work and prayer in accordance with the prescriptions of the Rule. In principle, it produced nothing superfluous, unless the needs of other communities required it. With the permission of the bishop, they accepted lay brothers, whom they treated like themselves in life and in death; these helped with the agricultural work and stockbreeding and managed the granges. Cîteaux was the first order to produce an effective organized structure for the life of the lay brothers; in doing

so, it integrated them as much as possible into the life of the order, while keeping them separate in some areas, as seemed suitable.

Bernard often used Tertullian's image according to which the cloister is to Christians what the desert was to the prophets: a prison freely chosen, a prison with open doors. He also repeated his conviction that Clairvaux embodied the vision of the new Jerusalem. The fundamental conception of the monastery and its social organization were inseparable from its mystical dimension: the ideal city of the sons and daughters of Benedict prefigured the heavenly Jerusalem in which all the children of the heavenly Father will find a place.

Due to the Reformation and in order to better meet the expectations of the faithful, the Cistercians became increasingly involved in parish life, especially in Germany. Almost all Cistercian houses of men assigned members to pastoral ministry, and the chapter of 1601 determined the legal status of parishes administered by the order. In the 18th century, as the monarchs of the Enlightenment applied their religious policies, this pastoral life of the Cistercians became the reason why many of its abbeys were not suppressed.

4. THE REFORMATION AND MONASTICISM

409

410

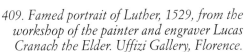

409. Famed portrait of Luther, 1529, from the workshop of the painter and engraver Lucas Cranach the Elder. Uffizi Gallery, Florence.

410. Portrait of Henry VIII of England, ca. 1540, by Hans Holbein the Younger. National Gallery, Rome.

In countries or regions that had fallen under the influence of Protestantism before or after the Peace of Augsburg (1555), the rulers completely abolished monastic life, the reason being that in his teaching Luther rejected monastic vows as contrary to the law of the gospel. In fact, he says in his *On Monastic Vows (De votis monasticis)* that these vows are contrary to the Word of God, faith, evangelical freedom, the precepts of God, charity, and natural reason: "There is no doubt that monastic vows are inherently dangerous because they cannot claim the authority and example of the Scriptures, nor do we find them in the New Testament or in the very early Church. . . . They are a pernicious human invention." As a result, he denied monasticism any spiritual value and called for the abolition of religious vows and religious orders, while emphasizing the value of the lay calling.

In addition to accusing the orders of laxity and inability to follow their rules, the Reformers made two new kinds of attack, both clearly brought up by Wycliffe a century before in England. One was a theological attack on the very principles of monasticism. According to the Reformers, the gospel provided the sole rule of Christian life; everything else was purely human addition and therefore evil. Monastics were wrong when they taught that salvation was to be found in fasts, penances, and set prayers, instead of the simple, basic, evangelical virtues. They said, secondly, that monastics were idlers in society, they wasted money on their own comfort and did no work of social value. From 1520 on, the attack on monasticism was an important element in Protestant culture.

The fact is that at that period there were too many monasteries and many of them were excessively rich and perhaps of little value to society, although this last phrase is debatable. Moreover, in many monasteries there was no real desire for reform at a time

when reform was needed. The decline of the religious orders in the years before the Reformation has been amply demonstrated, although it is only honest to say that even at that time a strong and fervent movement of reform was to be seen in a number of monasteries of women and not a few religious orders.

Generally speaking, after the Reformation, monastic life reflected the principle that the ruler decided the religion to be practiced in his or her territories and imposed it. Monastics remained wherever there were Catholic rulers or municipalities, and they disappeared wherever those in authority had gone over to Protestantism. In practice, this means that the northern half of Germany lost most of its monasteries, while in the south most of the abbeys remained in existence. Some monasteries of women resisted all the attacks and demands, especially where the abbess belonged to a royal family. Some even accepted Lutheranism provided they could retain their Catholic spiritual practices. In Sweden, submission to King Gustave I Vasa (1523–1560) resulted in a slow confiscation of properties over the course of several decades; in Norway and Denmark, the process was equally slow. In Holland, nuns fled from Lutheran areas.

In England, monasteries were violently destroyed between 1535 and 1540 by Thomas Cromwell, who wanted funds for royal expenses and the defense of the realm. Henry VIII gave his approval to this policy because he needed money and because not a few monks had opposed his divorce from Catherine and the act of royal supremacy. Some monasteries that were still deeply spiritual resisted stubbornly. Some Carthusians and other religious were executed for their resistance. The same process was repeated in Ireland a few years later. In Scotland, the laicization of the monasteries took place slowly over a period of 50 years. It is

411–412. Ruins of two English abbeys, a proof of the decline of monasticism since the Reformation. Above: view of the ruins of St. Mary of Buildwas, where one sees windows, doorways, the chapter room, and the remains of the church, which are glimpsed above the cloister.
Below: view of the remains of the great abbey of St. Mary at Fontains; on the left, one sees the facade of the church and on the right, the main body of the monastic buildings.

thought that in all of Europe there remained a little more than half of the monastics who had been there before the Reformation.

In German-speaking lands that remained Catholic the ancient monastic congregations, especially the Benedictines, experienced a considerable revival and growth. Thanks to their reorganization, a good formation and education, and a faithful observance of the Rule, German monks became an integral part of what was at that time, and continued to be, one of the most devoutly Catholic regions of Europe. Their great baroque abbeys were not only part of the landscape but also, and above all, influences in spiritual and ecclesial life.

In France, there were various successful attempts to form regional Benedictine congregations which were able to thoroughly reform existing monastic life and also produce new energy for expansion. The two new congregations of Saint-Vanne and Saint-Maur were at the heart of the cultural history of these centuries.

The congregation of Saint-Vanne introduced a substantial novelty into Benedictinism: centralization. Its monks made a vow of stability to the congregation and could be transferred from one monastery to another. It had a single center for the formation of the monks, who devoted themselves, in addition to the choral praying of the Liturgy of the Hours, which took up a good part of the day, to parochial ministry, teaching, and study. They were also outstanding for their historical researches, especially in French ecclesiastical history.

The Maurists, for their part, required that their candidates have a solid humanistic education before they entered and, after their entrance, gave them an excellent monastic training. After these monks had made their monastic profession, they continued to receive an intense religious training, but also an intellectual formation in which the ancient languages played a large part. For this they relied on excellent libraries. The specializations that marked out the Maurists were patristics, liturgy, and history.

5. THE TRAPPISTS

413. *Armand-Jean le Bouthillier de Rancé (1626–1700), the French nobleman who through the strange circumstances of his life found himself commendatory abbot of the monastery of La Trappe and afterwards effectively became its head by conducting a radical reform, more severe than the 12th century Cistercian rule itself. Criticized of course for the radical character of his work, he in fact restored life to monasticism by an extremist spirit which the period in which he lived justified.*

414. *Interior of a building for production of commercial goods in La Trappe. The problem of self-sufficiency remained fundamental for the monastic reform which gave birth to the Trappists.*

In the 17th century, due in part to the exhaustion of the impulse and enthusiasm engendered by the Council of Trent, the life of religious and of the church in general was not in one of its better periods. There were not lacking, of course, religious who preserved and strictly followed their foundational ideals and monasteries that continued to be important spiritual lights. There were also, however, numerous examples of profligacy and laxity, largely because of the baneful practice of the commendam, by which monasteries were put into the hands of priests or laypeople outside the community, whose main concern was to acquire its revenues. In truth, the general atmosphere in Europe was quite worldly and this fact undoubtedly found expression in a laxity in the ecclesiastical organization and in religious life both lay and clerical.

It was in this atmosphere that Jean Bouthellier de Rancé (1626–1700) found himself. He was the godson of Cardinal Richelieu, had been ordained a priest in 1651, and had St. Vincent de Paul as his adviser. Among the many benefices he possessed because of his family's influence was that of commendatory abbot of the Cistercian abbey of La Trappe, which had been founded in

1120. Located in Normandy, this monastery was in a ruinous state and contained six monks who only approximately observed the Rule. Rancé, who had been living an irregular and dissipated life, changed his ways and underwent a profound conversion following the death of a dear friend; he gave up his titles and benefices and decided to reform the little monastery, which until this point had meant nothing to him. The consequences of this decision soon became evident. Vocations multiplied as men were drawn by the spirit of penance, the strict observance that was imposed and observed, although the original six members were incapable of following the new pace and left the monastery. The fiery abbot, the "Stormy Abbot" (*L'Abbé Tempête*) as he would become known to historians, started with nothing, but as a man of passionate faith and steadfast in his resolve to remain faithful to his unalterable religious vocation, he devoted himself to a fervent quest of God by following the ideals of the gospel. La Trappe reflected the spiritual development of its reformer and the extreme asceticism of some 17th-century French thinkers.

The rules were very strict. No fish, eggs, or cheese; no wine, no mattress to lie down on at night. The monks kept perpetual si-

415

415. Exterior of the same building pictured on the left. Western monasticism continued with the intent of establishing an autonomous monastic world to avoid making compromises with the surrounding political reality.

lence, gave little time to recreation, limited their correspondence, lived a common life to the point of sleeping together in a single dormitory, reintroduced the chapter of faults, and restored manual labor as well as the Lenten fast in its completeness. Their life was regulated by the diurnal and nocturnal liturgical offices and by physical work that was often exhausting. In a way, La Trappe resurrected the heroic spirit of the first Cistercians, although in the view of some authors Rancé substituted the gloomy rigorism of his age for the vibrancy of Bernard's contemplative spirit.

This reform was approved by Innocent XI in 1678, and Rancé's example of a consistently sacrificial life was known and admired by religious and ecclesiastics. Rancé never thought of founding a congregation distinct from the Cistercians, nor did he accept an affiliation with other abbeys that had followed his example. In reality, this reform was a powerful blow against the worldliness of the clergy, which is the most dangerous and abiding temptation for religious and clerical life.

The disparagement of intellectual work that the educated Rancé cultivated and imposed on his monks brought him into vehement conflict with Mabillon and with Le Masson, the learned Benedictines of the Maurist congregation to which French culture owes so much. Their confrontation seemingly opposed solid devotion to authentic knowledge, but in fact both sides were correct in insisting on the importance of the religious tradition which each was defending. The controversy illuminated Rancé's character: bold, disdainful of the thinking of others, and absolutely certain that he was in the right. His style was aggressive, he was unjust in his attacks, he uttered fearless generalizations. Cardinal Bona said of him, "The ardor of this abbot was permeated by anger," but, we must add, also with generosity, gravity, and consistency.

In fact, the spirit of the two institutions (the Benedictines and La Trappe) was not the same during those years. The Benedictines had more than 400 splendidly built abbeys in France, but these contained few monks and generally little enthusiasm, with some exceptions such as the Congregation of St. Maur. The Trappists, on the other hand, were few, but they were consistently faithful to their vocation and to the ideas of their founder.

416

417

In a sense, the Trappists were a deeply religious answer to the pride of the Enlightenment spirit, which demanded a natural God and a natural religion, that is, one in harmony with reason and tailored to the human measure. It was an answer also to a worldly century in which moralists and apologists tried by every means to combine Christianity with comfort and pleasure. Rancé represented what the spirit of the Enlightenment scorned: complete abandonment into the hands of God, the creator and redeemer, and the necessity of the cross in God's plan of salvation. Rancé died in 1700 after resigning as abbot in 1695.

After the calamitous French Revolution when it seemed that all was lost in France, an organized effort was made at La Trappe to save a Cistercian nucleus that was viable for the future. A group of generous monks returned to their homeland and began to spread the order with surprising success. The fact that all of these men were enthusiastic followers of Abbot de Rancé led to an important chapter in subsequent history. Before the Revolution, Trappist observance was limited to a few communities. After 1815, Rancé's influence became a dominant force in the Cistercian renaissance in France and other countries. The Trappists would spread especially in Spain and the United States.

In 1813 there were two forms of Trappist observance, representing different interpretations of the Rule, and three congregations. In 1892 Leo XIII called all the superiors of the three congregations to Rome and formed them into a union, establishing "The Reformed Cistercian Order of Our Lady of La Trappe." Since 1903 the monks have been known as "Reformed Cistercians."

The abbot of the monastery of La Trappe wrote in a recent book: "Our generation had thoroughly committed itself to a profound renewal and to update itself in accordance with the decrees of Vatican Council II. What task awaits those whom we have trained and who will carry on the tradition in the near future? . . . The most obvious fact will be the decrease in the members of the communities . . . and the unsuitability of houses built for larger groups. No community, of course, is guaranteed immortality. . . . Our successors will see farther than we do, like the apostles whom the stained-glass windows of Chartres show lifted up on the shoulders of the prophets and thus able to see what their predecessors did not see."

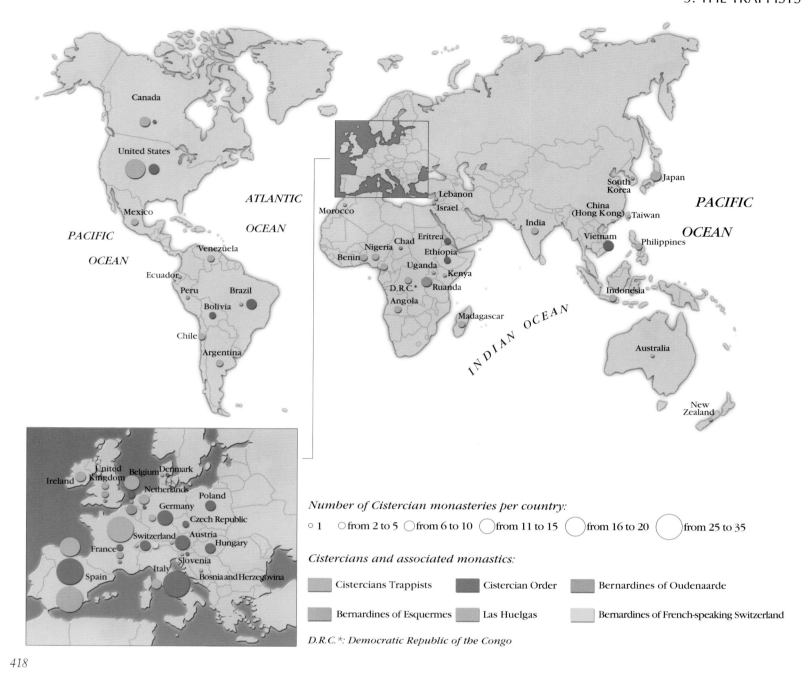

Number of Cistercian monasteries per country:

○ 1   ○ from 2 to 5   ○ from 6 to 10   ◯ from 11 to 15   ◯ from 16 to 20   ◯ from 25 to 35

Cistercians and associated monastics:

- Cistercians Trappists
- Cistercian Order
- Bernardines of Oudenaarde
- Bernardines of Esquermes
- Las Huelgas
- Bernardines of French-speaking Switzerland

D.R.C.*: Democratic Republic of the Congo

418

416. A monastic engaged in agricultural work. From La Vie Cistercienne, Cerf and Zodiaque, 1998.

417. The concentration on texts and other studies remain fundamental for the Trappist spirit. From La Vie Cistercienne, Cerf and Zodiaque, 1998.

418. The world expansion of the Cistercian and Trappist community, female as well as male.

6. EREMITICAL LIFE IN THE TWENTIETH CENTURY

The 20th century was a confused and agitated time that saw permanent revolutionary changes, a spiritual bewilderment. Monasticism in general and the eremitical life in particular were affected by this tempestuous whirl of ideas and circumstances, so that not only were the classical forms of religious life profoundly renewed but new forms also arose. Just as the church moved from an understanding of itself as a society to an understanding of itself as a communion, so too did the new communities rediscover the value of a communal life.

In fact, nothing in the modern world favored solitude: the speed of the communications media—radio, television, airplanes, the internet—the constant changes, and the theory or feeling that solitude was not good for the development of the human spirit.

Despite all this, in various environments there was a felt need of experiencing the eremitical life, a desire to return in some manner to the desert and to live in ways which modern thought considered unreasonable. Indeed, the impression could be given at times that these felt needs and experiments were elitist; they were, in any case, those of a minority.

Admittedly, the attempts to revive the solitary life in the Western church seemed to have had sparse results, while in the Eastern churches the solitary life practically disappeared. The monks and hermits of Mount Athos remained, but their numbers diminished and the age of the residents increased. Nevertheless, ongoing attempts were made to find new formulas for solitude and the search for God, while trying to remain faithful to the original charism without succumbing to stagnation.

The Camaldolese retained their cells on Monte Corona, Italy, opened a community at Caxias, Brazil, and in 1958 settled in California, facing the Pacific at Big Sur.

At the beginning of the 20th century there were twenty Carthusian monasteries: eleven in France and nine in other European countries. A century later, the same spirit and the same spiritual dedication are still being lived in charterhouses: four in France, two in Italy, five in Spain, and one each in Switzerland, Slovenia, Germany, England, Portugal, the United States, and Brazil, with seven hundred Carthusians in all.

The Carmelites, both Calced and Discalced, followed their age-old tendency in imitation of Elijah and founded some "deserts" as places for a life of solitude, withdrawal, and more intense spiritual experiences. The "desert" of Batuecas (Salamanca) is perhaps the best known, but there are others in France, Italy, Austria, Hungary, and, again, in Spain.

The American Benedictines permitted members to live an eremitical life in one of their monasteries. In fact, this was an attempt to renew the medieval Benedictine custom of having some hermits living near a monastery, on which they depended. In 1956, three Belgian Benedictines founded a fraternity at Les Landes, France, desiring to go back to the simplicity and poverty of primitive monasticism; this brotherhood has given rise to cells in other countries.

419

419. A characteristic photo of the Little Brother Charles de Jésus, Charles de Foucauld, taken in 1912.

420. View of one of the rare places where water is found in the region of Tassili-n-Ajjer in Algeria. It is in this desertic world frequented for millennia by nomadic populations that Charles de Foucauld decided to live his experience of the "desert" and of monasticism in full dialogue with the religiosity and culture of those who lived in, or passed through, the region, by devoting himself, like his brothers and disciples, to the works of those who live on the margins of consumer society.

421

422

421. The tent in Abiodh-sidi-Cheich in Algeria used by Madeleine de Jésus, the foundress of the Little Sisters. Attracted by the example and the spirituality of Charles de Foucauld, Madeleine Hutin left France in 1936 and went to Africa, where she experienced love for the little Jesus and the desire for friendship between persons of different religions. She returned to Europe, and her congregation, approved in 1964, established its center near the Fraternity of Three Fountains in Rome.

422. The last part of the life of Madeleine de Jésus was dedicated to Russia and the dialogue with the Orthodox Church. We see here a photo of her, taken in 1972, in the door of her van, called "Shooting Star," a real fraternity on wheels in which she traveled in the countries of Eastern Europe still under Stalinist regimes.

Charles de Foucauld was one of the most notable 20th-century searchers for the desert. After an irregular life as a soldier and after being a Trappist and a gardener for the Poor Clares of Nazareth, he settled in Algeria, some five hundred kilometers south of Oran, where he lived in a hut, praying and meditating. In 1905, he moved farther south to the oasis of Tamanrasset. In 1916 he was murdered by a band of armed Tuaregs. Thus died the hermit of the Sahara, a monk without a monastery, a teacher without students, a penitent and solitary who exerted a surprising influence on the spirituality of the 20th century by his example and through the congregations that arose years later: the Little Brothers of Jesus and the Little Sisters of Jesus. These follow a rule which de Foucauld left behind him in writing; according to it, the members must be poor religious who, without devoting themselves to an external ministry, are able to contribute to the invisible apostolate of the Church by sharing, through prayer and sacrifice, in the redemptive work of Christ.

The ancient eremitical orders have the same purpose, but in order to achieve it, they flee the world and seek a place more favorable to prayer. The hermit of the Sahara did not want Little Brothers and Sisters to isolate themselves in a cloister but rather live, in small groups, in the world with the poor whose life of hard work they share. This conception of the solitary life was truly revolutionary, yet its influence has not ceased to grow and to affect contemporary spirituality.

The well-known writer Divo Barsotti founded near Florence two eremitical communities, one of men and one of women, who live a contemplative life that shows a degree of Eastern inspiration. Earning their living by manual labor and as artisans, they have given a salutary shock to a world dominated by consumerism and technology and have become a focus of attention and imitation.

There are many other instances of Christians, individually or in groups, who have withdrawn to the solitude of "desert islands" and cities in order to make their Christianity whole again and to live it in depth without losing their concern for the salvific proclamation of Jesus Christ.

A monastic is someone who adopts a critical attitude toward the contemporary world and its structures, an attitude of protest toward society as it is, just as back in the 4th century the dwellers in the Egyptian desert did when they fled the Roman culture of their day. At the same time, however, monastics are aware of their obligation to bear witness to the gospel and be its shining lights.

All this is to say that in our time and throughout the history of Christianity, there are men and women who believe that the deeper meaning of their spiritual life can develop adequately only in silence and real solitude. The special task of monastics in today's world is to keep alive the contemplative experience and to keep open the way by which modern men and women may integrally experience their own interior depths. This mystical need of personal encounter with the Transcendent seems to have greater meaning in an age dominated by technology, an age where in not a few environments the meaning and necessity of the church had disappeared.

425

423. *The motherhouse of the community founded by Don Divo Barsotti, called the house of St. Sergius, in Settignano, near Florence.*

424. *Don Divo Barsotti.*

425. *Glimpse of the central court of the monastic community of Bose in northern Italy. In this old farmstead Enzo Bianchi, founder of the community, wanted to effect a reorganization adapted to both cenobitic and solitary life. Today, Bose gives one the opportunity to encounter monasticism and early Christianity—and, as at the beginning, is a sign as well as a spiritual and cultural presence in society.*

On the following page:
426. *Present-day monasteries in Africa.*

427. *Wooden crucifix. Congo, perhaps from the 16th century. In the land of Bakongo, Christian iconography began in the 16th century, the work of the Portuguese. The forms show the strong influence of Europe while the facial features are African. Later on, these crucifixes were also used according to African tradition as propitiatory figures for successful hunting and medicinal purposes.*

7. MONASTICISM IN AFRICA

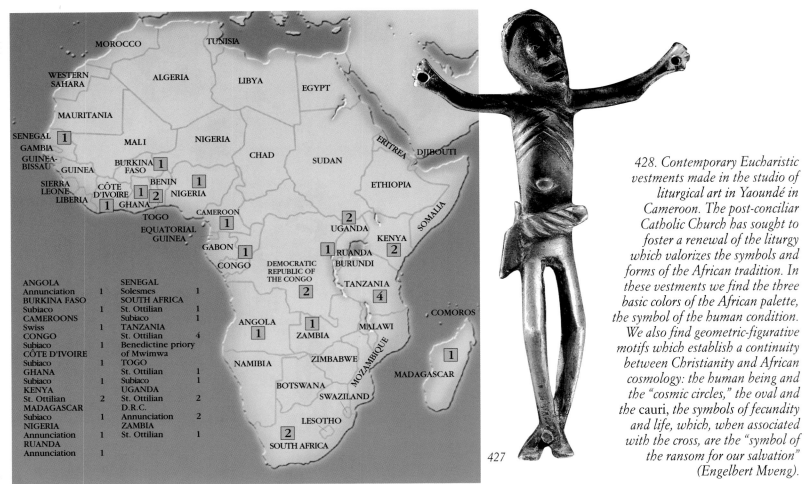

426

ANGOLA		SENEGAL	
Annunciation	1	Solesmes	1
BURKINA FASO		SOUTH AFRICA	
Subiaco	1	St. Ottilian	1
CAMEROONS		Subiaco	1
Swiss	1	TANZANIA	
CONGO		St. Ottilian	4
Subiaco	1	Benedictine priory	
CÔTE D'IVOIRE		of Mwimwa	
Subiaco	1	TOGO	
GHANA		St. Ottilian	1
Subiaco	1	Subiaco	1
KENYA		UGANDA	
St. Ottilian	2	St. Ottilian	2
MADAGASCAR		D.R.C.	
Subiaco	1	Annunciation	2
NIGERIA		ZAMBIA	
Annunciation	1	St. Ottilian	1
RUANDA			
Annunciation	1		

427

428. *Contemporary Eucharistic vestments made in the studio of liturgical art in Yaoundé in Cameroon. The post-conciliar Catholic Church has sought to foster a renewal of the liturgy which valorizes the symbols and forms of the African tradition. In these vestments we find the three basic colors of the African palette, the symbol of the human condition. We also find geometric-figurative motifs which establish a continuity between Christianity and African cosmology: the human being and the "cosmic circles," the oval and the* cauri, *the symbols of fecundity and life, which, when associated with the cross, are the "symbol of the ransom for our salvation"* (Engelbert Mveng).

In this chapter we shall take a particular case, the monastic communities in Benin, as an example of what is happening in some African communities and of the spread of monastic life in young Christian communities that are still in process of formation.

These monasteries are always real oases of spirituality and encounter, to which bishops, priests, the laity, families, and the young can retire as to the only available place of silence and recollection. The archdiocese of Cotonou has two Benedictine communities and one of Poor Clares. Two Cistercian communities exist in the diocese of Parakou.

In 1958, Msgr. Gantin, the archbishop of Cotonou, asked the Benedictine nuns of Vanves (France) to establish a monastery in the heart of the tropical forest. The first two women flew into the country in 1965 in order to learn the language of the country and to acquire some knowledge of the local church. Some years later, the arrival of four more monastic women marked the beginning of a history of witnessing and growth in a little village called Toffo. In 1972 they accepted their first African vocations, who foreshadowed the way in which the nuns' presence in that village could expand. Today, this monastery has nine professed, seven of them Beninese, as well as three postulants, and one novice.

Prayer and manual work are the basic occupations of these nuns. Toffo is known for the artistic quality and excellence of the liturgical vestments made there (stoles, chasubles, albs) and also for its clothing, tablecloths, and bedspreads. The nuns also cultivate some orchards and from their fruit make jams that are much appreciated by the people around.

Hospitality to visitors has a central place in the life of the community. The first to be welcomed are the inhabitants of the village in which the monastery is located, but the majority of visitors come from all countries, their purpose being to participate in the nuns' life of silence and prayer. Seminarians gather there for spiritual exercises and to prepare for priestly ordination; also seminarians from various dioceses are often seen at formation sessions or days of more intense prayer.

A little further south of Toffo is the monastery of Mount Tabor with its Benedictine monks. This monastery has had a complicated history. Its origin, in fact, was in another monastic community founded in the center of Benin in 1963. Various problems compelled the monks of French origin to abandon the foundation in 1989 and return to France. Those who were novices at the time were sent to Burkina Faso to complete their formation and when they returned in 1998 were welcomed to Cotonou; they then established the new foundation (Mount Tabor) with six professed and two novices. These numbers are small but they are enough to serve as a call and point of reference for those who feel drawn to the contemplative life and a more demanding spirituality.

The Poor Clare monastery, founded in 1993 from Marcatello in the Italian Marches, now numbers five professed, three postulants, and one novice. At the heart of the local church, they devote themselves to eucharistic adoration and to contemplation, in the spirit of St. Clare and St. Francis of Assisi, that is, they follow and imitate the poor and crucified Christ. In this community, too, the welcoming of guests is regarded as an important work; this

428

429

429. *Extraordinary pilaster from the church of Saint-Michel in Libreville, Gabon, the work of the sculptor Zéphyrin Lendogno. The decoration of Christian architecture becomes laden with the tradition and culture into which it is inserted.*

welcome is given especially to priests and laypersons who need a place adapted to a renovation of spirit. A special mark of this community is the care given to abandoned children, who are by no means rare in some African countries. The monastery tries to find homes in which the children are welcomed and adopted.

Two Cistercian communities, likewise of French origin, are 700 kilometers distant from the Poor Clares. The Trappist community of Our Lady of Kokoubou, begun in 1973, has ten solemnly professed monks (of which four are Beninese), two professed with temporary vows, and three novices. To be emphasized is the impact of the life of these men on a very young local church that must assimilate traditions which took shape in Europe over many centuries. Bishops, missionaries, and the Beninese clergy rely on these monks and regard the witness of their lives and their ceaseless prayer as an important spiritual support for their own evangelizing activity. The abbey provides a place to which those who are looking for a source of authentic spirituality can withdraw; it is an active laboratory of religious inculturation and a place that welcomes those in search of truth.

The Cistercian abbey of Our Lady of the Star, founded in 1960, elected the first African abbess in 1999. The members come from seven countries and number twenty-five solemnly professed, two novices, two postulants, and one oblate. The monastery has become a place of spirituality, attentive welcome, and the search for God by those who desire and want him. On the other hand, the common life lived by persons of such different cultural heritages requires that priority be given to essential values in order to deepen unity. These nuns have it in mind to found a monastery in the Democratic Republic of the Congo, although the difficult situation in that area is complicating the attempt.

In 1984 the Benedictine monks of Belloc founded the community of Saint-Benoît-des-Sources.

Something similar has been occurring in many other countries of this continent. As has always happened in the life of the church, the gradual maturation of the African churches calls for places of silence, more than ordinary austerity, and continual prayer. The monasteries are such places. It is for this reason that, little by little, the traditional orders and some new ones are founding monasteries, which are all the more necessary where the African secular clergy are only slowly making their way and developing their own way of life. The life of monastics is an attraction, a witness, and an opportunity for exchanges of experiences and needs. This demands of monastics a greater availability and an exceptional dedication to welcoming, advising, and traveling the road together with those who come to them.

The number of monasteries in the third world rose from thirty in 1950 to almost three hundred by the end of the century. In these monasteries and especially in those of Africa we find three important elements of religious life: a degree of commitment to the temporal liberation of the people, a receptive dialogue with monastics of other traditions, and a degree of departure from tradition when the previous two and connected goals require it, all this while keeping alive the emphasis on prayer, contemplation, and withdrawal from ordinary and permanent active ministries: in short, a return to Benedictine origins.

8. ANGLICAN MONASTICISM

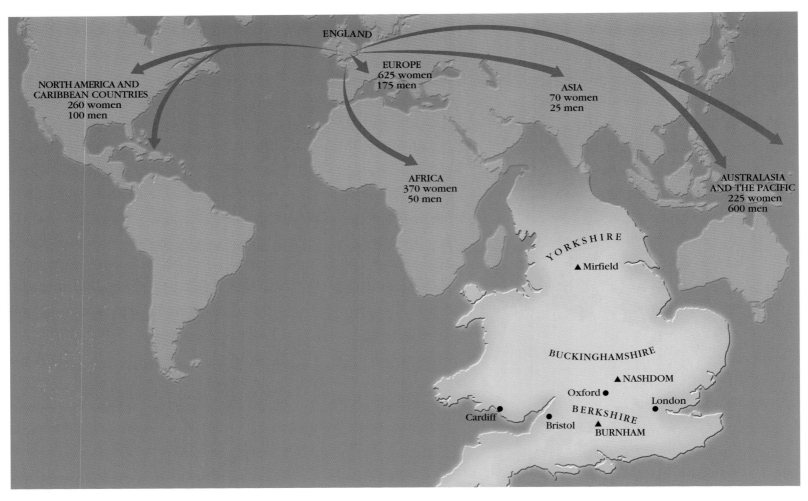

430

430. Number of Anglican monastics in the world.

In general, the Protestant world rejected monasticism, but beginning in the 17th century, there was no lack within Anglicanism of expressions of respect for this traditional religious phenomenon, especially among those Anglicans who were closer to Catholicism and more influenced by the religious fervor of the Counter Reformation.

Nevertheless, the rebirth of interest in monasticism was due fundamentally to the Oxford Movement, which began in 1833. In fact, the only experiment in this area prior to the 19th century was the community of Little Gidding in which some thirty persons lived for almost twenty years (1626–1646) according to a rule that imitated the life of the first Christian communities. The way of life, the charity, and the work that were typical of this institution earned the admiration of Charles I.

Two hundred years later, in 1842, John Henry Newman attempted to found a quasi-monastic community at Littlemore, near Oxford, in keeping with an idea that had come up frequently in his conversations with Edward Pusey. Under Newman's guidance a group of young men gathered in Littlemore to live a very austere life in an atmosphere of prayer and strong community spirit, but this experiment did not continue. In fact, from the outset many members of the Oxford Movement thought it necessary that the Church of England have monastic establishments and

that to bring this about it was necessary to speak publicly of the subject.

Indeed, from this point on, those influenced by the Oxford Movement produced a constant stream of foundations (the majority for women) that has continued down to our time.

The purpose of these communities of women was charity. Some adopted the rules and spirit of the Daughters of Charity, founded by St. Vincent de Paul, but not a few were marked by a greater degree of enclosure and recollection. Many of them spread to Australia, Canada, and some countries of Asia and Africa.

Of the 34 monastic experiments made between 1842 and 1961, five ended by converting to the Catholic Church and 19 died out. This left but ten surviving in the Anglican Communion, of which only four have lasted more than 50 years.

These communities are built on the traditional pillars of religious life: chastity, poverty, and a common life lived under obedience. They have adopted, completely or partially, the monastic form of the Divine Office and the Roman Missal. All are engaged in missionary and social work outside of England, and have produced notable fruit.

Perhaps the best-known community of women is the Community of the Sisters of the Love of God, which was founded in Oxford in 1906. Its spiritual goal has been a contemplative life of

431

431. *John Henry Newman at a young age, sketch by George Richmond. National Portrait Gallery, London.*

432

432. *St. Benedict. Newman's conversion to Catholicism was, according to his own statement, due to his assiduous study of the Fathers of the Church and their texts from the Cappadocians onward. Among Western figures, the one whose influence is most evident in Newman's writings is Benedict. This wall painting is by Master Conxolus (13th century), lower church of the monastery of the Sacro Speco, near Subiaco, Italy.*

prayer, intercession, and reparation. The nuns pray the nocturnal hours of the Breviary at two o'clock in the morning, and they practice a permanent form of intercession during the day and part of the night. They live in a strict and continual silence.

Something worthy of note happened to another community of women, the Community of the Servants of Christ. The bishop of Chelmsford stopped them from keeping the Blessed Sacrament in their chapel, with the result that the women religious decided to change their diocese. This action shows, on the one hand, the importance of the changes that went on in one sector of Anglicanism and, on the other, the complementarity of the contemplative life and the Christian sacramental tradition. In our time, these religious are firmly settled in their House of Prayer in Burnham.

The number of monks, meanwhile, is small because in fact there exists only one monastery in the traditional and historical sense of the word: the abbey of Nashdom, where the liturgy is impressively celebrated according to the Roman monastic rite. It can be said that Nashdom is an authentic Benedictine monastery which strictly adheres to the three elements of common life that St. Benedict so strongly emphasized: prayer, study, and manual work. Many of its members devote themselves to study and writing, while others preach, give retreats, and attend to the spiritual needs of the nearest towns.

The Church of England contains some communities that more closely resemble Catholic religious congregations. We may mention as an example the Community of the Resurrection, which is perhaps the best known and tries to live a life like that of the first Christians. Laymen, who have a job or a profession, and priests are alike members of the community in the fullest degree. Prayer, study, and work are the three pillars of their life, and one of their most esteemed occupations is the training of candidates for the priesthood. Another well-known community of the Anglican world is the Society of the Sacred Mission, which devotes itself basically to the instruction of the young and especially of those attracted to the priesthood.

In its beginnings the monastic movement in Anglicanism developed against the wishes of the bishops, so that mutual relations between the two were infrequent. But the situation has evolved in the course of time, and today there is a consultative council, made up of six members of the communities and six experts appointed by the bishops, and having a diocesan bishop as its president.

We find monasteries and, especially, religious houses in many other countries in which the Anglican Communion exists: Australia, New Zealand, and especially North America.

9. CONTEMPORARY PROTESTANT MONASTICISM IN EUROPE

433

433. A rare representation of Luther wearing his religious habit. The sketch is the work of Lucas Cranach.

434

434. A sketch of Søren Kierkegaard by Johan Vilhelm Gertner. Royal Library of Copenhagen. Monasticism, according to the Danish philosopher, was seen as a help to recovering the basic Christian existential position.

The decisive steps taken by the Reformers in both word and deed against religious vows and the forms of monastic life in their time did not encourage later resumption of this form of religious life in the Reformed Churches. Yet these same communities never lacked experiments in what can be called, to some extent, semi-monastic life. In any case, it was in the 20th century that such experiments arose in explicit forms, although these experienced difficulty in winning official recognition from their churches.

The origin of the new foundations was the extraordinary spiritual experiences of some individuals or small groups, especially amid the unique and tragic circumstances of life during the World Wars and in the problematic atmosphere of magnanimity in which the evangelical youth movement developed (the majority of the founders of the new communities belonged to that movement). These young people were often deeply pessimistic toward the existing state of spirituality, strongly critical of the ways of life in present European society, and critical in radical ways of the institutional churches. In one way or the other there was a re-echoing of the prophetic words of Søren Kierkegaard in the previous century, "Let us return to the monasteries from which Luther came," in the conviction that such monastic experiences could be an occasion of purification and renewal.

In fact, there was no real question of a return to the past, and indeed the word "monastery" was avoided because it retained too many echoes of an age which no one wanted to revive. People preferred to use the term "community," which, while traditional, had a good measure of indefiniteness. This was an age in which the church was rediscovered as being, hopefully, a fellowship in which pietistic movements proliferated and in which there was also a generous openness and positive evaluation of the possibilities present in the modern world, despite its being seemingly so opposed to Christian values. We must also take into account the influence of Dietrich Bonhoeffer and his book *Life in Community,* which is markedly incarnational and based on a strong christological foundation. In a lecture Bonhoeffer said: "No one can have God as Father who does not have the earth as mother." He was offering a conscious variation on a sentence in which St. Cyprian, bishop of Carthage, pointed to the close connection between the fatherhood of God and the motherhood of the Church.

It is not easy to discern the deeper meaning and organizational requirements of this fellowship and community, or to determine the secrets of its internal organization. There have been celibate brother/sisterhoods and others that were more open and changing. Some communities supposed a common life according to some specific vows, while others lived a common life only at certain times for the sake of particular tasks. Today there exist about sixty stable communities and many more that appear and rapidly disappear.

Depending on the various ways in which they are organized and their various objectives, we find communities that are parochial or contemplative, deaconal and social, or missionary and evangelical.

In 1913, forty evangelical pastors met and decided to devote themselves with special fervor to prayer and the study of the Bible. Today there are about a thousand such groups in the German-speaking area.

435. *Dietrich Bonhoeffer, the Protestant minister who was executed in 1945 in the concentration camp of Flossenbürg. Once more, in the thought of a Protestant thinker, the exigency of radical reform in the life of the churches recaptured elements of the monastic dimension.*

436. *In the years after the Second World War of the 20th century, the monastic community of Taizé, France, was for many youths a return to the perception of the communitarian dimension of Christianity. The existence of a monastic community, albeit a small one, became for many an invitation to rediscover a fundamental dimension of Christianity. In the photo, Brother Roger Schutz is speaking to a vast assembly of those who had gathered at Taizé.*

The contemplative communities, for their part, had a dedication to the spiritual life as their specific task. Such communities began in Sweden in 1919 and have been spreading through various European countries. Hamburg, in 1957, saw the rise of some communities inspired by Benedictine spirituality and others that adopted practices closer to the Cistercian tradition.

Other communities have devoted themselves to divine worship and prayer. For example, the Brothers of the Common Life (1905, Switzerland) and the Johannites, a community on Iona (Scotland), where once again there are so many admirable examples of the mystical life and of work to restore the culture of the medieval monasteries.

All these communities have come into existence separately, using their own autonomous rules and drawing hardly any inspiration from the ancient orders. Their common life and spirituality are focused basically on the Divine Office and the Eucharist. In keeping with the Reformed tradition, they reject any kind of personal merit for adopting this way of life. All of them have introduced a period of novitiate and testing before any more permanent commitment can be made. We find in these communities a generalized preference for the life of devotion, although they do not exclude theological work; in fact, we find some interesting theologians in these groups.

The communities' relations with the institutional churches are not very clear; however, they often have an ecumenical orientation that in one way or the other departs from that of the various churches.

A special example of this new attention to monastic spirituality is to be found in the well-known community of Taizé with its emphasis on a monastic life that is the fruit of influences from various spiritual traditions: the Franciscan, the Benedictine, that of Charles de Foucauld. Taizé is located, in fact, in Burgundy, not far from the ruins of the great monastery of Cluny. At Taizé, with its profoundly ecumenical spirit, there is, in addition to the service of the handicapped, the marginalized, and Third World peoples, a surprising dedication to the youth of Europe, with the distinct purpose of offering a meaning for their lives; this dedication has won acceptance to an exceptional degree from the young of all countries and every social condition.

In the life of the Taizé monks we find two key elements, essential to monastic life: prayer and work. As for asceticism, beyond any personal austerities, the form of apostolate adopted by the monks leads them constantly to help carry the burdens of others, to seek an interior understanding of all human beings, and, as far as possible, to promote their joint progress, while keeping alive their own concern for the poorest.

Taizé did not have an easy beginning, given the reservations stirred by its ecumenical calling, which in fact was quite undefined at the start. Taizé is also a community that feels itself called to live to a high degree the values of communion. As such, it sees itself as a place of reconciliation and unity, given that the heart of its religious experience is communion with God and communion with every human being.

10. MONASTICISM IN NORTH AMERICA

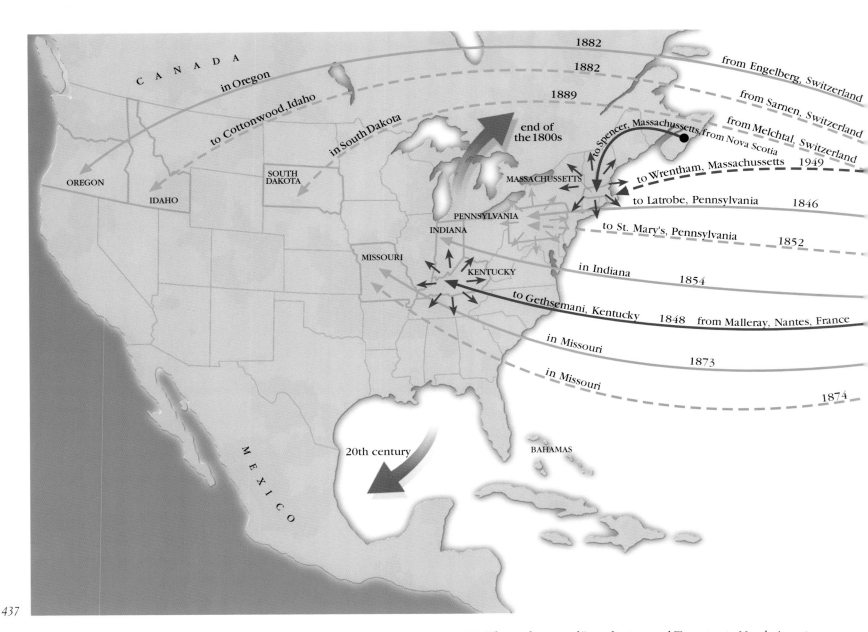

437

437. The settlement of Benedictines and Trappists in North America.

Monastic men and women originally came to North America for the same reasons other settlers came: refuge, opportunity, and mission. The extraordinary diversity of American monasticism is explainable by that array of factors as well as the national origins of the major American monastic families. In the second half of the 20th century the European foundations and their offspring undertook the renewal called for by Vatican Council II even as new communities emerged.

The history of American monasticism began in the late 16th century in Brazil (1581 at Bahia). In North America there were Benedictines in Mexico City at the very end of the 16th century, sent from Montserrat in Catalonia. Their priory would survive until 1863. The first English-speaking American Benedictines were those from the Catholic colony of Maryland who joined the exiled English communities in France and the Low Countries

(beginning in 1705). They did not return to establish monasticism in the American colonies. The first Benedictines actually to live in what had become the United States were French monks exiled after the dissolution of monasteries during the French Revolution. A lone Benedictine came in 1790 and devoted his remaining years to pastoral work, while Trappists came in 1803. Their efforts to establish Cistercian monasticism in Kentucky, Illinois, New York, and other sites were heroic but unsuccessful. A monk accidentally stranded in Nova Scotia in 1815 eventually established a precarious community there in 1823, but the real start of stable Trappist monasticism would be a quarter-century later.

The first successful monastic establishment in the United States was the Bavarian foundation at Latrobe, Pennsylvania, in 1846. The extraordinary figure behind this endeavor was Boniface Wimmer, a former diocesan priest who entered the Bavarian monastery of

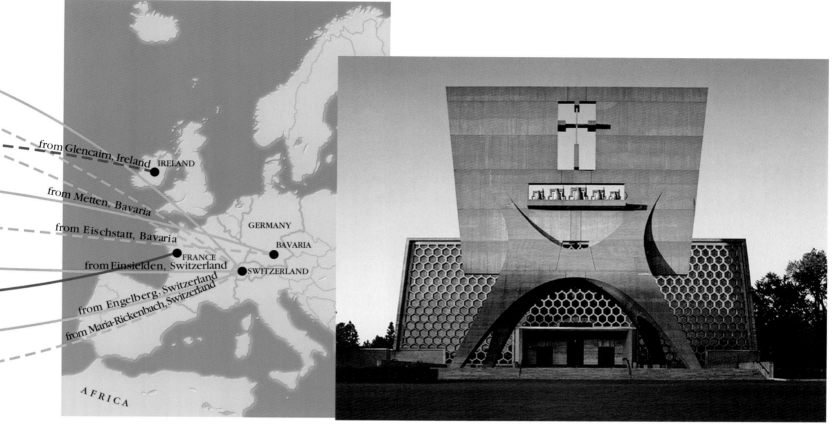

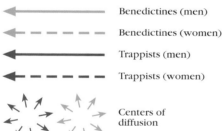

Benedictines (men)

Benedictines (women)

Trappists (men)

Trappists (women)

Centers of
diffusion

438

438. The church of St. John's Abbey in Collegeville, Minnesota, USA. The seat of an important monastery and famed university, St. John's called upon one of the masters of modern architecture, Marcel Breuer, to build the church; the work is an impressive achievement, a proof of the monastic resolve to be present within the culture of the time.

Metten in 1832 and developed a zeal for mission and a strong sense of destiny. Wimmer finally managed to secure permission to travel to America in service of German immigrants, taking with him 18 aspirants. In 1852 three Benedictine nuns from St. Walburga's in Eichstätt came to Pennsylvania to assist with the mission. Their leader, Benedicta Riepp, was Wimmer's match in determination. From Wimmer's male community at Latrobe and Riepp's monastery for women at St Mary's would come an astonishing series of foundations that would, by the mid-20th century, number thousands of professed members in the United States, Canada, Mexico, the Bahamas, and elsewhere.

The other major European monastic influx was Swiss. Benedictine monks came from Einsiedeln to Indiana (1854) and from Engelberg to Missouri (1873) and Oregon (1882). From these monasteries developed the Swiss-American Congregation, the

second-largest family of monasteries for men in the United States today. Like the Bavarians, the Swiss came to work with German-speaking immigrants, and Benedictine women from the monastery of Maria Rickenbach came to Missouri in 1874 to share the tasks of providing pastoral, educational, and medical care. They were the basis for two major groups of American monastic women, the Benedictine Sisters of Perpetual Adoration and the nuns of Sacred Heart Priory in Yankton, South Dakota, and their daughter houses. Two other Swiss monasteries of women established American foundations in the 1880s at Cottonwood, Idaho (1882, from Sarnen) and in South Dakota (1889, from Melchthal).

Benedictine men and women faced incredibly difficult conditions on the American frontier, sharing fully in the hardships of the immigrant farmers they served. Traditional monastic observance was impossible despite heroic effort. Many of the men spent

439

439. *Library of the Trappist abbey of Snowmass in Colorado, USA.*

440. *Blessed Sacrament chapel in the Trappist abbey of Mepkin, South Carolina, USA. Monastic architecture often seeks to create spaces for meditation by using light in simple and aniconic surroundings.*

440

considerable periods of time away from the monasteries on pastoral assignment, often alone. Monastic women were obliged to ease the customary observance of strict cloister and suffered the canonical penalty of losing their traditional solemn monastic vows and independence from subjection to the local diocesan bishop. For both Benedictine men and women in the United States the 20th century has seen much effort to reclaim monastic practices and identity.

The French Trappist monastery of Melleray, near Nantes, sent a party of monks, aspirants, and workers to the United States in 1848. They returned to Kentucky. This time their efforts were successful, and Gethsemani would be the mother of most male Cistercian houses in the United States. The struggling monastery in Nova Scotia founded a community in Rhode Island that later moved to Spencer, Massachusetts, and flourished. It was more than a century between Gethsemani's founding and the arrival in 1949 of the first Trappistines. They came from Glencairn in Ireland to Wrentham, Massachusetts, and several communities have been founded in turn from Wrentham.

By the end of the 19th century Benedictine monasteries in the United States had made foundations in Canada and begun missionary work in the Bahamas. The 20th century has seen the reestablishment of monasticism in Mexico by Benedictines from the United States and several foundations in Central America. European monastic colonization continued with the addition of English

Benedictine men in three communities in the United States and French Benedictines in Canada. There have been two new foundations of Benedictine women from Eichstätt in Bavaria, motherhouse of the original female Benedictine mission in 1852.

The original reasons that monasticism was brought to North America have changed. Religious persecution in Western Europe has ceased, though refugees from Communism in Eastern Europe and China established monasteries in the United States in the mid-20th century. The original missionary impulse of Bavarian and Swiss Benedictines has adapted to the assimilation of immigrant communities to American culture. The monasteries have seen a greater emphasis on community life and a reduction of external commitments, owing also to a decline in membership. Vatican Council II challenged all monasteries to examine traditional practices and assumptions. The process of renewal has affected monasticism like other forms of religious life and the priesthood, with a severe drop in the number of entrants to most Benedictine and Trappist communities. There has been some shifting of congregational affiliation as community identities have shifted. The Italian Olivetan Benedictine tradition, for example, has supported experiments in "double" monasteries of men and women.

While older North American communities have shrunk in size and questioned their purpose and future, new communities have been founded to emphasize a less apostolic kind of monasticism. Some were established as a new wave of European monastic colo-

441

442

443

441. Evocative light over a holy water font in the chapel of the abbey of the Virgin of Curutaran, Mexico.

442–443. View of the buildings and of the fields of the farming operations at the Trappistine abbey of El Encuentro in Mexico.

nization, such as the foundations of contemplative nuns by French and Bavarian monasteries, the Camaldolese foundation at Big Sur in California, and the Carthusian house in Vermont. Others were American initiatives in response to a desire for a more contemplative way of life, such as Mount Savior in New York, Weston Priory in Vermont, and the Monastery of Christ in the Desert in New Mexico. Several of these communities have attracted many new members. One may be seeing in North America a pattern familiar from European monastic history. Communities have cycles of growth and contraction, renewal and stasis. Some survive and flourish again; others do not. After more than 150 years, monasticism in North America has come to maturity and to new challenges.

257

11. MONASTICISM IN LATIN AMERICA

444. Old church and Benedictine monastery of Nostra Senhora do Monte Serrat in Salvador, Bahia, Brazil. The monastery was built between 1650 and 1679 by the abbot Fra Marco do Desterro.

445. Trappistine monastery of Quilvo, Chile, founded in 1981 from Vitorchiano, which in recent years has founded six monasteries in various countries.

444

445

The Benedictines and, generally speaking, the other monastic orders had little to do with the Spanish and Portuguese evangelization of the Americas. They came from Portugal, entered the continent through Brazil, and did not move into the other parts until the end of the 19th century. Since the 16th century there had been but a single monastery of Cistercian nuns, located in Lima; this has today been renewed by the addition of Spanish nuns from the monastery of Las Huelgas in Burgos. The kings of Spain did not allow monastic orders into the New World because they did not think these useful for the direct evangelization of the native peoples. This was probably a major mistake in light of the fact that the Benedictines were in large measure responsible for the evangelization of Europe.

At the present time, except for a few individual monasteries, Benedictine monastic life has not managed to take root and effectively produce autonomous houses in the Spanish-American sections of the continents. The majority of the foundations are still supported or governed by monks from the founding houses; moreover, after years of existence, some of these dependent foundations find themselves forced to close because the founding monastery is unable to continue sending new members, due to the scarcity of vocations in Europe. Monks of the Benedictine family have a presence in 18 Spanish-American countries, with a total of 870 monks.

The Benedictines reached Brazil in 1581 and there founded the first Benedictine monastery in the Americas at Bahia (today, Salvador). After that, the order spread to the main cities of the Portuguese colony.

In Brazil, a Portuguese group became an independent congregation in 1827, but in 1855 an anticlerical government forbade every form of proselytism, so that the congregation was on the edge of extinction. In 1895, at the request of the survivors, Maredsous (Belgium) sent out a colony of monks from Beuron; these monks quickly produced a notable resurgence in numbers and activities.

Brazil is still the South American country in which Benedictine monasticism has its deepest roots: 56 houses and 277 monks. Generally speaking, these monasteries carry on a good deal of pastoral and social activity: parishes, theological centers, colleges, libraries, social advancement of the most needy, and so on.

In the Spanish-American countries, many monasteries depend on European congregations. Mexico, for example, has two monasteries founded by the Spanish abbey of Silos, which belongs to the French Congregation. Martinique and Trinidad, French- and English-speaking respectively, have houses of the French and Belgian Congregations, and in Trinidad there is also a monastery of women that depends on St. Ottilien in Augsburg. Meanwhile, many other monasteries depended on North American abbeys. Thus the Mexican abbeys of Tepeyac (20 kilometers from Mexico City), Nuestra Señora de los Angelos (Cuernavaca), Nuestra Señora de la Soledad (Guanajuato), and Todos los Santos (Veracruz) were founded by the North American abbeys of St. John's, Mount Angel, and Christ in the Desert respectively.

446. *The diffusion of monasticism in Central and South America.*

446

BELIZE	
Swiss-American	1
GUATEMALA	
Swiss-American	2
Olivetan	1
Solesmes	1
ARGENTINA	
Cono-Sur	6
BRAZIL	
Brazilian	14
Subiaco	1
Hungarian	2
American-Cassinese	2
Camaldolese	2
Vallombrosan	1
Olivetan	2
CHILE	
Cono-Sur	2
COLOMBIA	
American-Cassinese	1
St. Ottilien	1
Subiaco	2
PARAGUAY	
Cono-Sur	1
PERU	
English	1
TRINIDAD	
Annunciation	1
URUGUAY	
Cono-Sur	1
VENEZUELA	
St. Ottilian	1

Venezuela has three houses founded from St. Ottilien; Chile has two founded from Samos and one from Beuron. Colombia also has one from Samos. Argentina has an sizable priory that is dependent on Subiaco, a daughter house of Silos in Buenos Aires, and a little colony from Einsiedeln in the Pampas.

In Chile, in the shadow of the Benedictine abbey of La Santissima Trinidad de las Condes (Santiago), there has come into existence an important Benedictine apostolic movement of the laity, the purpose of which is to introduce the basic values of the Rule of St. Benedict into the world of education. This movement has developed very effectively in Chile and is spreading to other countries of the continent. Its mission is the Christian education of children and young people in the perspective of the gospel and the Rule of Benedict of Nursia. The movement presently has 900 members, men and women, married and celibate.

The Charterhouse of Nuestra Señora Medianeira in Brazil had its beginning in 1985. The first Trappist monks came from the United States and founded houses in Argentina and Chile, while Cistercian nuns came from France and Italy.

The Cistercian Abbey in Azul (Argentina, 1984) is the first abbey of the strict observance in South America, but there are also priories in Chile, Argentina, Mexico, and Brazil. In these houses, the balance between contemplative vocation and missionary vision has led to the conviction that the future of this region of the Americas depends on its being built up in both the temporal and the spiritual realms. Given this outlook, the contemplative reli-

gious spirit must both compensate for and support the active work of evangelization.

The Premonstratensians have nine houses in the Spanish- and Portuguese-speaking Americas, out of which they work effectively as missionaries among the native peoples. The Cistercians of Germany, France, and Italy, whether of regular or strict observance, have founded some monasteries. These are young communities but they have certain typical traits that distinguish them within the order; they are characterized by the simplicity of their liturgy and by their effort to find a satisfactory contemplative expression that is adapted to the traditions of their vocations from among the original peoples. Since these are small communities, they do not engage in large-scale industries. They look for the right adaptation to the social setting of their respective houses, and are doing so without prejudice to their contemplative side.

The majority of the new monastic houses were endowed with resources and personnel so that no excessive productive activity would be required of all the members of the community. In these American houses there has also been a reaction against too close a connection between priesthood and the monastic vocation; emphasis has been placed on the movement toward the contemplative life, simplicity, manual work, and the importance of *lectio divina;* and there has begun to appear a mentality less attached to traditions and very free in its interpretation of the Rule, with the result that creativity is combined with a fidelity to the essentials of each order.

The monasteries are in very frequent contact with one another by way of ongoing meetings for the purpose of responding to the challenge of a Christian world whose members are very numerous but which is passing through a grave social and cultural crisis. There is no doubt that solidarity with the surrounding people in their social and political problems causes difficulties, although there is an effort to face these without departing from the ways of traditional Benedictine hospitality. In the liturgical movement the monasteries are trying to take over and incorporate elements of the local people's religious customs, with special attention to the Native American population. There is, for example, the Paraguayan foundation of Tupassy María by the monastery of Toldos.

Women's monasticism has spread widely and, in this case, in continuity with the rich tradition of the colonial past, for, while monks had hardly been present during those centuries, except in Brazil, contemplative religious women were a constant presence, although not from the Benedictine family. As a result, we find many monasteries of Cistercian, Trappist, and Benedictine nuns in almost all the countries of this vast Spanish- and Portuguese-speaking region of the Americas.

It can be said that in these countries there is a profusion of small communities, not a few of which are being called upon to divide even further. At first sight, this may seem rather chaotic, but in fact the situation is hardly different from what monasticism was in many periods of the Middle Ages. Moreover, this state of affairs seems to meet the needs of the current situation in this region of the Americas as it searches for itself in a process of permanent and creative development.

12. MONASTICISM IN OCEANIA AND ASIA

447. *Cloister of the monastery of Matutum. The Trappistine monastery was founded in 1995 by ten monastics from Vitorchiano, a monastery in the vicinity of Rome.*

448. *A dance performed in the monastery of Matutum, Mindanao, the Philippines, in honor of the nuns from Vitorchiano who had come to visit.*

449. *Benedictine monks of the monastery of the Holy Trinity Yatsugatake, Fujimi Machi, Nagano Ken, Japan (St. John's Abbey, Collegeville, archives).*

450. *Monastery of the Holy Trinity Yatsugatake, Fujimi, Japan (St. John's Abbey, archives).*

The Benedictine presence in Oceania is very limited. Ever since Australia became an English colony, the country has always had English Benedictines working as missionaries and in the service of the bishops. The most important house is the monastery of New Nursia, which was founded by Rosendo Salvado, a Spanish Benedictine, in 1846. This house, built in the middle of a forest, became an important center of evangelization and inculturation among the original inhabitants of Australia. In its shadow there developed a sizable city, an important center of culture and Christian life, just as happened in Europe in earlier centuries.

Benedictine and Trappist monasteries also exist in Australia and New Zealand (Aotearoa), although vocations among the Aboriginal Peoples and Maori continue to be few and the monks from these countries have not yet surpassed the Irish in numbers. On the other hand, the influence, especially throughout Samoa and Tonga, of the Trappists of Kopua in New Zealand has led to numerous vocations in these places. Furthermore, for the profession of novices in Tonga, the traditional ceremonial has been adapted to the culture

of their island, thereby creating impressive and widely accepted liturgical rites.

There are Benedictines today in five countries of Oceania; 120 men and 460 women.

The first monks of the Benedictine family who took up permanent residence on the continent of Asia were the French Cistercians of the Strict Observance, who came to China in 1883. Today Benedictine monasteries of men are to be found in other Asian countries, with a total of 1300 men: 40 monasteries with 600 members; 6 with 500 Cistercians; and 9 with 190 Cistercians of the Strict Observance.

Benedictine men are in Sadhu Benedicti Math (Bangladesh); they have 6 houses in Korea, 12 in India, 2 in Israel, the monastery of the Holy Trinity in Japan (founded by the North American abbey of Saint John's in Collegeville in 1947), 4 in Sri Lanka, and 2 priories in Taiwan (founded by North American abbeys in 1966 and 1964). In Vietnam there is Thien An Abbey, founded from the French abbey of La Pierre-qui-Vire in 1940. The Benedictines and

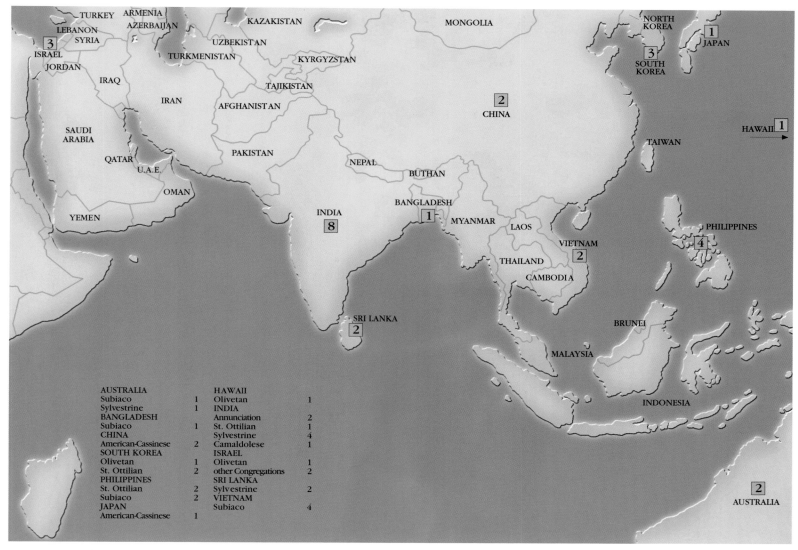

AUSTRALIA
Subiaco   1
Sylvestrine   1
BANGLADESH
Subiaco   1
CHINA
American-Cassinese   2
SOUTH KOREA
Olivetan   1
St. Ottilian   2
PHILIPPINES
St. Ottilian   2
Subiaco   2
JAPAN
American-Cassinese   1

HAWAII
Olivetan   1
INDIA
Annunciation   2
St. Ottilian   1
Sylvestrine   4
Camaldolese   1
ISRAEL
Olivetan   1
other Congregations   2
SRI LANKA
Sylvestrine   2
VIETNAM
Subiaco   4

451

451. *Today's diffusion of monasticism in Asia, Australia, and Hawaii.*

Cistercians suffered terribly in Vietnam under Communist rule, but the communities have deep roots in the country and an abundance of vocations. Thien An Abbey has in turn established three new monasteries. The main apostolic activity of these communities is the welcome of visitors and spiritual direction.

In the Philippines, Benedictine men were represented by the monastery of Montserrat in Manila, which combined deep roots in the Spanish tradition with an integration into Philippine culture. More recently, however, foundations more representative of the local cultures have arisen in large numbers. The Montserrat community operates Saint Bede, a prestigious secondary school with 6000 students, while the abbatial church is the center of a sizable parish. In 1981, Montserrat founded the monastery of the Transfiguration (Malaybalay City), which is an important center of spirituality for the entire southern Philippines.

In 1983 the house of St. Benedict in Digos on the island of Mindanao was established; it was thought that, since the people were untutored in religious matters compared to the remainder of the archipelago, the most needed task there was to help them deepen their faith. The monks are the pastors of a parish of over 65,000 widely scattered inhabitants and also of 50 chapels since they must also serve the tribal people in the mountains. In 1991,

this abbey established St. Anselm, a study center and a house of formation and studies for young monks.

The Cistercians of the Strict Observance (Trappists) succeeded in establishing three important monasteries in China, with some communities counting over 150 members. The rise of Communism put an end to these foundations and thirty monks suffered martyrdom, but a small group managed to survive until today in secret and amid great suffering. At the present time some young men are joining them. Under the secret direction of the monks a group of young women asked to become Cistercian monastics and succeeded in leaving the country in order to make their profession at an abbey in Japan; they, too, are now living in secret in China.

In Asia the Trappists have 9 monasteries of men and 8 of women, with 190 men and 265 women in all.

Women's monasticism is very well represented in the Philippines, especially by the Benedictine nuns of Tutzing (Germany), with the priory of St. Scholastica in Manila having around a hundred sisters widely scattered throughout the islands. The women direct and attend to many apostolic undertakings, for example, radio broadcasts for teaching the catechism to remote populations not easily visited.

13. ECUMENISM

453. The Trappist monk Thomas Merton has become one of the symbols of ecumenism. His work extended itself to dialoguing with other religions and to fostering the reciprocal spiritual contribution between the monastic experiences of other religions. The dialogue between religions did not begin by verbalizing its doctrinal themes but by plumbing the depths of religious experience. As has been said, the monastic experience is the model of every Christian's religious experience. Dialogue between monastics of various religions is therefore an important contribution to the dialogue between believers of various religions.

452

453

452. Sister Maria Gabriella Sagheddu, the Trappistine nun from Sardinia who dedicated the last years of her monastic life to praying for ecumenism.

As the ecumenical movement developed in the churches of the 20th century, Western monasticism emerged with it as a privileged locus for ecumenical encounter and reflection. Monasticism arose before the final division between Eastern and Western Christianity in 1054 and the fragmentation of the Reformation. Therefore, Western monasticism looks in two directions in its ecumenical regard: to the Eastern churches, with whom it shares a spiritual and monastic heritage, and to the churches of the Reformation, which share monasticism's emphasis on a biblical spirituality. Roman Catholic monasteries today are natural venues for ecumenical gatherings since all can participate fully in the Divine Office. At the same time, monasticism of various kinds has arisen within churches of the Reformation, and members of those communities have a natural affinity with their brothers and sisters in the Roman Catholic and Orthodox churches. There are also explicitly ecumenical communities, like that of Taizé in Burgundy, which include both Roman Catholic and Protestant members.

Western monasticism of the 19th century looked to the Middle Ages for inspiration, but monasticism of the 20th century participated fully in the revival of patristic and liturgical studies. This rediscovery of early Christianity and the fundamental sources of monastic spirituality led inevitably to a keener appreciation of the spirituality and traditions of Eastern Christianity where the patristic and liturgical orientation was preserved more faithfully. This look to the East was a particular interest of Dom Lambert Beauduin (1873–1960). In 1925 this Belgian Benedictine founded the bi-ritual monastery at Amay (it moved to Chevetogne in 1939) and its famous periodical, *Irénikon*. Beauduin had also participated

in the Malines Conversations with Anglicans between 1921 and 1926. Beauduin was a pioneer in ecumenism and an innovator in monastic life and suffered both misunderstanding and negative reaction to his work. Although Vatican Council II and its decree on ecumenism came after his death, it vindicated his convictions, and Chevetogne continues to witness to a fuller vision of a church drawing equally from Eastern and Western traditions.

Sister Maria Gabrielle Sagheddu (1914–1939), a Sicilian Trappistine beatified in 1983, was another kind of monastic ecumenical witness. She and her abbess were influenced by the call of the French priest Paul Couturier to prayer for Christian unity, and shortly after her first profession in 1937 she asked to offer her life of prayer for the sake of unity. Although she lived only two more years, her devotion to ecumenism became known even during her lifetime. Her beatification in 1983 recognized the importance of prayer in ecumenical work, an emphasis especially suited to monastic communities.

The most famous ecumenical monastic initiative is surely the community of Taizé. The project began in 1944 when a young Swiss Protestant, Roger Schutz (b. 1915), settled with friends at this Burgundian site not far from the ruined abbey of Cluny. Earlier in the war he had lived at Taizé to be in solidarity with the French experience of Nazi occupation. When he returned with his companions, their intention was to become a "parable of community." In 1949 they took lifetime vows of commitment to celibacy, community, and simplicity of life. Soon they were joined by Roman Catholic brothers, and over time the community became international as well as ecumenical. Taizé is known most for its outreach

454

455

454. An ecumenical encounter in 1961, promoted by the monastic community of Taizé. In the background, the village church of Taizé.

455. The Benedictine monk Kilian McDonnell, founder and president of the Institute of Ecumenical and Cultural Research in Collegeville, standing in front of the Institute.

to the young and its contemplative chant, popularized in prayer groups around the world, but the ecumenical focus has remained central to the founder's vision and the life of the community.

Another member of the Trappist branch of the Cistercians, Thomas Merton (1915–1968), made a vital contribution to the nascent American ecumenical movement in the 1950s and 1960s through his published writings and correspondence. Merton described a contemplative Christianity that had much to offer to the global and national challenges of the Cold War and the Civil Rights Movement. Many Protestants were intrigued by Merton's vision of church and society and became his friends through visits to the monastery of Gethsemani in Kentucky or through letters. As Merton evolved from his hyper-Catholicism of the 1940s and early 1950s to a more comprehensive view of the Christian spiritual tradition, integrating particularly patristic and Eastern perspectives, he developed a naturally ecumenical outlook. Toward the end of his life Merton's interests expanded to non-Christian religions, especially Asian Buddhism. Remaining anchored and faithful in his Christian monastic life, Merton was able to be hospitable to other spiritual traditions without being threatened in his own.

After the encouragement of formal ecumenical dialogue by Vatican Council II, in 1965 the Benedictine monks of Saint John's Abbey at Collegeville, Minnesota (U.S.A.), established a center for dialogue and scholarship on ecumenism. Now known as the

Institute for Ecumenical and Cultural Research, the center sponsors consultations on topics of common interest and provides housing and research facilities for visiting academics and church leaders. The monastery itself attracts individuals and groups from other churches, and invited the Episcopal Diocese of Minnesota to build its retreat house on the Abbey's property. Monks of Saint John's participate in national and international ecumenical dialogues as well.

Small monastic communities dedicated particularly to ecumenical experimentation or understanding continue to emerge. Though often short-lived, they make a real contribution to grassroots ecumenism. Meanwhile, the traditional monastic emphasis on hospitality is increasingly understood as including an emphasis on welcoming Christians of other churches. Monastic retreat houses provide an opportunity to explore the breadth and depth of Christian forms of prayer, and the "marginal" nature of monastic communities can make them safer ground for retreatants from other churches. Spiritual programs such as Centering Prayer, Dom John Main's work on Christian meditation, and Taizé prayer have had great appeal across formal ecclesiastical boundaries, tapping as they do the spiritual riches of the early, undivided Church. Monasticism's greatest contribution to ecumenism, as to everything else, is prayer.

14. THE MONASTIC INTERRELIGIOUS DIALOGUE

456

456. *Phase 7 of the Interreligious Monastic Dialogue. A Conversation between monastics of the different religions at Dzongsar Institute of Bir, India (Aaron Raverty, O.S.B., Collegeville).*

FROM INTERRELIGIOUS DIALOGUE TO MONASTIC DIALOGUE

The interreligious dialogue grew out of the Second Vatican Council (1962–1965). Pope Paul VI in his first encyclical, *Ecclesiam Suam* (1964), emphasized the need for interreligious dialogue; but it was the council document *Nostra Aetate* (1965) on "The Relationship of the Church to Non-Christian Religions" that set genuine interreligious dialogue in motion. In 1974, the president of the secretariat established to promote the Catholic Church's relationship with other religions asked the Abbot Primate to urge that Christian monastics, both men and women, seek to become bridges for promoting mutual understanding between Christians and persons of other faiths.

In 1968, the world's Benedictine abbots sponsored their first Asian East-West Intermonastic Conference in Bangkok to explore the way of dialogue with other religions. It was this conference that brought Thomas Merton to the East and eventually to visit with the Dalai Lama. It was a watershed beginning for East-West intermonastic dialogue. Two other Asian conferences followed, sponsored by Aide Inter-Monastères (AIM), an organization of the Benedictine Confederation, which was given the responsibility of facilitating interfaith dialogue: Bangalore in 1973 and Sri Lanka in 1980.

In 1978, at AIM's invitation, the organization "AIM's North American Board for East-West Dialogue" was formed; it later took the name Monastic Interreligious Dialogue (MID). Some months later, a European monastic group chose the name Dialogue Interreligieux Monastique (DIM). The purpose of these groups was to stimulate interest among Western monastics in the ideas and values present in Eastern religions and to assist in the development of intermonastic dialogue, especially between Buddhist and Christian monastics.

The Naropa East-West conferences, planned by the Naropa Institute in Boulder, Colorado, and MID, were held in 1980 and 1981. At the latter, the secretary of MID asked the Dalai Lama, at a semiprivate audience, if he was willing to send his monks to American Christian monasteries. His answer was yes and the Intermonastic Hospitality Exchanges between American Christian and Tibetan Buddhist monastics were set in motion. (DIM has also hosted exchanges with Tibetan and other Buddhist, especially Zen, monastics in Europe and Asia.)

There were several exchanges between 1982 and 1992, out of which came an intermonastic dialogue between the Dalai Lama, other Buddhist leaders, and members of MID, held during the

1993 Parliament of the World's Religions in Chicago. Following this encounter, the Dalai Lama proposed that MID invite 25 Buddhist and 25 Christian masters to live together for a full week of shared practice and dialogue on the spiritual life; he also asked if it might be held at Gethsemani Abbey, the home of his friend Thomas Merton. The first Gethsemani Encounter took place in 1996; the second in 2002.

Exchanges sponsored by MID continue to the present, and since 1996 they go beyond shared hospitality and friendship between Tibetan Buddhist monastics in exile and monastics in the United States. They seek to concretely help their Buddhist brothers and sisters in exile in creative ways, for instance, education in health care, computer skills, and English within a Christian monastic context.

The Monastic Interreligious Dialogue has been a journey of Eastern and Western monastics traveling together from communication to communion.

THE ANCIENT ROOTS OF TODAY'S COMMITMENT

Between Christian monastics and Hindu sadhu (poor), sannayasi (renouncers), and yogi, or Buddhist bhikku (beggars), arahat (worthy ones), thera (elders), and zen masters, or masters of the kabala and the hasidim (pious ones), or Muslim fakirs (poor ones), Sufi, and dervishes, there are potential points of contact, such as detachment from the cares of the world, the search for the Absolute, and reliance on a discipline or asceticism; all these were brought up in the early chapters of the present work. Merton wrote on the occasion of his journey to Asia: "Until now, my conversations with Buddhists have been open and frank, and there has been a complete communication at a truly deep level. It seems that we recognize in each other a certain depth of spiritual experience; this is beyond question."

The quest for this kind of dialogue about the religious experiences at the heart of each religious tradition inspired Fathers Jules Monchanin, Henri Le Saulx, and Bede Griffiths to establish Christian ashrams in India. In addition, not a few monasteries have experienced a stronger desire for dialogue with their brothers and sisters in other religions.

The desire for dialogue between monastics from various traditions could also be seen in Merton on the occasion just referred to: "I left my monastery to come here not simply as a university researcher or even as an author. . . . I come as a pilgrim desirous of obtaining not just information or 'facts' about other monastic traditions, but desirous rather of drinking from the ancient springs of monastic vision and experience."

This interest of monastics both Eastern and Western found concrete expression at the conferences of Bangkok (1966), Bangalore (1973), and Kandy (1980). In 1977, the abbey of Praglia (Italy) sponsored a series of meetings of Christian, Buddhist, and Hindu monks. Also in 1977, the Benedictines organized two study groups, in Europe and the United States, for the purpose of finding and promoting various possibilities for a profitable interreligious dialogue.

In 1979, twenty-nine Buddhist monks and two Shinto priests, all of them Japanese, took up residence for three weeks in European Benedictine and Trappist monasteries. In 1983, European monastics, fifteen men and two women, lived in Japanese monasteries. The final assessments of these ventures showed that the experiences were mutually enriching.

These were extraordinary experiences that, going far beyond study and doctrinal comparisons, went to the level of spiritual search in silence, prayer, and shared meditation, in daily work and meals taken in common. Through this sharing of life and spiritual aspirations at the most personal level it became possible to achieve a communion between the two parties.

THE GIFTS OF MONASTICISM

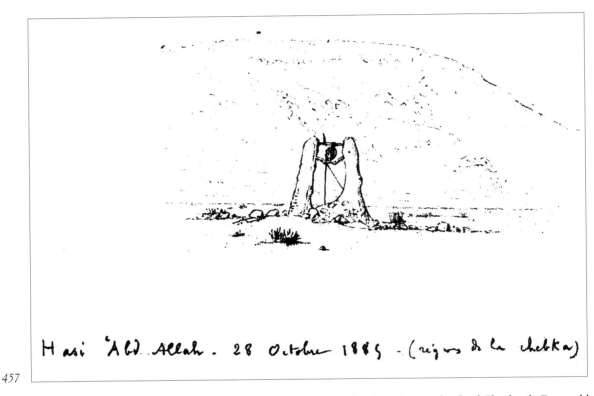

457. A well in the desert. Sketch in the notebook of Charles de Foucauld made in 1885. Two symbols of the monastic dimension: the desert into which one withdraws and the water (the well) which gives life.

Monasticism is one of the most instructive, brilliant, and impressive aspects of Christian history. Its manifestations are numerous and colorful; it is closely linked to the daily vicissitudes of the Christian people, and very dependent on the personality and characteristic traits of each nation and each culture. At the same time, however, it is a direct expression of the fundamental core of the gospel's teaching and demands.

Down through the centuries, monastics, both women and men, have concerned themselves with God alone, in the most complete solitude, by means of regular prayer and ceaseless penance. St. Benedict wrote in his rule that "the life of a monk ought to be a continuous Lent" (49, 1; *RB 1980: The Rule of St. Benedict* [Collegeville: The Liturgical Press, 1981] 253), although, in fact, it is a way of life led at every moment with the joyous hope of Easter. Monastics are by definition contemplatives; they seek the living God in history, which is shot through with Jesus Christ; in nature, which is a magnificent expression of the divine beauty; and in the depths of their own being; and they long constantly for heaven. The words of Exodus 33:18, "Show me your glory, I pray," would be an adequate summation of monastic spirituality.

At the same time, however, Monastics are concerned with human beings, their brothers and sisters, and with their needs and concerns. Education and the economy, manuscripts and agriculture, schools and distilleries have been some of the occupations and objects of dedication by Western monastics of markedly different congregations, but the works were inspired by the same motives. The love of Christ impelled and moved them not only to pray constantly for their fellow human beings but also to advise as they traveled the roads of this always complicated and confused world; this was especially the case when these fellow human beings did not have clear goals. Evagrius Ponticus defined a monastic as one who "lives separated from all and united with all," while St. Anthony never hesitated to leave his cherished solitude in order to relieve the needs or solve the problems of others who asked for his help.

The life of monastics, in its deepest and essential meaning, is a journey of conversion and turning to God, a continual weaving of ties and relationships with God. Although there is no doubt that their ultimate goals are those of every Christian who tries to live the gospel message in its fullness, monastics fervently and constantly seek to grasp the deepest meaning of the fact that they are children of God; they bring into clear light the contradiction involved in sin and its bitter consequences; they make clear in word and work how one can be liberated from evil in this "vale of tears." These new soldiers of Christ, who are poor with the poor Christ, scorn the riches of this world; they have put off the old self and rejoice to be clad in the new (Ephesians). In their view, their life and their activity are always works of love.

In this personal search and pilgrimage, monastics seek to have an undivided heart, incapable of serving two masters; a heart that is placed wholly at the service of God, without any division; a heart that is not drawn in several directions by the world or by the passions. Their control of the body by sometimes radical methods, their austere life, their renunciation of whatever can weaken their commitment and complete self-surrender, all these have but one purpose: to enable them to love and serve the only Lord of life and death.

If the goal of monastic life is union with God and the authentic search for the divine through purity of heart, then monastics must seek God where God can be found, and know the divine in the measure granted to the limited human intellect. God is a hidden God who makes the divine self known in the degree to which God is truly sought. But God manifests the divine self in a special way in sacred Scripture, which is God's own written word. Consequently, reading and study, whether on one's own or by following the interpretation of this word that is given by the Fathers, will inevitably grant us a better knowledge of God and, as a result, bring us closer to the divine, increase our love, and make us better disposed for prayer and union with the divinity. It is not possible to understand monastic life without taking into account this devout veneration and following of the sacred books.

The consecrated life is at the service of the mission of the Church or, better, at the service of the mission of Jesus, which the Church continues in time until the second coming of the Lord. For this reason, monastics have a twofold relationship: with Christ and with the Church. Even in the deepest solitude or on top of the highest pillar, they have a strong awareness of the Church and of their own obligation to evangelize, to be witnesses of Christ, and to help their brothers and sisters in their temporal and spiritual needs. The surprising scenes of monastics preaching the good news to peoples outside the Christian tradition provide some of the most extraordinary pages of Christian history.

Monasticism offers mental health and hope. Those who live in tranquility without agitation, without complaint or back talk, without apathy or reluctance; those who are not attached to or worried about earthly possessions, and are not mastered by the passions of body or spirit, but at every moment preserve control of their actions, their movements, and their thoughts; those who love God in whom they trust and whom they serve, conscious as they are of being the daughters and sons of God and the sisters and brothers of Christ who took flesh in order to be our brother and save us, under the beneficent action of the Spirit: these enjoy peace of spirit and live by hope.

Monastic community life offers standards and practices of civility and living together. It teaches its members to bear patiently with the weaknesses of their neighbors, those of both body and spirit, as well as with their own weaknesses, which are always with us as a constant source of distress. The purpose of this patience is to avoid inconveniencing others with useless complaints and to remain resolute in always accepting one's own limitations, one's own frailty.

The main purpose Benedict had in imposing manual work on his monks was not social usefulness or poetical experience, but partly asceticism. The work of monastics is, nevertheless, all these things. Western monastics have worked patiently and fervently, transforming places, improving the land, perfecting agricultural methods, and discovering the secrets of the grape. They love God but also human beings and nature, and they have obtained its gifts.

In fact, in the eyes of Christians, the monastic institution is an integral part of their spiritual world. Monastics are not deserters from the world and the Church, although from the beginning they have constituted a mute protest against a worldly Christianity and a hardly Christian world. They do not contribute to the gross national product, but without them the world would be a more turbulent and self-centered place, less thoughtful and generous.

INDEX OF PERSONS

INDEX OF PLACES

PHOTOGRAPH CREDITS

Aaron Raverty, O.S.B.: 456
Abbey of El Encuentro, Mexico: 442, 443
Abbey of La Trappe, France: 413, 414, 415
Abbey of the Virgin of Curutarán: 441
Angelo Stabin: 5, 10, 11, 14, 40, 49, 97, 98, 99, 100, 101, 102, 106, 153, 189 191, 367
Apostolic Library, Vatican: 24
Archives of Arte Luciano Pedicini, Naples: 223, 224
Athenon Publishing: 157, 167, 239, 296, 318, 321, 364
Axinia Dzurova/Fabio Gentili: 247, 249, 255, 365, 366
BAMS Photo Rodella: 152, 171, 301, 302, 382, 408
Belzeaux-Zodiaque: 124
Bozidar Babić: 265
Bruno Fert: 416, 417
David Tellazzi, drawings: 60, 61, 67
Dúchas, The Heritage Service: 121
Emmanuel Anati: 19, 33, 420
Ermanno Leso, drawings: 3, 14, 17, 32
Fernando Lanzi: 95, 170, 220, 396
Giraudon/Alinari/Condé Museum: 403
Isber Melhem: 40, 41, 44, 53, 53, 55, 64, 71, 72, 77, 78, 80, 159, 267, 374
J. Stoikvić: 266

Jaca Book Archives/Adriano Alpago Novello: 1, 73, 184, 186, 268, 269, 270, 275, 176, 277, 282–285, 288, 289, 290, 292, 293, 375
Jaca Book Archives/E. V. Gippenreiter: 150, 308, 310, 325, 326, 328, 329, 331, 332, 334, 336
Jaca Book Archives/Iskusstvo: 30, 31, 79, 145, 160, 303, 304, 309, 311, 314, 327, 330, 333, 351, 356, 359
Jaca Book Archives/La Prova: 82, 83, 84, 86
Jaca Book Archives/Mauro Magliani: 47, 48, 108
Jaca Book Archives/Radu Mendrea: 20, 22, 23, 26, 27, 179, 337, 338, 339, 342, 343, 346, 347, 355, 369
Jean-Louis Nou: 9
Little Sisters of Jesus, Tre Fontane, Rome: 419, 421, 422
Lunwerg Archives/Isabel Valls: 111, 112, 113, 117
Lunwerg Archives/Pedro de Polol: 114
Lunwerg Archives/Ramon Manent: 183
Massimo Capuani: 43, 46, 50, 54, 58, 59, 62, 65, 68, 151, 254, 155, 173–177, 228, 230, 231–238, 240, 241, 244, 252, 260, 262, 280, 283, 316, 317, 320, 340, 350, 353, 360, 361, 363, 370, 376–379
Medici Laurentian Library, Florence, with the permission of the Ministry for Cultural Heritage and Activities: 74

National Library, Paris: 126, 209, 210
Paoline Publishing, Milan/Patriarchate of Moscow (Antiono Tarzia): 363
Photothèque André Held, Ecublens: 2, 29
Rapuzzi, Brescia: 107
RMN (photo Hervé Lewandowski): 70
Roger-Viollet: 105
Romano Zardi: 148
SANU (Serbian Academy of the Sciences and Arts): 256, 257
Scala Archives, Florence: 410
St. John's Abbey, Collegeville, Minnesota: 438 (by Greg Becker), 449, 450, 455
Stiftsbibliothek (Abbey Library), St. Gall, photo Kal Künzler: 92, 142, 196, 197, 198, 212
Swiss Mission of Coptic Archaeology, Geneva: 56, 161
Terryl N. Kinder: 404–407, 439, 440
Trappist Monastery of Vitorchiano: 445, 447, 448, 452
Vlado Kiprijanovski, Skopje: 169, 245
Vasari Archives, Rome: 187
Zodiaque: 201, 219, 222, 294, 297, 298, 381, 411, 412

Selection of illustrations
Franco Strada, La Fotolito, Milan

Printing and binding
D'Auria Industrie Grafiche S.p.A., Ascoli Piceno